THE M. & E. HANDBOOK SERIES

BUSINESS AND FINANCIAL MANAGEMENT

THE M. & E. HANDBOOK SERIES

BUSINESS AND FINANCIAL MANAGEMENT

SECOND EDITION

B. K. R. WATTS, B.A., A.M.B.I.M.

MACDONALD AND EVANS

MACDONALD & EVANS LTD
Estover, Plymouth PL6 7PZ

First published as *Industry and Finance* 1971
Reprinted 1972
Reprinted 1973
Second edition 1975
Reprinted 1977

©

MACDONALD AND EVANS LIMITED
1975

ISBN: 0 7121 0243 4

*Printed in Great Britain by Butler & Tanner Ltd
Frome and London*

PREFACE TO THE SECOND EDITION

THIS book is intended for students preparing for the Institute of Chartered Accountants' and for the Association of Certified Accountants' examinations which require a detailed knowledge of a wide range of subjects relating to business and financial management. In addition, it will certainly be of value to students taking other examinations at intermediate or final level, in particular those of the Institute of Bankers, Chartered Institute of Secretaries, Higher National Certificate and Diploma, Diploma in Management Studies, Institute of Administrative Management, C.N.A.A. in Business Studies, as well as for practising managers who wish further to develop their understanding of finance.

Methods of study. The HANDBOOK which replaces the author's successful HANDBOOK *Industry and Finance*, will be of value to students for revision purposes since the essentials of business and financial management are here combined under one cover. However, it is not intended to be an exhaustive textbook, for no single book can cover the demanding requirements of the final professional examination syllabuses in adequate scope and depth.

The student is advised to read quickly through the Chapter and section headings and the numbered paragraph headings to get an overall picture of the contents. Then he should read through each section in sequence. The Progress Tests at the end of each chapter are for self-examination and revision.

Keeping up to date. No textbook can tell the final-level student all he needs to know or replace the student's own judgment; if he finds it difficult to master any section he should not hesitate to refer to other books on the subject, particularly those on the recommended reading list. The student must keep up to date with current developments and, in particular, he is advised to read *The Financial Times, The Times Business Supplement, The Economist* and, of course, the appropriate professional magazines. It is also a good idea for the student to collect relevant press cuttings for future reference. The student will find that by diligent reading, by keeping up to date, by drawing from his own professional and business experience and

v

by working through these study notes, he will build up a considerable fund of knowledge and should have no difficulty in meeting examination requirements.

NOTICE TO LECTURERS

Many lecturers are now using **HANDBOOKS,** as working texts to save time otherwise wasted by students in protracted note-taking. The purpose of the series is to meet practical teaching requirements as far as possible, and lecturers are cordially invited to forward comments or criticisms to the publishers for consideration.

P. W. D. REDMOND
General Editor

CONTENTS

LIST OF ILLUSTRATIONS

LIST OF TABLES

PART ONE

THE STRUCTURE OF INDUSTRY

CHAPTER I

THE FIRM AND INDUSTRY

THE CONCEPT OF INDUSTRY

1. The establishment or plant. This is the business premises at a particular address. Since it is readily identifiable, it serves as a basis for official statitistics.

2. The firm. The accountant regards the firm as an unincorporated business whereas the economist, recognising this legal distinction, regards a firm as the "planning unit" where economic decisions are taken, *e.g.* what is to be produced, in what quantities and qualities and how. Frequently the firm coincides with the plant; however, large-scale industry is made up of multi-plant firms in a variety of organisational structures.

3. The industrial group. This occurs where a single firm exercises financial and policy control over other firms, *e.g.* I.C.I., formed in 1926 by the merger of four chemical firms for the purpose of "co-ordinating and developing their business on broad imperial lines." Today it employs more than 199,000 workers in the U.K., has 161 subsidiaries and a group turnover exceeding £1,600m per annum.

The main units in the organisation are the eight manufacturing divisions and two main subsidiaries, which are responsible for its other companies and for I.C.I.'s interests in numerous associated companies. Although each division is run by a divisional chairman, ultimate authority rests with the main board consisting of sixteen executive and six non-executive directors who formulate overall policy and exercise functional and operational roles (*e.g.* responsibilities for personnel, R. & D. and paints division respectively). In this way, this

1

vast organisation is decentralised; considerable authority is given to the divisional chairman, while decisions are made consistent with the overall strategy through a system of functional and operational control.

4. The financial group. This exists where a parent company exercises financial control over a number of otherwise autonomous subsidiaries. A requently cited example is the Thomas Tilling Group, which was created when the parent company sold its interests in transport at the time of nationalisation and bought shares in companies and became an industrial holding company or "conglomerate." Today it has widespread interests in mining, vehicle distribution, "Pyrex" glassware, publishing and engineering. Such extensive diversification makes intervention by the parent company in the day-to-day management in its subsidiaries impracticable. It concerns itself rather with matters of investment expenditures, appointment of executives and group strategy.

5. The joint venture. This is where two or more companies co-operate to overcome a common problem or exploit a market opportunity. They may establish a jointly owned company, *e.g.* in 1951 the United Sulphuric Acid Corporation was established by I.C.I., Fisons and nine other companies to produce acid from domestic resources.

6. The cartel. This is a defensive arrangement where companies agree to limit individual freedom regarding output, price and capacity. The cartel tends, however, to be short-lived as success depends on the loyalty of its members and this cannot be guaranteed for ever. Ambitious members may find the restrictions frustrating, while any success in maintaining high prices will induce members to exceed their quotas. Since the war monopoly and restrictive practice legislation has in any case limited the scope for collusion.

The various Government-sponsored Marketing Boards, which set quotas and standards and undertake to market members' produce, are examples of cartels which have enjoyed varying degrees of success. The following are the chief ones which have been set up at various times:

(a) The Milk Marketing Board.
(b) The Potato Marketing Board.

(c) The Hops Marketing Board.
(d) The Egg Marketing Board.

7. The need for industrial classification. Firms and plants need to be classified for the following variety of reasons:

(a) Similar firms wish to associate because they:

(i) produce similar goods;
(ii) employ similar techniques;
(iii) employ similar types of labour; or
(iv) have common interests.

Through their trade association, an interchange of information helps them overcome their common problems and advance their interests in negotiations with unions and the Government.

(b) Economists require information to advance theories and examine industrial problems.

(c) The State needs information for control and economic planning, e.g.:

(i) the National Plan set targets and outlined the main problems facing specific industries;

(ii) The Regional Employment Premium is based on industrial classifications.

8. Methods of classifying industries. The task of classifying industry is made difficult by its diversity and its tendency to change. Ideally, an industry consists of a group of firms producing identical products, which they sell in the same market, all with a common technology and labour types. However, the immense variety within industry makes this criterion inpracticable and a more sophisticated classification in terms of products, resources and activities may be thought necessary. Thus an industrial group may be demarcated by:

(a) products (e.g. vehicle and aircraft industries);
(b) raw materials (e.g. rubber and chemical industries); or
(c) processes (e.g. spinning and weaving industries).

9. Indicators to industrial groupings. The various trade associations provide a guide to industrial groups (e.g. the Society of British Aircraft Manufacturers), although many vertical amalgamations (e.g. the Society of Motor Manufacturers and Traders) and lateral mergers of product associations make trade association membership a less meaningful indicator of narrow industrial classes.

10. Standard Industrial Classification. By using the Standard Industrial Classification (S.I.C.), produced in 1948, the Government secures uniformity and comparability in official statistics on production, distribution and employment, etc.

The S.I.C. consists of "establishments," classified into industries according to their principal activities or products, so that if the Government requires statistics on production or employment in a particular industry it can survey the establishments of that classification. Clearly the "firm" is too imprecise to be the unit of industrial analysis because a firm may own or control many establishments specialising in different trades.

It consists of twenty-seven major industrial groups or orders of industry, covering extractive (1–2), manufacturing (3–19), construction (20), public utilities (21–22), and commercial, private and public services (23–27). Each order is then subdivided into minimum list headings or specialist trades (total 181).

EXAMPLE:

Order 1: Agriculture, forestry, fishing

*Minimum
    list
 heading*

   001   Agriculture and horticulture

          1. Farming and stock-rearing

All types of agricultural holdings, including those of 1 acre or less, except market gardens and holdings used mainly for the production of fruit, flowers or seeds.

          2. Agricultural contracting.

Services such as ploughing, ditching, field draining, hedging, crop spraying, etc.

          3. Market gardening, fruit, flower and seed growing, etc.

   002   Forestry, etc.

   003   Fishing

          1. Sea fishing, etc.

          2. Fishing in inland waters.

THE SIZE OF FIRMS

11. Criteria for measuring size of firm. Several criteria are available for measuring the size of firms:

(a) *Output.* If statistics of output volumes are available, they provide a satisfactory guide to the size of firms, but only when firms are producing similar goods. Value-of-output figures (quantity produced multiplied by price) permit comparisons between firms whose products are more dissimilar, but they are less satisfactory for comparisons between industries, where values are certain to reflect differences in costs and market forces.

(b) *Raw materials.* The consumption of raw materials in real or money terms indicates the relative sizes of firms, but the same limitations apply as for (a).

(c) *Employees.* The numbers on the payroll are commonly used, although it should be noted that not all companies publish details and this method neglects other factors, particularly capital, which is more important in capital-intensive industries (*e.g.* petroleum and chemicals). Nor does it distinguish between types of workers and skills.

(d) *Capital.* This standard is widely used for inter-firm comparisons. Capital employed is the most useful measure since it is supplied by all companies. It may be either:

(*i*) gross capital employed (*i.e.* the value of fixed and current assets); or

(*ii*) net capital employed (*i.e.* the value of fixed and current assets less current liabilities).

Even so, this method may understate the relative importance of a highly labour-intensive firm.

(e) *Profits.* Profit figures are provided by all companies but are less suitable as a consistent yardstick because of their volatile nature.

(f) *Market capitalisation.* This is a possible method of judging, although it is impracticable for consistent comparisons between firms because it is volatile and eliminates the several large private companies and British subsidiaries of foreign companies.

The relative size of a firm will depend on the criteria adopted, so that a firm highly ranked on one basis may be lower ranked and seemingly less important on another. However, any disparity is unimportant, for a firm is certain to be either large, medium or small whatever basis is used.

TABLE I. LARGE BRITISH INDUSTRIAL COMPANIES RANKED BY
SIZE (VARIOUS CRITERIA) (1974)

Company	Capital employed (£m)	Rank	Turnover (£m)	Rank	Employees (000)	Rank
Shell Transport	2·363	1	3·184	2	—	—
B.P.	2·293	2	3·431	1	26·4	68
I.C.I.	1·936	3	1·694	4	199·0	2
Rio Tinto	1·057	4	0·588	19	10·8	149
Br. American Tobacco	0·913	5	2·037	3	110·0	5

Source: The Times 1000, 1973–4

The Times survey surprisingly reveals that these industrial companies are relatively small compared with the biggest enterprises when measured by capital employed, which consist of nationalised industries (*e.g.* the Electricity Council and the Electricity Boards, the biggest with £5,185,400), and British and overseas banks.

THE SMALL FIRM

12. What is a small firm? Although definition is necessarily arbitrary, the small firm may be indicated by the following criteria:

(*a*) *The number of employees.* The C.B.I., for example, has defined the small firm as a firm employing less than 200, but the Rural Industries Bureau defines it as a firm employing less than ten.

(*b*) *The turnover.* In the discussions preceding the *Companies Act* 1967, the C.B.I. considered the small firm to be a firm whose turnover was less than £1m. The Government's figure was £50,000.

It has been estimated that 97 per cent of manufacturing establishments employ less than 500 workers, representing some 50 per cent of the total manufacturing labour force, and produce 45 per cent of total industrial sales. These establishments also show a higher average increase in profits than industry generally.

13. Reasons for the survival of the small firm. Although the mortality rate is high for small firms, they survive in large numbers as a group for the following reasons:

(*a*) The optimum size of firm (*i.e.* the best or most efficient firm which has lowest production costs per unit of output), may be small in an industry because:

(*i*) technical process may favour small scale, *e.g.* power looms in weaving.

(*ii*) the market may be small if customers prefer personal services and variety, rather than impersonal, large-scale organisations and standardised products.

(*b*) There may be the following obstacles to further growth:

(*i*) Difficulties of raising finance for expansion.

(*ii*) Active competition or restrictive practices or monopoly legislation.

(*iii*) The lack of ambition, self-interest or managerial ambition of the original entrepreneur.

(*iv*) Many small firms are content with the non-monetary advantages of independence and prestige.

(*v*) Risks increase with growth; further growth may become unacceptable to the management.

(*vi*) Administration may become less efficient because of inertia and low morale.

(*c*) Industry is not static and a small size is a transitory stage between "birth," large scale success and "death."

(*i*) There seems to be an unlimited supply of would-be entrepreneurs possessing experience and capital who are prepared to start in business on a modest scale. Many eventually succeed to a large extent.

(*ii*) Unsuccessful firms decline and are eventually wound up.

14. Are small firms needed? Small firms may be defended on the following grounds:

(*a*) They are frequent sources of new products and processes (*i.e.* they are inventive).

(*b*) New firms have initiative and ambition and stimulate industry.

(*c*) They are more flexible than larger firms and react quickly and less violently to the activities of the market and Governments, with less effect on, say, employment, or production.

(*d*) They perform tasks unsuited to large-scale industry often more efficiently.

15. Problems facing small firms. Those who recognise the value of small firms argue that Government policy is orientated towards large-scale industry, and disregards their problems. Small firms are unable to overcome these problems themselves, and so they are perpetuated and efficiency is impeded. They indicate that, in the U.S.A., West Germany and Japan, offices have been set up to assist them and they argue that a corresponding body is required for the U.K.

16. Nature of assistance. The main areas where assistance is needed are as follows:

(*a*) Management and accounting techniques for staff and consultancy services.

(*b*) Sources and methods of finance.

(*c*) Marketing assistance in modern techniques, and assistance in exporting, purchasing and stock control techniques.

(*d*) General information, *e.g.* interpretation of statistics and legislation in non-technical language.

(*e*) Repeal of "oppressive" legislation, *e.g.* critics claimed that the *Companies Act* 1967 would inhibit the growth of the small firm. They objected to disclosures of trading details which larger firms might exploit to their disadvantage. Also, the *Finance Act* 1965 imposed a harsh tax liability on close companies and discouraged reinvestment of profits. Along with estate duty and capital gains tax, this could well discourage enterprise.

17. Present sources of information. Accountants, bank managers, merchant banks, N.E.D.C. and respective "Neddies," the industrial liaison service, the I.C.F.C., the B.I.M., the British Productivity Council, and trade associations are all useful sources of information.

Nevertheless, despite the valuable assistance provided by these groups, the main problem of the small firm is one of communication, *i.e.* how to get assistance, and who from and where from.

18. Possible courses of action.

(*a*) A bureau for small firms could be financed by members' subscriptions, although Government backing would be necessary to give such a bureau greater authority and continuity. Its work would be:

(*i*) to keep registers of consultants;
(*ii*) to give technical assistance;
(*iii*) to survey and report on common problems;
(*iv*) to represent members in negotiations; and
(*v*) to overcome communication problems.

(*b*) The Government could adopt the U.S. Government's policy of setting aside a proportion (*e.g.* 20 per cent) of contracts for tender to small firms ("set aside" contracts). Naturally, further orders would depend on past performance and tender prices.

(*c*) In 1968 a pilot scheme to help small firms was set up in the Bristol and Glasgow areas by the Government on the initiative of N.U.M.A.S. (a non-profit-making consultancy organisation for small firms, established by the Board of Trade in the 1950s). A fund of £500,000 was provided, from which half the small firms' consultancy expenses could be claimed (to a maximum of £5,000). This scheme received enthusiastic support; it could well be introduced on a more ambitious scale.

(*d*) The Bolton Report (1971) on small firms contained fifty-six recommendations. High on the list of priorities was the recommendation for advisory services to help overcome the small firms' communication problems mentioned above. Consequently, the government acted.

(*i*) The Small Firms Division was set up within the D.T.I. (now Department of Trade).

(*ii*) Small Firms Information Centres were established under the auspices of the D.T.I.'s Regional Development Centre to establish contacts between companies and suitable professional advisors, *e.g.* banks, accountants.

PROGRESS TEST 1

1. "Large-scale industry is made up of multi-plant firms in a variety of organisational structures." Comment on this statement. (1–6)

2. For what reasons are industrial classifications useful to the following?

(*a*) Firms.
(*b*) Economists.
(*c*) Governments. (7)

3. Discuss the problems of defining "an industry" and suggest various criteria which may be used to indicate some industries with which you are familiar. (8)

4. What do you understand by the Standard Industrial

Classification and what problems does such a classification overcome? (**10**)

5. Compare and contrast the various criteria for measuring the size of firms. (**11–12**)

6. How do you account for the survival of the small firm? (**13**)

7. "In view of the important role of small firms in British industry the Government should introduce remedial measures to help them overcome the serious problems which check their efficiency." Comment on this statement. (**14–18**)

8. It has been said that poor communication is a serious problem facing small firms. Outline their various sources of information and suggest practical measures to overcome this problem. (**17–18**)

CHAPTER II

ECONOMIES OF SCALE

1. Sources of economies of scale. The pattern of industrial concentration and the continuing trend towards larger plant capacities and firms may be explained by the following factors:

(a) *Internal economies of scale:*

(i) Economies of large-scale plant or economies of large outputs, *i.e.* technical economies which reduce unit costs of production at high levels of output (*see* **2-7**).

(ii) Economies of large-scale organisations, *i.e.* general economies which reduce unit costs of goods in large-sized organisations (*see* **8-12**).

(b) *External economies of scale.* These are economies enjoyed by large and small firms that arise from the large size, growth or concentration of the industry (*see* **13** and **14**).

ECONOMIES OF LARGE-SCALE PLANT

2. Introduction. If factors of production (*i.e.* materials, labour and capital) are increased by, say, x per cent, then total output in a large-capacity plant may increase by more than x per cent. The extent of these economies depends on the technological nature of individual industries. The processing industries, for example, employ methods of production which realise considerable savings in unit costs of production when large outputs are handled, while other industries (*e.g.* the textile and clothing industries) necessarily employ different technologies which cannot effect such savings. However, a technological principle can be identified in all productive operations. Larger plants tend to be more efficient than smaller plants up to a certain level of output.

It is possible to identify the factors responsible for these savings, as follows:

(a) Certain processes require proportionally fewer factors of production for a given output (*see* **3**).

(b) Other processes involve factors of production which are less than perfectly sub-divisible (*see* **6**).

11

3. Non-proportional inputs and outputs. Certain processes require proportionally less inputs for a given output.

(a) Economies of scale operate when demand is random. For example, a small-scale TV rental firm employing a maintenance electrician may discover that he is working below capacity, but because TV sets break down at random, his services will be demanded more frequently and eventually continuously as the firm's scale of operation increases. Evidently, the cost of maintenance does not increase in proportion to the number of installations.

(b) A firm may be using a process which benefits from the mathematical relationships between length, area and volume. For example:

	Building A	*Building B*
Perimeter	400 ft (122 m) (*i.e.* length and breadth is 100 ft (30 m)	800 ft (244 m) (*i.e.* dimensions are doubled)
Area	10,000 sq. ft (930 m²	40,000 sq. ft (3,720 m² (*i.e.* area is quadrupled)

Apparently construction costs per sq. ft (m²) are reduced, as total costs are unlikely to increase in proportion to area. However, in practice builders quote a standard price per sq. ft (m²), perhaps to subsidise smaller, less economic projects and to insure against contingencies of idle time, wastage, etc.

4. Economies of scale. The trend towards larger aircraft operated by airlines on short, medium and long routes from the 100+-seaters of the 1950's to the 150+-seaters and now

TABLE II(A). COMPARISON OF COST AND CAPACITY

	Standard VC10	*Super VC10*
Date of purchase	*1964*	*1965*
Cost	£2·3m	£3·0m
Inflation index	100·0	102·5
Cost (1964 base)	£2·3m	£2·9m
Certified seat capacity	151	169
Certified cargo capacity	1,350 cu. ft	1,950 cu. ft.
Cost *per* seat	£15,231	£17,159
Cost *per* cu. ft of cargo	£1,703	£1,487

the 250+-seater Jumbo generations reflects the significant economies of scale in construction and operation of large-capacity aircraft. For instance, let us consider two directly comparable aircraft: the standard VC10 and the super VC10.

The above table shows that for an additional capital expenditure of £600,000, eighteen additional seats and 600 cu. ft of cargo space were obtained. Consequently, capital cost *per* cu. ft of cargo space fell from £1,703 to £1,487, a significant economy of scale, while cost *per* seat actually increased from £15,231 to £17,159. However, one should bear in mind that this extra capacity obtained by stretching the fuselage fore and aft of the wings necessitated an extra 10 per cent increase in power which was achieved by adding one extra stage to the engines. In addition, fuel tankage had to be increased from 65k kilos to 70k kilos. In summary, the greater technical sophistication of the enlarged aircraft meant additional costs that limited the capital benefits derived from the larger scale.

5. Economies in operating cost.

TABLE II(B). OPERATING ECONOMIES

	Standard VC10	Super VC10
	pence per capacity ton mile	
1967–68	6·50	4·50
69–70	6·25	5·00
71–72	7·00	5·00
73–74	8·50	6·50

The rapid increase for the period 1973–4 was due to the fuel price increases: however, the Super VC10 clearly outperformed the Standard in terms of operating costs throughout the period 1967–74. In addition, it provided management with a more flexible aircraft because of its larger carrying capacity and increased operating range.

6. Indivisibility of factors of production. Production may be more efficient on a large scale because some factors of production cannot be varied in proportion to output, as follows:

(*a*) The principal factor in the production process may not be sub-divisible. This is particularly true of heavy plant, which some industries require in large units for efficient operation. For example, a car-body manufacturer incurs a considerable yet non-repeating expense when he installs a press which will later realise economies in the form of reducing fixed costs per unit of output (A.F.C.) over long production runs, thus:

Fixed cost—one car body press .   .   .   £100,000
Fixed cost *per* body if 1 produced   .   .   £100,000
Fixed cost *per* body if 100 produced   .   .   £1,000
Fixed cost *per* body if 1,000 produced   .   £100

(*b*) There may be several plants of different capacities which are not sub-divisible. In these cases, production is most efficient when all plants are fully utilised, *i.e.* when the optimum rate of throughput is equal to the lowest common multiple of their capacities. Imagine a production process which consists of three activities:

(*i*) Operation	(*ii*) Capacity per hour	(*iii*) No. of factors	(*iv*) Total outputs per hour (L.C.M.)
Pressing	20	20 presses	400
Machining	16	25 lathes	400
Packing	25	16 packers	400

Here the optimum rate of production is 400 units per hour, with no idle time for machinery or packers, so that, ideally speaking, the number of machines and packers indicated in column (*iii*) should be employed. However, in practice some other combination may be employed for the following reasons:

(*i*) Reserve machinery is necessary in the event of break-downs and extra men in case of absenteeism. But the choice and number of reserves will depend on the anticipated work-load, their comparative costs and their versatility. Usually occupational mobility varies inversely with specialisation; general-purpose equipment can usually perform a number of operations, unlike specialised equipment. On the other hand, efficiency usually increases with specialisation, so that a firm is forced to compromise between the conflicting objectives of flexibility and efficiency when dealing with the problem of factor combinations and reserves.

(*ii*) Firms may be unable to afford the optimum number of machines. Instead, they may concentrate on one process, buying semi-finished goods outside and selling or sub-contracting their output to specialists.

(c) Specialist employees are not sub-divisible, as they each have work capacities. For instance, designers and accountants may be under-employed initially when the scale of activity is low, but, as the firm expands, work-loads increase to realise economies in the form of lower salary costs *per* unit of output.

This is true also of any team of specialists. A design group is to some extent an indivisible unit, so that if one member leaves a team of three then the firm may well lose more than 33 per cent of its results.

7. Limitations of economies of scale. There are circumstances when capital-intensive industry cuts back investment expenditure on new larger-scale plant or equipment and instead devotes more to modernising existing plant. The reasons for this may be summarised as follows:

(a) Large-scale plant takes longer to build and frequently raises technological problems. However, a number of smaller-capacity plants, although eventually less efficient, satisfy demand and realise profits in the short term.

(b) If the large-scale plant breaks down, then a big proportion of total capacity is out of commission. Once orders are lost it is difficult to restore goodwill.

(c) Large-scale plant requires a large market for efficient operation. However, although exporting offers a solution, it is the most uncertain and competitive market, especially when there is excess world capacity.

(d) A technically inefficient firm may be protected in its local market by transport costs which will be high for certain products, *e.g.* bricks.

(e) It may protect itself in the market by appointing exclusive dealers (*e.g.* tied public houses) so as to ensure adequate outlets.

(f) Small firms may specialise in one aspect of production, but they may buy know-how and designs instead of pursuing all the benefits which large-scale organisation offers.

ECONOMIES OF LARGE FIRMS

8. Advantages of large firms. The large organisation possesses several advantages over the small firm, *e.g.* a better calibre of management and staff, power and finance, all of which realise economies.

(a) *Management.* Good managers, who can make correct decisions, delegate responsibility, communicate effectively, select suitable staff and provide leadership, are rare. That this is recognised is shown by the emphasis placed on training in management skills in colleges, business schools and industry.

Large organisations, by the nature of their special problems, need good managers and they are probably better placed to attract them with their offers of superior prospects, salaries, working conditions and fringe benefits (*e.g.* non-contributory pensions, a company car, etc.). Thus, they can be more selective than small firms in their choice of managers.

The larger organisation may also be more conducive to the development of management performance. There are many different departments and subsidiaries which can provide all-round experience and which can enable them to exploit the opportunities offered by inter-group comparisons, to bring the efficiency of the whole up to that of the most efficient unit and thereby to extend the size and market share of the organisation.

(*b*) *Staff.* There are four advantages claimed for the large firm in this respect:

(*i*) Often there is a better chance of success in terms of career prospects and salary in a large organisation. A large firm thus has a wide choice of candidates.

(*ii*) Internal appointments avoid the friction and resentment which external appointments often cause.

(*iii*) Company staff records provide useful and perhaps more reliable information than application forms from outsiders.

(*iv*) It may be less costly in terms of salary to promote staff internally. Outsiders generally demand considerable financial compensation for losing their present security and to make up for the difficulties in settling into a strange job.

9. Finance. The large firm has the opportunity of economising in financial matters, as follows:

(*a*) *Internal.* Large organisations, whose capital requirements are more stable, have an advantage over smaller ones whose requirements are likely to exceed retained profits.

(*b*) *External.* Although the minimum charges of issuing houses are high, administration costs do not increase in proportion to the size of issues, so there may be considerable economies for a large issue. Furthermore, an established public company may draw upon existing market goodwill for a successful issue of securities. Smaller firms on the other hand may be forced to offer more attractive and more costly coupons to secure the investors' approval.

(*c*) *Working capital.* Compared with smaller firms, large firms need smaller amounts of circulating capital in proportion to turnover (although they are larger, of course, in absolute terms).

10. Benefits accruing from finance. The large firm probably has a large cash flow as well, which secures for it the following powerful advantages:

(a) *Risk-spreading.* Large firms have finance available to spread the risks of the market by diversifying their interests. Rather than depending on one product and the vagaries of the market, they may enter new industries possessing ideally counter-cyclical characteristics, *e.g.* Imperial Tobacco Ltd. have interests in the food and cosmetic trades.

(b) *Research.* The large firm is more able to afford expenditure for research. This often leads to new materials, products and processes.

(c) *Development and innovation.* It can also better afford:

    (i) to develop discoveries for commercial production;
    (ii) to introduce more efficient methods of production.

Consequently patent rights and royalties are secured and the firm's overall competitiveness is improved.

(d) *Advertising.* The large firm can better afford expenditure for advertising its products, to build up its market share.

11. Power. It has been suggested that very large companies have "advantages of power" over the following groups:

(a) *Local government.*

(b) *The Press.* Large companies are sometimes able to secure sympathetic or preferential treatment.

(c) *Suppliers.* Large firms may be able to secure attractive terms from suppliers, because:

    (i) lower prices may in part be due to economies in production;
    (ii) suppliers may be tempted to quote lower prices to keep important customers; or
    (iii) large-scale customers may use their strong bargaining power to demand lower terms.

(d) *Customers.* After the second world war, manufacturers' restrictive agreements effectively reduced consumer choice. However, the *Restrictive Practices Act* 1956 outlawed collective action and, although it permitted resale price maintenance by individual manufacturers, the position changed radically with the *Resale Prices Act* 1964. Today, R.P.M. has virtually disappeared in the High Street. Nevertheless, there is some concern that the present trend towards concentration places greater power in the hands of manufacturers and reduces consumer sovereignty.

(e) *Employees.* In theory, a monopolist employer can force down wages. However, it is doubtful that this would happen in practice for there are unlikely to be many monopolist employers within one locality. Abuse of power is unlikely for other reasons, as follows:

(i) Trade unions would use their collective power to resist such action.

(ii) Such a policy is certain to fail in conditions of full employment. Workers will move elsewhere.

(iii) Large firms are anxious to uphold their reputations as good employers. Many have been wage pace-setters for industry and have voluntarily provided additional facilities by way of canteens, social clubs, etc.

12. Disadvantages of large-scale firms. The main problems arising from large organisations are due to:

(a) inertia;
(b) low morale;
(c) poor co-ordination; or
(d) reduced flexibility.

There is a danger within a large organisation that workers lose their identity, that conflicts of interest arise between workers or between sections of the firm, that delays in communication increase, and co-ordination deteriorates.

However, it would be a very weak firm which suffered from all these problems at once. Moreover, most large organisations only suffer from them because they use procedural rules which are certain to introduce some inflexibility into their operations. Future policy becomes less flexible since these firms are committed by past decisions (*e.g.* the location of specific plant will necessarily limit the scope of future company policy).

For this reason, since the second world war many large British firms have followed the example set by General Motors and have become decentralised. They have been split into virtually independent divisions, each with responsibility for trading and investment policy. Each division is responsible to the main board for general policy only. In this way, decentralisation of authority has helped to overcome the problem of inflexibility in large organisations.

EXTERNAL ECONOMIES OF SCALE

13. Geographical integration. In areas of localised industrial concentration firms tend to specialise. They concentrate on a limited number of standardised products, processes and services on a larger scale than would be possible outside the localised area. This is due to *external economies of scale*. Firms benefit from limited activies in much the same way that large integrated firms benefit from internal economies of scale. They operate large-capacity plant, meeting orders from numerous other firms who individually cannot afford to use such plant efficiently. Also, close contact improves production planning, reduces uncertainty and the burden on management while realising economies in communications and transport. Thus in such areas the tendency is towards localised disintegration by small, efficient specialists.

14. Sources of external economies. Firms making up the Lancashire cotton industry benefit from the proximity of the following:

    (*a*) Local specialist cotton markets.
    (*b*) The skilled labour force.
    (*c*) Specialist machinery manufacturers.
    (*d*) Specialised services.
    (*e*) Research facilities.

PROGRESS TEST 2

1. Distinguish between internal and external economies of scale and indicate the main economies of large-scale production. **(1)**

2. "In all types of productive operations, larger plants are always more efficient than smaller plants up to a certain level of output." Identify and explain the factors responsible for these economies. **(2)**

3. Explain the term "internal economies of scale" and describe its operation in any one industry with which you are familiar. **(4–5)**

4. Explain with examples what is meant by "indivisibility" of factors of production and its relevance to the concept of economies of scale. **(6)**

5. A manufacturer employs several machines of different capacities:

        Machine A . . . . 16 units *per* hour
        Machine B . . . . 8 units *per* hour
        Machine C . . . . 25 units *per* hour

What advice can you give him on the optimum rate of through-put and the number of machines of each type? (6)

6. For what reasons may a firm be smaller than the optimum size of firm that is indicated by the economies of scale principle? (7)

7. "The bigger the better." Under what conditions is this true of industrial undertakings? (8–11)

8. Discuss the advantages and disadvantages of large-scale organisations. (8–12)

9. Explain how it is that geographical disintegration realises external economies of scale. (13)

CHAPTER III

THE INTEGRATION OF ECONOMIC ACTIVITIES

INTEGRATION BY ADMINISTRATION

1. Types of integration. The various stages of the complete production process (raw material, manufacture and distribution), may be linked by markets or by administration, as follows:

(*a*) A firm which bridges these markets by controlling the necessary factors (materials, labour, plant and premises) at different stages of production is said to integrate its operations *vertically*:

(*i*) *backwards*, if it expands to the raw material stage;
(*ii*) *forwards*, if it expands towards the consumer.

(*b*) If the firm expands by amalgamating with firms at the same stage of production it integrates *horizontally* (*see* 2).

(*c*) If it diversifies into other trades, it integrates laterally (*see* 5 and 6).

These forms of integration may be visualised as in Fig. 1

2. Horizontal integration. A firm may expand by horizontal integration for offensive motives for the following reasons:

(*a*) It may desire to absorb its competitors' share of the market and profits.

(*b*) It may wish to realise the advantages of large-scale plant and organisation. It is unlikely that a firm wishing to double its output will need to double its labour force, fixed and working capital, administration, purchasing and selling departments. In this way administration and manufacturing costs *per* unit of output may be reduced. Efficiencies may be further realised by the employment of specialists in management manpower and equipment and from using maintenance and repair services to capacity.

The optimum size of the firm's technical unit is probably larger than its administrative unit so that economies may be less marked at higher levels of output because of problems

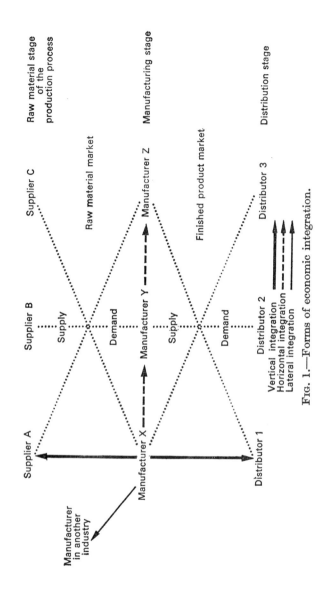

Raw material stage of the production process

Manufacturing stage

Distribution stage

Supplier C

Raw material market

Manufacturer Z

Distributor 3

Supplier B

Supply   Demand

Supply   Demand

Finished product market

Distributor 2

Vertical integration ————▶
Horizontal integration ----▶
Lateral integration ·······▶

Supplier A

Manufacturer Y

Manufacturer X

Distributor 1

Manufacturer in another industry

FIG. 1.—Forms of economic integration.

of co-ordination and communication in administration and management. Nevertheless, the technical economies are often considerable and are usually sufficient to outweigh uneconomical tendencies elsewhere, especially in process industries and manufacturing industries employing flow production techniques.

The typical relationship of costs to the size of plant is illustrated in Fig. 2 by the curve AC. This shows that economies of scale cause unit costs to decrease until the curve reaches the minimum optimal scale, A, where AC is lowest. If constant returns to scale are then experienced the firm may employ multiples of this scale to secure these minimum unit costs until the maximum optimal scale, B, after which expansion causes diseconomies to set in so that AC rises.

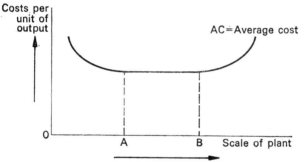

FIG. 2.—Typical relationship of costs to size of plant.

3. Vertical integration (1).

A firm may expand its operations vertically if it has offensive motives, as follows:

(a) A firm may desire to eliminate the profits of enterprises operating forwards or backwards in the production process.

(b) It may wish to secure economies of scale of non-manufacturing processes. For example, research and development units, production planning, marketing, purchasing and management organisations are less than perfectly divisible and probably have different capacities. But as the principle of multiples shows, common costs of these activities at different stages in the production process are reduced when used to capacity, *i.e.* they are spread over a larger range of activity, as follows:

(i) *Research and development.* The minimum size of unit necessary for significant contributions to know-how is generally large and expensive so that R. & D. are usually the prerogative of large firms who can finance them and utilise them to capacity.

(*ii*) *Production planning.* Efficient production demands efficient production planning. However, difficulties may arise in assembly industries where independent suppliers are linked by the market. Obviously, close liaison between the specialist component producers is essential to decide on job specifications, prices, deliveries and future development. However, breakdowns in communication do occur, and these may induce firms to by-pass the market. They may integrate these operations by administration and build up a team of specialists who collectively can work more effectively.

(*iii*) *Purchasing.* A centralised buying department for a group will realise economies if used to capacity. It may also secure large order discounts. However, stock control problems may be aggravated.

(*iv*) *Marketing.* A single selling department will reduce the duplication of effort and costs.

(*c*) It may wish to secure technical economies of scale. For example, in an integrated steel works, heat from the blast furnace which would be otherwise wasted, is used to work the metal into tubes and sheets.

(*d*) It may wish to control the demands for its product more directly and thereby more effectively by by-passing the wholesaler. Large-scale breweries and petrol companies with their tied outlets are examples of this.

4. Vertical integration (2). A firm which is expanding its operations vertically may be motivated by defensive objectives, as follows:

(*a*) It may desire to reduce risk by bridging the uncertainty of the raw material market. The manufacturer who integrates backwards is assured of supplies which may be scarce and costly when demand is high, or they may be controlled by a monopolist.

(*b*) It may desire to secure adequate outlets for its products.

In summary, there is no general rule that vertical integration realises economies. It may in certain cases but in others it may be uneconomic (*e.g.* detergent manufacturers do not integrate forward into retailing since their sales would be below the minimum optimal scale necessary for efficient retailing). Alternatively vertical integration may have a neutral effect on costs, although it may be attempted if some other advantage outlined above is anticipated.

5. Lateral integration (1). A firm which is expanding its operations laterally may have offensive motives, as follows:

(*a*) It may desire to benefit from existing goodwill by transferring the firm's brand name or image to new products.

(*b*) It may wish to expand turnover by entering new industries while employing common techniques, skills, raw materials or by-products from other activities. However, strong competition from specialists is to be expected.

(*c*) To employ spare capacity profitably.

(*d*) To exploit a profitable opportunity.

6. Lateral integration (2). A firm which is expanding laterally may have defensive motives, as follows:

(*a*) It may wish to secure stability of profits, especially in those trades which are prone to cyclical fluctuations. Profits may be maintained if more stable "bread and butter trades" or "counter-cyclical" industries are entered.

(*b*) It may wish to maintain its share of the market by offering distributors and customers a choice from a comprehensive range of goods.

INTEGRATION v. STANDARDISATION

7. Problem of inflexibility. A manufacturer's attitude to vertical integration depends partly on the present and expected state of the market.

Where supply exceeds demand and where this buyer's market is expected to last for some time, vertical disintegration can be expected because of low returns on capital in the depressed supply industry. However, the decision to disintegrate will be influenced by the likely capital loss from the sale of these investments and by considerations of group loyalty and pride.

However, in the long run the issue is determined by the comparative merits of integration and standardisation.

8. Integration and standardisation. The more a firm of given resources is integrated, the smaller is its scale of operations and efficiency in each activity. Thus integration may militate against scale, thereby encouraging disintegration, although large firms possessing sufficient resources can integrate several activities, performing them on the optimum scale if the market allows.

The smaller firm seems to have a choice between two courses of action, as follows:

(a) The firm can integrate and use small-scale plant. This is less efficient and will produce lower returns than for specialists, but this course may be preferred for the following reasons:

(i) It may overcome monopoly situations.

(ii) Integration of the complete production process, as compared with market integration, reduces uncertainties.

(iii) The firm may already have spare capacity suitable for the integrated activity.

(iv) It may be larger than the specialist and perhaps more credit-worthy, which with (ii) might make capital issues cheaper.

(b) It can perform fewer activities, each on a larger scale.

9. Limitations of standardisation. Firms may be prevented from exploiting the maximum economies from the large-scale standardisation of products, even though it is technically feasible, because of the following constraints:

(a) The market for the product may be limited. This is influenced by the following factors:

(i) The level of disposable incomes.

(ii) The propensity to save.

(iii) The size of population.

(iv) The age distribution of the population.

(v) Tastes, habits and fashions.

(vi) The success of competitors.

(vii) Advertising.

(b) The high costs of distribution.

(c) The shortage of capital.

(d) The risks associated with standardisation may be unacceptable to the management; they may feel they are putting "all their eggs in one basket."

For these reasons firms and plants may not necessarily be organised for the largest possible scale of production which their resources or technology permit.

INTEGRATION BY THE MARKET MECHANISM

10. Reasons for market integration. We have seen that vertical integration may offset scale, inducing firms to specialise in one process, while using the market to obtain other necessary goods and services. Other firms might prefer to administer consecutive processes but may be forced to use the market if they lack the necessary know-how, expertise or finance. Firms may find it advantageous to use the market in the following circumstances:

(a) *Infrequent purchases.* They may occasionally buy items of specialised plant, equipment and buildings rather than make them themselves. It is probably more reliable and cheaper to use the services of specialist suppliers, who possess know-how and experience and whose prices may reflect economies of large-scale output.

(b) *Frequent purchases.* Firms often find it preferable to buy regular supplies of raw materials, components and semi-finished goods and services from specialist suppliers rather than attempt to make them themselves. They do this for the following reasons:

(i) Specialist suppliers usually offer the trade a range of goods.

(ii) Goods may be produced on a scale large enough to secure economies of production.

(iii) Suppliers' prices may reflect other economies which may accrue through specialisation in management, laboratories or equipment.

(iv) They economise in working capital from lower stock levels.

(v) Historical reasons, as in the building and shoe trades.

11. Limitations of market integration. Despite the obvious benefits of wider choice, high standards of product design and quality, general flexibility in purchasing and pecuniary advantages, there are circumstances when on balance the market as an integrating device is unsatisfactory, as follows:

(a) Firms are ultimately responsible for the performance, price and delivery of the end-product and they may be unprepared to share this responsibility with suppliers, who may let them down by delivering late, or wrong or poor-quality goods. Obviously, firms who fail once in these respects will not be used again, but the risk always exists, although it can be reduced by late delivery penalty clauses and stock-holding.

(b) Firms may wish to perform the work themselves for security reasons.

INTEGRATION BY CO-OPERATION

12. Objectives of co-operative arrangements. An important feature of British industry is the co-operative or collective organisation, where firms work together to forward their economic activities. They do this:

    (*a*) to combine the financial strength of several companies for large-scale investment projects;

    (*b*) to share a project's risks or its benefits;

    (*c*) to avoid unnecessary duplication of resources; or

    (*d*) to exploit an opportunity more quickly and effectively than by market or administrative means.

13. Loose co-operative arrangements. These arrangements usually take the form of cartels and consortia. Some may be established temporarily for large-scale investment projects, or for sharing the costs of sales campaigns. An example of such an arrangement was the consortium of ten building-supply merchants who joined J. H. Sankey in 1967 for an export drive in Europe and the E.E.C. Examples of more permanent co-operative arrangements can be found in the consortium of insurance companies who supply capital to finance British exporters, in the groupings of companies engaged in atomic power-station construction, and in industrial "pick-a-back" schemes, where national companies allow smaller firms, who cannot afford export departments, the use of their facilities.

14. Joint projects. Where a project requires co-operation in investment and production a company specially designed for the purpose is usually established. Several examples can be found in the capital-intensive industries, *e.g.* the United Sulphuric Acid Corporation established in 1951 by I.C.I., Fisons and other companies to manufacture sulphuric acid from domestic resources in an attempt to reduce their dependence on foreign supplies.

15. Trade associations. There are more than 1,500 regional and national trade associations representing employers. They are organised on a single product, process and industry basis which are represented nationally by federations. Most of these federations were members of the British Employers' Confederation (B.E.C.), which was concerned with general labour matters, until 1965 when it merged with the Federation of British Industries (F.B.I.), which negotiated for industry on economic and commercial matters, and the smaller National Association of British Manufacturers (N.A.B.M.), to form a single national organisation, the Confederation of British Industry (C.B.I.).

The main aims of employers' organisations may be summarised under the following headings.

(a) The general protection and advancement of members' interests.

(b) The collection and dissemination of information on taxation, patents, raw materials, demand and other statistics useful to members.

(c) The promotion of legislation favourable to the interest of members.

(d) The standardisation of contracts for the trade.

(e) The organisation of trade fairs.

(f) Negotiation with the Government.

(g) Negotiation with trade unions.

(h) Formulation of price and output policies.

PROGRESS TEST 3

1. Explain the term "integration of economic activities" and the possible ways this integration may be accomplished. (1)

2. Discuss the possible motives of a firm which decides to expand its activities by horizontal integration. (2)

3. Discuss the possible motives of a firm which decides to expand its activities by vertical integration. (3–4)

4. Discuss the possible motives of a firm which decides to expand its activities by lateral integration. (5–6)

5. "A manufacturer's attitude towards vertical integration or disintegration depends on the present and expected state of the market." Discuss this statement. (7–9)

6. A manufacturer of limited resources asks your advice as to whether he should specialise in production or use them to integrate vertically. What is your advice? (8)

7. Discuss the various factors which may prevent firms from exploiting the maximum economies of large-scale standardisation although they may be technically feasible. (9)

8. Explain why manufacturers use the market mechanism to integrate their economic activities. Illustrate your answer with two industries which are characterised by "market integration." (10)

9. Discuss the advantages and disadvantages of "integration by the market mechanism." (10–11)

10. Discuss the possible ways in which firms may co-operate to integrate their economic activities. For what reasons is this co-operative arrangement preferable to administrative and market solutions? (12–15)

11. Discuss the nature and purpose of trade associations. (15)

CHAPTER IV

INDUSTRIAL CONCENTRATION

NATURE OF INDUSTRIAL CONCENTRATION

1. Evidence of concentration. Concentration is indicated by the concentration ratio. This measures the percentage share of output or of employees in one industry accounted for by the biggest firms, usually three.

The following evidence suggests that concentration has steadily increased in British industry:

(a) There have been several studies to measure the extent of concentration in particular industries. These include the following works:

(i) Leak and Maizels, *The Structure of British Industry* (Journal of the Royal Statistical Society, 1945). Leak and Maizels used the 1935 Census of Production figures to calculate the extent to which output was concentrated in the hands of the three biggest firms in a number of industries. They also compared these concentration ratios (C.R.) with those for similar American industries and discovered that the patterns were alike. Also size of industry and degree of concentration in both countries generally varied inversely and the highest and lowest C.R. values were in similar industries.

(ii) Little and Evely, *Concentration in British Industry* (C.U.P., 1960). This book compared industrial concentration ratios for 1935 and 1951. This showed that while a number of industries were not directly comparable because technological changes and diversification had altered their character, concentration had increased in those industries highly concentrated in 1935. However, there was little evidence to suggest that concentration had increased throughout British industry generally.

(iii) Armstrong and Silverston, *Size of Plant, Size of Enterprise and Concentration in British Manufacturing Industry, 1935-58* (Journal of the Royal Statistical Society, 1965). The authors concluded that in terms of employment, the average size of the largest plants had increased since 1935 and in 1958 accounted for a higher proportion of total employment in nearly all manufacturing trades.

31

(b) Table III indicates that although small enterprises are still responsible for a large proportion of total employment, large enterprises have increased in number and are responsible for a larger share of total employment in manufacturing industries.

TABLE III. THE STRUCTURE OF BRITISH MANUFACTURING INDUSTRY

Number employed by enterprise	Number of enterprises		Share of employment (%)	
	1935	1958	1935	1958
1–499	—	—	50·5	35·9
500–1,999	1,549	1,481	18·0	18·3
2,000–9,999	358	395	17·8	21·0
10,000–49,000	50	66	11·9	17·5
50,000 and over	2	8	1·8	7·3

(c) A Board of Trade survey based on quoted companies with more than £0·5m of net assets at 1961 revealed that the number of such companies fell from 1,312 in 1961 to 908 in 1968, a reduction of 31 per cent. This reflected merger activity. Furthermore, concentration had proceeded in terms of net assets.

In 1961, the largest 28 companies accounted for 39 per cent of net assets.

In 1968, the largest 28 companies accounted for 50 per cent of net assets.

2. Factors causing concentration.

(a) Industry has moved towards more capital-intensive production methods, a process which has consolidated the position of large firms in industry. Smaller firms find such methods an obstacle to growth, while newcomers find them an effective barrier to entry.

(b) State activity has contributed as follows:

(i) Direct participation in developing certain industries, e.g. aircraft.

(ii) Financial assistance in "rationalisation schemes", e.g. cotton and shipbuilding.

(iii) High import tariffs of the 1930s insulated British industry from overseas competition. Consequently several giant foreign companies located factories in the U.K., e.g. Proctor & Gamble.

(*iv*) Nationalisation Acts.

(*v*) The Industrial Reorganisation Corporation facilitated amalgamations both directly (*e.g.* G.E.C. and A.E.I.) and indirectly through the "educational effect" of making industry more aware of the advantages of amalgamations.

(*c*) Changes in the pattern of demand, as follows:

(*i*) In a stagnant, declining industry, only the strongest firms survive.

(*ii*) Innovators may secure a larger share of an expanding market despite the tendency of new firms to reduce concentration.

(*iii*) Successful advertising and sales promotion, *e.g.* detergent and petrol "giants."

(*d*) Major technological changes or technical improvements may influence the degree of concentration within a trade and certainly the innovator's share of the market, *e.g.* Pilkington's flow-glass technique and Wilkinson's introduction of the stainless-steel razor blade.

(*e*) Industry's attitudes towards mergers and take-overs.

(*f*) The optimum technical size of firms may have increased.

(*g*) Highly concentrated industries may have grown more rapidly than the rest.

(*h*) Restrictive practice legislation may have encouraged mergers and concentration as an alternative to collusion.

3. International comparisons of concentration. An authoritative source of information is the Fortune Directory of the 200 largest industrial companies outside the U.S.A., which is published annually. Amongst other things it indicates their nationalities and their industrial diversification (*see* Table IV).

TABLE IV. INDUSTRIAL CONCENTRATION (BY COUNTRY)

	Number of companies ranked 1–200				*Industrial spread*	
	1965	*1966*	*1967*	*1973*	*1967*	*1973*
Britain	57	58	55	38	38	31
Canada	14	12	11	7	12	7
France	23	23	23	22	17	22
Germany	30	26	25	30	15	17
Italy	8	7	8	5	14	14
Japan	34	38	43	54	24	24

One possible interpretation of these figures is that, except for the combined food, drink and tobacco industries, in which Britain has fourteen companies specialising (more than all the other countries combined), her industry is generally diffused, especially when compared with the limited industrial spread of other industrial nations. Japan and Germany both have particularly large concentrations in various engineering-, electrical- and chemical-based sectors.

4. Implications.

(a) Diversification militates against economies of scale. Industrial concentrations, on the other hand, help to produce such benefits.

(b) However, a diffused economy is less susceptible to structural change and its consequences, e.g. structural unemployment.

(c) The growth rates of those sectors in which Britain is to a degree concentrated compare unfavourably with the technically advanced industries in which her competitors specialise. The poor performance of these highly concentrated industries naturally affects the rate of overall economic growth. This is shown by comparing the percentage annual increase in sales, as follows:

	1966	1967	1973
Food products	5·1	6·5	24·2
Electrical equipment	12·2	13·6	31·6
Automobiles	16·9	9·6	30·9
Chemicals	14·7	9·3	43·6

5. Advantages of rationalisation.

(a) It is claimed that enlarged corporate groups will yield economies, as follows:

(i) They may benefit from synergic advantages, with economies in management, finance, purchasing, marketing, design and, in particular, economies resulting from the use of modern plant for long production runs. Lower unit costs should improve competitiveness, which is especially important if Britain is to secure a permanent equilibrium in its balance of trade. The limited size of the domestic market, which may be less than the minimum optimal level of production of modern large-scale manufacturing plant, further underlines the need for success in international markets.

(*ii*) Corporate groups may more easily afford the R. & D. funds which are vital in technology-intensive industries. This is borne out by evidence from the U.S.A. and Britain where a handful of giant firms are responsible for the bulk of private R. & D. expenditure.

(*iii*) They can better afford to exploit discoveries.

(*iv*) There are savings in scarce R. & D. resources, as duplication of competitive research is avoided.

(*v*) There are savings of scarce factors of production as wasteful competition is avoided. Stacey (see *Mergers in Modern Britain*, Hutchinson, 1966) stated that at one time in the U.K. there were 169 manufacturers of electric fires producing 1,113 different models, an average of seven models per manufacturer with annual sales of only £1,211 each! Fortunately the situation has since improved.

(*b*) Concentration in industry centralises decision-making and thereby facilitates Government planning and control of the economy.

6. Take-over and merger activity. The estimated values of mergers and take-overs in the U.K. between 1966 and 1972 were as follows:

	Manufacturing industries (£m)	*Manufacturing, commercial financial companies* (£m)
1966	443	—
1967	756	—
1968	1,666	—
1969	722	1396
1970	674	1,406
1971	372	1,165
1972	—	2,938

The increase in merger and take-over activity may be attributed to the following factors:

(*a*) The role of the Industrial Reorganisation Corporation 1965–70.

(*i*) The I.R.C. actively encouraged mergers.

(*ii*) It had an "educational effect," in that it increased industry's awareness of the advantages of mergers.

(*b*) The merger and take-over boom of 1968–9 affected the attitude of potential bidders and the underlying sentiment of the market (*i.e.* one bid generated others).

(*c*) Companies may find that comparable returns can be obtained by buying up competitors or by acquiring diversification interests as against investments in new projects.

(*d*) Asset-stripping. An increasing number of companies have been acquired by asset-strippers who implement reorganisation and rationalisation schemes and then dispose of surplus or undervalued assets.

(*e*) Underlying expansive and defensive motives.

THE REGULATION OF TAKE-OVER ACTIVITY

7. Criticism of take-over activity. Increased take-over activity in the 1950s and the development of questionable tactics revealed the inadequacy of the financial authorities to control events. The chief criticisms were as follows:

(*a*) The shareholders of offeree companies were not always kept fully informed, so as to enable them to make an independent judgment.

(*b*) Occasionally there were leakages of information regarding imminent bids which unsettled the market for the company's shares.

(*c*) Some defensive tactics were of doubtful merit and not always in the interest of shareholders and employees.

8. The Take-over Code 1959. As a result of criticism, a City working party consisting of representatives from the Issuing Houses Association, the Acceptance Houses Committee, the Association of Investment Trusts, the British Insurance Association, the Committee of London Clearing Banks and the Stock Exchange endeavoured to regularise the methods of take-over activity. They established the Notes on Amalgamations of British Businesses, or the "Queensberry Rules."

9. Revised Notes 1963. After unanticipated developments in take-over activity the Revised Notes on Company Amalgamation brought the rules up to date. However, this Code proved ineffectual for the following reasons:

(*a*) The A.I.T., B.I.A. and other institutions whose financial strength suggested that they commanded a considerable influence in the market were seldom prepared to intervene when the code was broken.

(*b*) The Stock Exchange rarely suspended quotations.

(*c*) Some merchant banks apparently took advantage of the Code's loose wording, for the benefit of clients.

(*d*) The Code was breached in 1966 when Philips bought control of Pye through friendly institutions. Because official action was not forthcoming this set an example for institutions who bought shares while take-over bids were in progress in order to sell them at a profit. In 1967 the take-over battle for Metal Industries brought matters to a head. A merchant bank bought sufficient shares to give Aberdare Holdings control of the share capital of Metal Industries. However, Metal Industries reacted by successfully issuing enough new shares to Thorn Electrical to give it control of the enlarged share capital. The result was renewed demands for the revision of the "Queensberry Rules" and for a stronger, more comprehensive code. The panel was then reconvened, with representatives of the C.B.I. for the first time attending.

10. Revised Code 1968. This Revised Code closed the breaches made since 1963. However, it was again backed only by moral sanctions, although it was hoped that the spirit of the Code, as well as the precise wording and the authoritative rulings on interpretation by a new Panel on Take-overs, would be observed.

11. A summary of the Code. The Code's ten principles were embodied in thirty-five rules. The basic idea behind the Code was that all parties concerned in a take-over deal should consider the interests of shareholders. They should not discriminate between shareholders nor do anything to frustrate them from making a choice, and should treat the information in documents sent to shareholders with the same probity which prospectuses demand.

The thirty-five rules may be summarised as follows:

(*a*) An offer must be made to the board as a whole on behalf of an identified principal.

(*b*) Shareholders must be informed at once.

(*c*) Secrecy must be observed before any announcement is made.

(*d*) The offeror must be identified and his holding in the offeree given.

(*e*) The board must justify its motives for rejecting a bid.

(*f*) Documents sent to shareholders must be treated with the greatest care.

(*g*) Trading and profit projections must be substantiated and confirmed by a financial adviser.

(*h*) Documents must be forwarded to the panel.

(*i*) A formal offer cannot be made unconditional without at least a 50 per cent acceptance.

(*j*) An offer is made for twenty-one days and then the offeror must state his intentions and his holdings.

(*k*) The Stock Exchange may suspend quotations if these are not forthcoming.

(*l*) Partial bids are generally undesirable but when necessary they should be made *pro rata* to each shareholder.

(*m*) Separate offers must be made for different classes of share.

(*n*) No inside dealings are permitted between the approach and the offer announcement.

(*o*) Shareholders who accept the bid price may receive further payment if the offeror or associates buy shares above the bid price.

(*p*) The board anticipating or faced with a bid must not change the company's assets or share structure without a general meeting.

12. Effectiveness of the Code. The main disadvantage of the City Code remained: it was a voluntary set of rules administered by a Panel possessing inadequate disciplinary powers. This was shown in the following cases:

(*a*) It appeared reluctant to censure offenders and where this was done it was seemingly without effect.

(*b*) It might be inequitable to suspend a broking house which acts on instructions from merchant banks.

(*c*) Suspension of an institution for a single breach of the Code might be too severe.

(*d*) Suspension of quotation would hit the individual shareholders whom the panel was designed to protect.

(*e*) Foreign companies could not be disciplined.

To the year ended March 1969, the Panel dealt with issues arising from eighty bids. On only five occasions did it make any public announcements and it issued public criticism only twice: once of Courtauld's offer for International Paints and once of the merchant bank's handling of American Tobacco's bid for Gallaher. Allegations of breaches within months of the Revised Code's promulgation and dissatisfaction with the Panel's indecisiveness led to demands for a new regulatory body, perhaps an equivalent of the American Securities and Exchange Commission. These unsatisfactory experiences certainly brought the prospect of such a commission being created in England closer than ever before.

13. Take-over Panel 1969. An attempt was made to overcome the Panel's problem of sanctions regarding its rulings on the revised code. The Panel was supported by the Board of Trade, the Stock Exchange and the I.H.A. It still had no powers of punitive sanction, but reported on offences to the appropriate professional body, who might suspend or expel members. Similarly the Board of Trade, acting under the 1958 Act, might suspend a licensed or exempted dealer in securities and the Stock Exchange might suspend dealings in a company's shares if asked by the Panel. Finally, the Bank of England could exercise its authority over non-resident bidders through exchange-control regulations.

The Revised Code, published in April 1969, introduced a new procedure for profit forecasts in bids. Forecasts were to be prepared by the company's accountants and its advisers (if any) and published in the offer document. In addition, there were a number of alterations in wording, for clarification or emphasis.

The Panel made a highly promising start when in the Pergamon–Leasco affair (1969) it obtained a suspension in dealings of Pergamon shares, carried out a thorough investigation and requested an enquiry by the Board of Trade, authorised, according to Press reports, by the *Companies Act* 1948 (165 (B)3), on account of the fact "that its members have not been given all the information with respect to the affairs which they might reasonably expect."

In March 1974, the Panel was again subject to criticism when having issued a statement "the City Panel considers that a change in economic, industrial or political circumstances would not normally justify the withdrawal of an announced offer," it reversed its rulings two months later under pressure in three take-overs, saying that companies need not go through with their bids.

However in July 1974 it overcame such criticism and scored perhaps its greatest triumph in showing it was prepared to use sanctions, when in the case of the Ashbourne take-over it stated "it had no alternative but to recommend that the facilities of the securities market should be withheld from the consortium companies and their respective groups until such time as the (Panel's) statement of July 23rd had been complied with" (*i.e.* to reduce its voting powers on the Ashbourne board).

14. Regulatory powers of the U.K. system. In order to afford adequate protection for investors, there is:

(*a*) *Company law.* Companies Acts appear about every twenty years as a result of investigations by Royal Commissions or Committees that recommend legislation to bring current law into line with best accounting practice and with developments in commerce and industry and to plug loopholes in current legislation.

    (*i*) Shareholders and debenture holders are provided with financial details prescribed by the Acts in the company's annual reports which are subject to independent audit.
    (*ii*) Prospective shareholders are similarly supplied with financial information signed by the auditor or independent accountant in all company prospectuses and similar documents.

(*b*) *Prevention of Fraud (Investments) Act 1958.* This requires dealings of securities to be handled by dealers licensed by the Department of Trade. Furthermore, this Act provides the Department with control over unit trusts' operations.
(*c*) *Protection of Depositors Act 1963.* This regulates advertisements and provides for publication of audited accounts for depositors.
(*d*) *The Stock Exchange.* The Stock Exchange requires compliance with its rules on disclosure as a condition for quotation.
(*e*) *The City Panel on Take-overs and Mergers.*
(*f*) *The Bank of England* has powers over banks under the *Nationalisation Act* 1946.
(*g*) *The Treasury and Bank of England* have powers over foreign exchange transactions and therefore take-overs involving foreign companies.
(*h*) *The Department of Trade* has wide powers to investigate any company's affairs, usually by appointing inspectors.
(*i*) *The fraud squad* has expertise in investigating company frauds.

15. Regulatory powers of the U.S. system. The Securities Exchange Commission (S.E.C.) was set up in 1934, empowered by the *Securities Act* 1933 and *Securities Exchange Act* 1934 to "protect the interests of the public and investors against malpractices in the securities and financial markets."

The S.E.C. members, backed by a large permanent staff, are appointed by the President and exercise executive, judicial and legislative powers to police the securities and financial markets. Clearly, their powers are far-reaching.

(a) All companies selling new securities, or whose securities are publicly traded, must file registration documents and periodic reports disclosing financial and trading details demanded by the Securities Acts.

(b) Financial statements certified by independent public accountants that they conform to the accepted professional accounting standards are reviewed by the S.E.C.

(c) To improve disclosure, the S.E.C. is empowered to formulate rules stipulating the content and basis of valuation of data in financial statements and procedures for their presentation. In summary, the requirements of the American system are not radically different from those demanded by British Companies Acts.

(d) It can act instantly:

(i) To make rules that apply to everyone including private individuals.

(ii) To hold investigations with judicial powers of subpoena of individuals and documents.

(iii) To threaten and institute civil and criminal proceedings.

(iv) To suspend quotations and suspend dealers.

Clearly, the American statutory system is in direct contrast with the self-regulatory system of the U.K. and it is a subject of endless debate whether a similar agency with executive, judicial and legislative powers should be established in the U.K. to police the financial markets.

16. An S.E.C. for the U.K.? The S.E.C. cannot be effectively transplanted into the U.K. financial system. Indeed, it is unique to the American system where some fifty varied systems of state laws and a Federal legal system, numerous stock exchanges and over-the-counter dealings operate. In addition to the geographical, legal and administrative problems were the excesses, abuses and trauma of the free-for-all system that culminated in the Wall Street crash: it is certainly not surprising that America should adopt a statutory system which concentrates on the prevention of fraud and proper disclosure.

It is argued that the U.K. already possesses adequate regulatory powers (*see* **14**). The main strength of the Panel that supervises the U.K. system is its flexibility in operation: rules can be framed to meet changing circumstances and practice notes amended in the light of the Panel's directives. However, the Panel still lacks legal sanctions. Certainly the threat of expulsion of offenders by the professional bodies and the loss of the offender's licence may be sufficient to ensure that professionals obey the spirit of the Code, but there appears to be little the Panel can do when directors ignore its directives or even challenge its authority.

MONOPOLY LEGISLATION

17. Background to legislation. The United kingdom was a free-trading nation prior to 1931 but with the spread of "economic nationalism" in the depression, it was forced to follow the rest of the world and impose tariffs to safeguard employment levels. This transformed the economy into a highly protective one, and in this defensive environment restrictive agreements and monopolies appeared. After the war, however, Government attitudes towards monopolies hardened for the following reasons:

(*a*) Public attention was focused on the "harmful abuses of monopoly power."

(*b*) The Government had restructured industry through its rationalisation schemes in the 1930s and redirected it between 1939 and 1945. It reconsidered Britain's role in the post-war period and realised that an offensive attitude was needed to succeed in developing overseas trade. Consequently the Government took positive action to make British industry more competitive.

18. Monopoly powers. The dangers inherent in monopoly power may be summarised under the following headings:

(*a*) The exploitation of customers (in the form of higher prices) to earn excessive profits.

(*b*) Unfair competition to prevent competitors from entering the industry.

(*c*) The suppression of innovation.

(*d*) Reduction in choice.

19. The Monopolies Commission 1948. The Monopolies Commission was established to investigate and report on matters referred to it by the Board of Trade, *i.e.* to find out whether a firm or group responsible for supplying, processing or buying more than one-third of an industry's trade was in the national interest. Its findings suggested that this was best served when competition is encouraged. Occasionally, however, the Commission allowed oligopoly situations to develop to balance the power of monopoly buyers.

20. Criticisms of the Monopolies Commission. The Monopolies Commission has been criticised for the following reasons:

(*a*) It was originally too small and this delayed its operation, *e.g.* the report on the supply of electrical equipment for motor vehicles took six years to complete.

(*b*) It had no powers to implement decisions but relied on Government action. However, only in the case of dentist goods and imported timber were "cease and desist" orders made. The Government preferred to negotiate changes and hoped that "publicity will operate to cause a monopoly to change its habits."

(*c*) Because it lacked authority, its findings did not always command the respect of industry. Some industries even published pamphlets defending their actions, presumably in order to influence public opinion prior to possible Government action.

(*d*) Its findings set no judicial precedents to deter others, as each case was decided on its facts.

(*e*) It was not always completely consistent. The absence of judicial procedure has allowed Government economic policies to influence its findings.

21. An important recommendation. In 1955, the Commission published its most important report: "A Report on exclusive dealings, collective boycotts, aggregated rebates and other discriminatory trade practices." This drew on information from its investigations and from the reports of various Government departments. Its recommendation for legislation to deal with these practices was accepted and the *Restrictive Practices Act* was passed in 1956.

22. Restrictive Practices Act 1956. This changed the method of control of restrictive practices from investigation and recommendation by an administrative tribunal to control by statute law and the Restrictive Practices Court. The Monopolies Commission was left to deal with straightforward monopolies.

It was now necessary to register restrictive agreements and they were then submitted by the registrar to this High Court for decision. Careful selection of cases quickly established matters of principle, with the result that by June 1963, 1,505 of the total of 2,430 agreements registered were ended voluntarily because of the precedents set in the twenty-four cases which had been heard.

This law differed from the other law in that the burden of proof was on the defendant. There was a presumption that the agreement was against the public interest and therefore void and the onus was on him to show the court otherwise. This might be done by successfully passing through one of the seven "gateways" and the "tailpiece."

23. The seven gateways and tailpiece. The defendant had to prove to the court that the agreement produced one or more of the following beneficial effects (or "gateways"):

(a) The restriction was necessary to protect users of the goods from physical injury. This was argued unsuccessfully in the chemists', vehicle distributors' and tyre-makers' agreements because the court held that either the chance of public injury was only slight or, if it was likely, the public should be protected by Government legislation, and not by private agreements.

(b) The removal of the restriction would deny the public specific and substantial advantages. Black bolts and nuts, cement, magnets, books and other agreements were allowed as they resulted in substantial benefits by way of lower prices, standardisation, convenience and co-operation in research and development.

(c) The restriction was necessary to counter the action of a group which restricts competition.

(d) It was needed to enable parties to negotiate fair terms with monopolists. Gateways (c) and (d) are obviously linked and have not been used outside the boilermakers', transformers' and sulphuric acid cases.

(e) Its removal would cause serious and persistent unemployment. This was successfully pleaded by the yarn spinners in 1959 but the court held that this benefit was outweighed by the harm caused to the public, particularly as prices were higher than they might have been in a free market.

(*f*) Its removal would cause a loss of export revenue. This was successful in the boilermakers' case (1959).

(*g*) The restriction was needed to maintain other restrictive agreements already passed by the court. This then allowed it to support a restriction which was essential for the maintenance of another which was in the public interest.

However, it was not enough to prove one or more of these benefits to the satisfaction of the court. The court had to be satisfied that the benefits resulting from the restriction on balance outweighed the detriment its operation might cause in other respects (*i.e.* the "tailpiece").

Since 1968 the Board of Trade could exempt a proposed agreement from registration if the parties consulted the Board before it is made, and if:

(*a*) the project was of substantial importance to the economy;
(*b*) its object was to promote efficiency or improve capacity;
(*c*) the agreement was needed for its success; or
(*d*) on balance it was in the national interest.

24. Consequences of the Act. Punitive action was not available to the court against unsuccessful defendants (as in the United States, where individuals may be imprisoned), although parties to void agreements were unable to enforce them in the courts and might be fined for contempt of court. This would happen if they violated an order taken by the registrar to prevent parties from continuing agreements or making others to like effect. For example, in 1964 eight members of the Galvanised Tank Manufacturers' Association were fined £102,000 for breach of the 1959 decision.

In 1962 the registrar noted that when price agreements ended, parties frequently entered into "information agreements" where they sent their trade associations price lists. This effectively stifled competition, so that legislation was tightened to make "information agreements" registerable. However, manufacturers could plead in defence that such agreements did not restrict competition.

MONOPOLIES AND MERGERS

25. Monopolies and Mergers Act 1965. A Royal Commission investigating the Press in 1961 recommended public scrutiny of all future concentrations. In 1965 the *Monopolies and Mergers*

Act subjected concentrations in other fields to scrutiny in order to safeguard the "national interest." This Act empowered the Board of Trade to refer to an enlarged Monopolies Commission for investigating mergers which would create or strengthen a monopoly situation or where the total taken-over assets exceed £5m. It was also empowered under such references to hold up and dissolve mergers if recommended. For example, the Board of Trade and the Monopolies Commission allowed the acquisition of Pressed Steel by B.M.C. in 1965, although the Imperial Tobacco/Smiths Crisps and Ross Group/Associated Fisheries mergers were blocked.

The Act also strengthened Government control over monopolies. The Board of Trade became able to regulate prices, demand price lists and prohibit or impose conditions on monopolists and oligopolists.

26. Criticism of current legislation.

(*a*) Some suggest that the Restrictive Practices Court is unsuited for economic planning decisions, *e.g.* when it considers the economic effects of removing restrictions on efficiency, employment, prices and distribution patterns. It is claimed that these are best left to Government policy or to administrative bodies, which are unhindered by judicial procedure and precedent.

(*b*) Others claim that "large firms should be more accountable to the public interest." Performance should be the criterion for the continuance of registered agreements, monoploies or conglomerates, which could be judged from confidential annual reports giving details of turnover, profits, return on capital and investment. An unsatisfactory performance by industrial and international standards might then render the agreement void or prompt Government counter-action, *e.g.* reduced import duties.

(*c*) Government policy regarding references under the 1965 Act to the Monopolies Commission has been criticised as inconsistent. Consequently, the Board of Trade (now Department of Trade) published in August 1969 an explanation of the criteria it uses when exercising its discretion for referring mergers but did not attempt to formulate guide lines.

27. Criteria for referment. The Department of Trade's criteria for deciding whether to refer an agreement are as follows:

(*a*) Does the merger come within the scope of the 1956 Act?

(b) If satisfied, the Board seeks factual information on:

(i) the companies involved (*e.g.* labour force, ownership);

(ii) the industry or market (*e.g.* products, degree of competition); and

(iii) the merger proposals (*e.g.* motives, methods, implications). "The task is to identify possible detriments to the public interest, which may arise from the merger and to assess whether the expected benefits from larger scale and rationalisation are likely to outweight these detriments. The crucial questions therefore relate to the facts of the individual case." (*Merger, A Guide to Board of Trade Practice*, H.M.S.O., 1969.)

28. Broad considerations. The Board of Trade booklet mentioned above classified mergers as horizontal, vertical or conglomerate, and examined in detail a merger's possible implications for each type, as follows:

(a) A horizontal merger's possible impact in the short and long run on:

(i) market power;

(ii) efficiency;

(iii) the balance of payments; and

(iv) regional policy and redundancy.

(b) A vertical merger's possible impact on the same factors, plus:

(i) competition;

(ii) efficiency in production and distribution.

(c) A conglomerate merger's possible impact on the same factors, plus:

(i) motives;

(ii) benefits;

(iii) efficiency in the different sectors within the conglomerate's sphere of activities;

(iv) the effect on monopolies within these sectors;

(v) the effect on the industrial structure of each sector;

(vi) in addition, separate accounting information for the different sectors is required.

29. Disadvantages of system of automatic reference. The present discretionary system is preferable to a system of automatic reference since this would have the following disadvantages:

(a) Problems of definition and interpretation. For example, how are the relevant geographical and industrial markets to be defined and what is to be the precise market share or taken-over value of assets that qualify for reference?

(b) Forgoing the flexibility which discretion under the 1965 Act allows, e.g. assurances from the firms, effect on export or import trade, effect on regional development.

(c) An increased work-load for the Monopolies Commission. More delay, uncertainty and expense.

(d) Major legislation, which would overthrow the whole basis of post-war legislation.

CONGLOMERATES

30. Definition. A conglomerate is a holding company with a number of interests widely diversified throughout different industries. It is "pure" where there is little relationship between the types or sequence of activities and "less pure" where they are related in some way, e.g. where a company integrates laterally forward, converting materials into diverse end-use markets. Its interests may be spread internationally (creating an international conglomerate).

31. Doubtful value of lateral integration. The term "cult of giantism" was coined in 1968 to describe the unprecedented level of take-over and merger activity, which in value terms amounted to £2,312m, of which some two-thirds was for concentration and one-third for diversification purposes. While many could appreciate the advantages of large-scale organisations which concentration might bring, the merits of diversification were less apparent. The increasing number of amalgamations of this latter nature, coupled with doubts about their economic value, placed the conglomerate at the centre of a controversy.

In January 1969, the Board of Trade referred two proposed conglomerate mergers, Unilever/Allied Breweries and Rank/De la Rue, to the Monopolies Commission to examine the issues involved. The Commission allowed the former to proceed but concluded that the latter would operate against the public interest and therefore refused to allow it. Its findings did not in fact clarify official policy on mergers and as a result of continuing uncertainty, the Board of Trade issued a guide to Board of Trade practice.

The Board of Trade surveys on which Table V is based indicated that between 1964 and 1968, the annual number of acquisitions of non-quoted (and smaller) companies was halved, while that of quoted (and larger) companies doubled. Furthermore, these were increasingly financed by equity and loan

TABLE V. ANALYSIS OF ACQUISITIONS AND CONSIDERATION GIVEN
BY LARGE* COMPANIES

	1964	1965	1966	1967	1968
Number of companies acquired					
Non-quoted	868	920	727	577	458
Quoted	71	75	78	84	140
Total	939	995	805	661	598
Total consideration					
(£m)	502	507	447	781	1653
Cash	304	243	183	260	271
Shares and loans	198	264	264	521	1382
Ordinary	164	206	201	338	1145
Preference	14	10	2	8	4
Loan stock	20	48	61	175	233
Average considerations					
(£m)	0·5	0·5	0·6	1·2	2·8

* *i.e.* those companies in the Board of Trade survey with net assets exceeding £0·5m in 1964 or annual income exceeding £50,000.

"paper," especially the latter. Cash, however, dropped dramatically over this period.

32. Disadvantages of conglomerates. The chief fears and criticisms of conglomerate mergers may be summarised as follows:

(*a*) These amalgamations were proceeding at an unparalleled rate and their economic consequences were unknown. Fears were expressed that:

(*i*) conglomerates possessed potential monopoly powers which might be used to dictate to retailers, consumers and employees;

(*ii*) the increased cost and inflexibility of their administration in the enlarged organisation might outweigh other expected economic benefits. Consequently diseconomies might result.

(b) Trade unions were concerned about redundancies resulting from large-scale amalgamations.

(c) Lateral integration hindered rationalisation of industries.

(d) Competition was constrained because:

(i) risk capital was used to buy established companies and not for investment in innovation or re-equipment in the parent company's business;

(ii) subsidiaries had disproportionate economic power when they drew on the group's resources;

(iii) the group was less responsive to competition in the various industries; and

(iv) the spread of conglomerates weakened the stimulus of competition in the economy.

(e) Diversification by any group of limited resources inhibited its economic growth in any industry compared with large-scale specialisation, although some economies in overheads, finance, R. & D. and marketing were probable.

(f) A group might, however, grow in financial terms when it used its shares which have a high profit earnings ratio to buy "victim" companies with lesser profit earnings ratios. This might lead to a false appreciation of the results of the merger and an over-evaluation of the company's shares which might be used for further acquisitions.

A company growing financially is less stable than one expanding by "organic" growth.

For example, if the earnings available for ordinary dividend of two companies A and B are equal and each has an earnings per ordinary share of £0·25, and A, the offeror, has a P/E ratio of 30 : 1 and B, the offeree, a P/E of 15/1, then after a merger financed by an exchange of one of A company's share for two shares of B, total earnings of the merged company have doubled immediately and earnings per share have risen from £0·25 to £0·30 without any internal growth whatsoever.

(g) The failure of a group precipitated by an excessive debt-capital burden, coupled with a bearish market, could seriously affect investors' confidence and the supply of capital.

(h) Conglomerates gave insufficient information about their different activities. It was therefore difficult for investors to assess the real profitability of the group.

33. Advantages of conglomerates. On the other hand there are conglomerates whose performance, whether measured in terms of return on capital, innovation or market growth, is superior to many other companies. Any interest by such companies in an industry is certain to ginger up competitors, perhaps forcing them to innovate, streamline their organisation and generally improve their efficiency, in order to maintain market shares or to resist acquisition. Furthermore, their emergence is to be expected for the following reasons:

(a) Any aggressive management will seize profit opportunities which are more numerous laterally than horizontally and vertically combined.

(b) The "conglomerate umbrella" gives small companies access to specialised management skills, personnel and finance, and allows cross-fertilisation of ideas.

(c) Companies tend to diversify when they find their original business expanding too slowly.

(d) Developments in management techniques mean that increasingly larger organisations may be controlled.

(e) Integration by means of a holding company is cheaper than by complete integration.

(f) Its structure allows constituent firms a high degree of autonomy which may realise benefits of decentralisation.

(g) This suggests that large-scale redundancy is not inevitable.

PROGRESS TEST 4

1. Outline the main factors responsible for the increased concentration in British industry. (1–5)

2. What do you understand by the Take-over Panel and Code? (6–11)

3. "The City Panel lacks adequate disciplinary powers and should be replaced by the equivalent of a Securities Exchange Commission." Discuss. (12–16)

4. Explain the circumstances which brought into being the Monopoly Commission, its purpose and objects in operation. (17–18)

5. Explain the term "monopoly power." (18)

6. A manufacturer could continue with a restrictive agreement after 1956 only if he could prove its worth by passing through the "gateways" and "tailpiece." Explain. (21–23)

7. Assess the effectiveness of the *Restrictive Practices Act* 1956, and its consequences. (22–24)

8. "The *Monopolies and Mergers Act* 1965, strengthened Government control over monopolies." Comment. (25)

9. "The present system for controlling mergers in Britain is essentially a pragmatic one." Discuss. (27–29)

10. (a) What is a conglomerate?
(b) Discuss the pros and cons of conglomerate mergers. (30–33)

PART TWO

FINANCE FOR INDUSTRY

CHAPTER V

LONG-TERM FINANCE FOR INDUSTRY

THE CAPITAL MARKET

1. The capital market. Generally speaking saving (making money available, for borrowers) and investment (using money for the purchase of capital goods or equipment) are undertaken by different parties, and some mechanism is needed to co-ordinate these forces of demand and supply. This is done by the capital market through its many different specialist institutions, which act as intermediaries and channel the savings of companies and individuals to borrowers. The main institutions are as follows:

(a) Commercial banks.
(b) Merchant banks.
(c) Discount houses.
(d) Insurance companies and pension funds.
(e) Investment trusts, etc.
(f) The Stock Exchange.

2. Categories of capital. In order to examine more closely the main sources of capital, and the roles of the financial institutions, it is convenient to classify these funds under broad headings. They may be grouped according to risk, e.g. low-, medium- and high-risk capital. However, it is more satisfactory to use liquidity as the criterion. In this way, the institutions are members either of the money market or of the capital market. The former provides industry, in the broadest sense, with very short-term loans for the financing of Treasury and commercial bills of exchange. The latter is concerned with longer-term loans but will include some institutions which also operate in the money market, *e.g.* the commercial banks, whose advances contribute towards industry's working capital. The main categories of capital are as follows:

(*a*) Long-term capital (*i.e.* "permanent" share, loan capital).
(*b*) Short- and medium-term capital (*i.e.* working or circulating capital).

Two other types of highly specialised capital merit special attention. They are:

(*c*) Export finance.
(*d*) Specialist finance.

THE NEW ISSUE MARKET

3. Advantages of private companies.

(*a*) Private companies are likely to be small enough to benefit from the following factors:

(*i*) Close contact between directors, staff and employees.
(*ii*) Greater flexibility.
(*iii*) The stimulus of members' self-interest.

(*b*) They possess the following privileges:

(*i*) Fewer documentary requirements compared with public companies.
(*ii*) Fewer procedural requirements.

(*c*) Control is exercised by members who can manage the company in their own interest, uninfluenced by public opinion, *i.e.* they are not in the public eye.

(*d*) They are secure from take-over bids.

(*e*) They can discount current profitability for longer-term development, which would reduce the market valuation of public companies and invite take-over bids.

4. Advantages of public companies.

(*a*) Public companies may invite the general public to subscribe capital and thereby raise more money than by private subscription.

(*b*) They may secure the advantages of quotation (*see* **5**).

(*c*) Their status lessens the impact of death duties on shareholders who may more readily sell shares to realise funds.

(*d*) Public subscription may avoid the "close company" status of the *Finance Act* 1965, and its special tax provisions.

Generally, these advantages outweigh those for private companies; hence the tendency for conversion at some stage in the development of firms.

5. Reasons for share quotation. Every year about 100 privately-owned companies seek a Stock Exchange quotation for their shares for one or more of the following reasons:

(a) Shareholders of unquoted companies may request a "flotation" which, while adding nothing to the capital resources of the company, does provide them with cash or marketable shares which may be used for a variety of purposes: the spread of investment risk, consumption, estate duty, etc.

(b) Capital commitments may outstretch net cash flow, in which case the new issues market may be the suitable source of new permanent capital or long-term loans. In addition, banks, a main source of working capital, may react more sympathetically to requests from quoted companies. On the other hand, companies wishing to reduce their dependence on bank finance, which may be withdrawn in times of severe credit squeeze, may be attracted towards the long-term finance of the new issues market.

(c) Quotation may lessen the impact and uncertainties of death duties and avoid the problem of valuation of unquoted shares.

(d) Quoted shares are readily marketable and acceptable and may be given as consideration in merger and take-over transactions.

(e) Quotation can avoid the tax disadvantages of "close" companies.

(f) Quotation seems to invest companies with a superior status. This may be important to customers, who often like to know the trading patterns and financial resources of their suppliers.

(g) The market tends to place a higher valuation on quoted companies than private investors do, and this is naturally to the benefit of shareholders.

6. Disadvantages of quotation. Against the above advantages must be set the following disadvantages:

(a) Quotation may be accomplished at a cost to some shareholders in the form of loss of control in the conduct of the business. However, it is not essential that equity should be made public, and it may be possible to raise capital by an issue of quoted loan stock instead, so that equity and control is retained, e.g. Ferranti.

(*b*) The exacting Stock Exchange requirements place greater responsibilities on the board of directors. Quotation also demands a fair distribution policy and consistent profits. Failure on the part of directors will damage the company's public standing.

(*c*) The disclosure of information for shareholders reviewing progress (*e.g.* growth prospects and circumstances which might materially affect share prices), may be useful to competitors. However, the *Companies Act* 1967 partly overcomes this objection since all limited liability companies are required to publish trading and financial details.

(*d*) Going public is expensive.

(*e*) The company is vulnerable to take-over bids.

7. Requirements for quotation. Generally speaking, a company seeking Stock Exchange quotation needs to fulfil the following conditions:

(*a*) It should be of reasonable size. The Federation of Stock Exchanges ruled that £500,000 corporate value was the minimal acceptance figure and most issuing houses are probably unwilling to put their name to an issue when corporate pre-tax profits are £50,000 or less. Radcliffe reported in 1959 that the "bar of size is rising not falling. The machinery of public issue is tending to become less and less available to the smaller industrial undertaking."

This was attributed to the increasing dependence of the market on the institutional investors, who prefer the more readily marketable securities and are reluctant to hold small amounts "because of the administrative difficulty." This virtually means large issues of high-grade securities.

Nevertheless, a company in this situation may take the following actions:

(*i*) It may exchange its unquoted shares for the shares of a quoted company by means of a "reverse take-over," although the Stock Exchange is certain to suspend quotation if the new company is materially different, until the necessary information about the new company is supplied.

(*ii*) It may merge with companies in a similar situation whose group valuation and collective pre-tax profits are sufficient for quotation.

(*b*) A sufficiently large proportion of shares must be made available to the public to create a market. Here, the Federation of Stock Exchanges states that the minimum market value for any one security for which quotation is sought should be £200,000. Furthermore it requires that some 35 per cent of an issue of equity securities and 30 per cent of fixed-interest securities should be made available to the public.

(c) The company must have a satisfactory trading record, and must be financially sound. Ideally it should have a record of profitable trading with adequate levels of fixed and working capital in relation to liabilities.

8. Types of issues. A company may make its securities available to investors by the following means:

    (a) An issue by prospectus:

        (i) a public issue by the company;
        (ii) an offer for sale; or
        (iii) an offer for sale by tender.

    (b) Placing:

        (i) a private placing;
        (ii) a Stock Exchange placing.

    (c) An introduction.
    (d) A Rights Issue.
    (e) A Bonus Issue.

All are methods whereby companies raise new capital (except the introduction and Bonus Issue) and all except the private placings by the issue of quoted securities.

9. An offer for sale. This method either permits a company to raise new capital by means of an issue of shares, or allows existing shareholders to realise their shareholdings in cash. In the former case, the issuing house buys the shares from the company and, in the latter case, from the shareholders. As principal, it offers them for sale to the public, either by offering the shares at the purchase price, charging the company a fee for the Stock Exchange quotation and administrative services, or by re-selling them at a higher price, and making a profit on the transaction, or it does both.

10. Preliminary work for an issue. The fifty-six members of the Issuing Houses Association play an important role in the new issues market, acting as intermediaries between companies seeking long-term capital and those who are prepared to supply it by investing. Companies desiring quotations seek the sponsorship of a specialist merchant bank whose high standing will inspire the confidence of investors. This is essential for a successful issue. However, before committing its name to the venture, the bank will naturally examine the company very carefully, its memorandum and articles of association, trading record, directors and management, shareholders and its true financial position.

If satisfied, it then works out a programme dealing with the following points:

    (*a*) Capital reorganisation schemes.
    (*b*) The size of the issue.
    (*c*) The timing of the issue.
    (*d*) Classes of securities, their terms and the estimated issue prices.

Once these proposals are agreed, then a detailed programme is planned for the preparation of reports by solicitors, accountants and stock brokers. These are required for the registrar of companies, the Stock Exchange, the prospectus (*see* **11**), publication and advertising.

11. Prospectus. This is the invitation to the public to apply for securities in the company. Prospectuses are probably familiar to most people, since they are widely advertised in the Press. Briefly the details they contain, which must conform to Companies Acts and Stock Exchange regulations, are:

    (*a*) The name of the company, its share capital, names of directors, bankers, solicitors, auditors, brokers and secretary, and the arrangements for application.

    (*b*) The chairman's report, which deals with the following points:

        (*i*) History and business.
        (*ii*) Management and staff.
        (*iii*) Premises.
        (*iv*) Net assets.
        (*v*) Working capital.
        (*vi*) Profits and dividends.
        (*vii*) Prospects.

    (*c*) The accountant's report, which contains the following information:

        (*i*) The company's profits (pre-tax and depreciation) for the previous ten years (five years since 1973).
        (*ii*) The company's assets and liabilities.
        (*iii*) The rates of dividends paid on each class of share for the past five years.

(*d*) General information, including the following information:

    (*i*) Directors' interests.

    (*ii*) Whether or not the company is a close company.

    (*iii*) Articles of association.

    (*iv*) Details of subsidiaries.

    (*v*) Details of the contract between the shareholders and the issuing house, and other contracts not in the ordinary course of business.

    (*vi*) Details of capital reorganisation.

12. Application and allotment. After the application lists are closed, work proceeds on allotment. If the issue is under-subscribed, then all applications can be accepted in full and the shortfall borne by the underwriters (*see* **13**). In the case of over-subscription, ballots are held or applications scaled down, usually to the advantage of smaller applicants (*see* Table VI).

TABLE VI. BASIS OF ALLOTMENT FOR SHARES IN SCOTTISH, ENGLISH AND EUROPEAN TEXTILES (APRIL 1969)

Application	*Allotment*	*Application*	*Allotment*
200– 2,000	200 ballot for shares	50,500–100,000	5,000
2,100– 5,000	200	100,500–200,000	10,000
5,500–10,000	500	200,500–300,000	15,000
10,500–25,000	1,000		
25,000–50,000	2,500	over 300,000	20,000

Letters of acceptance and allotment are posted so that they are received by the allottees before dealings commence.

13. Underwriting. For a fee, the issuing house underwrites the issue, guaranteeing a full subscription at the agreed terms. Thus the risk to the company, that adverse market conditions might endanger the issue, is removed, since any deficiency in public subscription is made good by the issuing house and its sub-underwriters (other merchant banks, insurance companies, pension funds and other institutional investors) in return for a sub-underwriting commission of about $1\frac{1}{4}$ per cent on the offer price. Thus, of the £20m Agricultural Mortgage Corporation

$9\frac{1}{2}$ per cent debenture stock 1983–6, applications were received for 7 per cent. The remaining 93 per cent were taken up by the underwriters.

In spite of this extreme case, sub-underwriters are apparently in a privileged position. If the issue is fully subscribed, they earn a commission without further obligation on their part, and if not they possess sound quoted securities which are marketable, perhaps eventually at a premium, in addition to their fee.

14. A public issue by the company. Here the company raises capital by offering shares directly to the public. The procedure is much the same as for the offer for sale outlined above. However, in this case the issuing house does not assume the role of principal and is not normally required by the issuing company to deal with advertising, allocation and allotment, although it usually arranges underwriting.

15. Offer for sale by tender. The procedure is similar to that for issuing Government Treasury bills. It has been used by a number of public utilities since 1945 and by other companies throughout the 1960s and 1970s.

The offer for sale quotes a minimum price to guide investors in tendering a price which they judge will secure for them the allotment they want. However, shares are finally allotted at a single "striking" price, which is the lowest price at which the issue is fully subscribed. Obviously, this is to the advantage of applicants who have quoted excessively high prices.

The extent to which this method has been used has varied according to the issue and the experiences of companies raising capital in this manner. When striking prices are necessarily set below the minimum offer and dealings open at a discount, the attitude of issuing houses and investors to further issues by tender is certain to be influenced. The approval of the Stock Exchange is always required.

16. Advantages of tenders.

(a) Tenders may be preferred by issuing houses in unsettled markets or where a company seeking quotation has no counterpart for comparison. By "charging what the market will bear," they are relieved of the full responsibility for pitching the terms of the issue exactly right and are spared the embarrassment of a large premium should they pitch the offer price too low in an offer for sale.

(*b*) In a buoyant market an optimistic valuation by the public will mean that vendors may get a better price for their shares. However, they should also consider that they may be driven up to levels which they cannot hold, which could jeopardise future issues.

(*c*) Tenders reduce stagging activities because the parties who tender and establish the likely striking price are generally the long-term investors.

In view of these changing conditions, tenders seem to come into vogue for short periods.

17. Stags. The difficulty of issuing successfully a large number of shares or loan stock over a short period is reduced by the activities of stags, who acquire shares for resale at a profit when dealings commence. However, they are most active when the risk of losses from unfavourable changes in market conditions is lowest and may be discouraged if the issuing house believes that permanent investors will subscribe sufficient amounts. Investors who must compete for allotment naturally wish them to be discouraged. They may be discouraged in the following ways:

(*a*) Since stagging is encouraged when part of the issue price is payable on application and the balance by calls, the issuing house can demand payment in full on application.

(*b*) Evidence of sufficient bank facilities to match total applications may be required. Alternatively all cheques may be "presented." Thus financial limitations and the threat of legal action (fraud) will prevent stags from applying for very large amounts beyond their means.

(*c*) Multiple applications, which increase their chances of reasonable allotments in ballots and drastic scaling-down arrangements, may be banned.

(*d*) Furthermore, short-term gains tax has discouraged this speculation.

(*e*) Banks are unlikely to provide facilities for these purposes in times of severe credit squeeze.

18. Private placings. Companies not requiring quotation or only limited amounts of capital may approach issuing houses with a view to private placings. Institutional clients may be more interested in the security of the investment, return and growth, rather than marketability of the securities. Alternatively, companies may place their shares or loan stock direct with interested finance houses.

19. Stock Exchange placings. The Stock Exchange may agree to a placing of securities which are likely to be of limited interest to investors. Small issues of fixed-interest securities which fall into this category are placed with institutional investors, brokers and jobbers on the Stock Exchange, from whom the general public may purchase.

20. Costs of new issues. The expenses of placings are substantially less than those for public issues and offers for sale, for the following reasons:

(a) Printing costs of limited numbers of application forms and prospectuses are lower.
(b) Bank charges for application and allotment are lower.
(c) No underwriting is required.
(d) Advertising charges are minimal.

The Stock Exchange introduction is certain to be the least costly method.

Costs vary not only between the method of issue, but according to the size of the issue. Naturally a large issue will incur higher charges than a smaller one. However, this is a source of real economies of scale, since costs do not increase in proportion to the size of the issue. Table VII shows the economies of large-scale issues.

TABLE VII. ECONOMIES OF LARGE-SCALE ISSUES

Value of offer for sale	Total cost of issue	%
£210,000	£24,000	11·4
£520,000	£30,000	5·8
£2,000,000	£90,000	4·5

21. Stock Exchange introduction. Where a company's shares are held by, say, 100 shareholders, quotation or "permission to deal" may be obtained by means of an introduction. This does not raise new capital and so does not require a prospectus, although advertisements similar to those for placings are needed. Information is also required by the Shares and Loans Department of the Stock Exchange, as for a quotation of shares by public issue.

22. Rights Issue. When raising new capital, companies very commonly give existing shareholders an opportunity to subscribe for shares at a preferential price in proportion to their existing holdings. For instance, in a "one for two" issue, a shareholder with 200 shares is entitled to a further 100.

23. Valuation of the rights. Assuming the information contained in 22 and that the market price of the share is currently £1·00 and the rights issue is made at 75p per share, then the value of rights is found by formula:

$$\frac{\text{Market price} - \text{Issue price of new shares}}{\text{No. of shares required for a right to the new share}}$$

$$= \frac{100p - 75p}{2 + 1}$$

$$= \frac{25p}{2 + 1}$$

$$= 8·3p$$

Thus an investor wishing to acquire shares in this company can either buy in the market at £1·00 or buy the rights of 12·5p per existing share and then subscribe at the issuing price of 75p.

24. Advantages to the company.

    (a) A Rights Issue is relatively cheap and simple.
    (b) It is usually successful.
    (c) It provides publicity.
    (d) Additional shares may create a more active market.

25. Disadvantages to the company.

    (a) The company may forgo higher premiums obtainable in the open market.
    (b) It must increase profits proportionally to maintain the dividend rate and share prices.
    (c) The extra supplies may in the short term depress the share price.
    (d) A Rights Issue may raise the problem of fractions.

26. Advantages to shareholders.

(a) They buy shares at a preferential price if Rights are taken up.

(b) They can sell Rights to third parties. Either way no loss is incurred. (Details of current Right offers are published daily in *The Financial Times*.)

(c) They may maintain their relative shareholding and control position.

(d) They can make up their mind whether to sell or accept on the basis of their past experience with the company.

(e) The lower share price may make them more marketable.

27. Disadvantages to shareholders.

(a) Those who fail to sell Rights or accept will suffer losses from lower share prices. For example:

<pre>
                    Already issued:
100,000 ordinary shares (market value £1) = £100,000
                    Rights Issue:
100,000 ordinary shares issued at 80p   =   £80,000
                    Total capital: ————————
200,000 ordinary shares   = £180,000
                                              £180,000
       1 ordinary share   = ————————
                                               200,000
</pre>

= 90p per share, compared with the original £1.

Shareholders who accept lose 10p per share on those held but gain 10p on new shares.

(b) They may lack funds.

(c) They face increased risks arising from their increased shareholding. Diversification may be preferable.

(d) They may incur capital gains liability on the sale of Rights.

28. Bonus Issues. A Bonus Issue does not raise fresh capital but represents a capitalisation of accumulated reserves, which

EXAMPLE: X Co. *balance sheets and bonus issues of shares*

Before bonus issue		*After bonus issue*
Authorised share capital	£250,000	£250,000
Issued share capital	50,000	200,000
Capital reserves	200,000	50,000
Revenue reserve	25,000	25,000
Shareholders' funds	275,000	275,000
Represented by:		
Assets	275,000	275,000

brings nominal capital into line with the value of capital employed.

Thus the bonus issue of 3 : 1 has not raised any additional funds; it has merely transferred £150,000 from capital reserve into shares. This is clearly seen by examination of the total shareholders' funds figure, which is unchanged at £275,000.

Assuming that the market price was £4·00 prior to issue, then the new price will be as follows:

$$\text{New share price} = \text{Market price} \times \frac{\text{Original no. of shares}}{\text{New no. of shares}}$$

$$= 400\text{p} \qquad \times \frac{50,000}{200,000}$$

$$= \underline{£1·00}$$

29. Share split. A split or subdivision of shares, like a bonus issue, does not provide the shareholder with any direct monetary advantage, for although he holds more shares, the average price falls (the extent depending on market sentiment) and total dividends are unlikely to change since corporate earning power is unchanged. Nevertheless, the smaller valuation tends to make them slightly more attractive to investors and therefore more marketable. Shareholders' relative voting powers are also unchanged.

30. Timing the issue. There is no set of rules for the timing of issues, a process which is so important for success. To companies this means the best possible price for their shares and the lowest fixed-interest charges on long-term loans.

They have to rely to a large extent on the judgment of the issuing house which can best interpret market trends. There are a multitude of factors which may influence the climate of the market and the success or otherwise of an issue. An issuing house will consider the following factors, in timing an issue:

    (a) The general level of prices of securities.
    (b) The general market trends and trade expectations.
    (c) Political and international crises.
    (d) Budgets.
    (e) Taxation changes and company legislation.

TABLE VIII. CAPITAL ISSUES BY QUOTED PUBLIC COMPANIES
ANALYSED BY METHOD OF ISSUE (£m)

	1968	1969	1970	1971	1972	1973
Public issues and offers						
for sale	30·6	112·3	28·6	102·3	293·7	93·3
Tenders	10·2	9·9	37·2	34·3	24·4	8·0
Placings	178·4	139·3	140·4	253·4	323·3	89·6
Issues to shareholders:						
(a) Ordinary shares	362·4	169·4	62·7	169·9	359·1	71·0
(b) Preference and						
loan capital	107·6	197·0	92·6	66·1	116·7	26·5

Table VIII indicates the relative importance of the main methods employed in the capital market to raise new finance by the issue of quoted securities. Note the insignificance of tenders in comparison with placings, Rights Issues and offers for sale and the decline in total capital issue in 1973.

ISSUING HOUSES

31. Types of issuing house. There are basically three types of issuing house.

    (a) *The merchant bank.* Originally specialising in merchanting business, these banks today deal in accepting bills of exchange and advising companies on share issues, *e.g.* Hill Samuel.

    (b) *The finance house.* These houses have taken on issuing house work in addition to their traditional role of financing companies themselves, *e.g.* Industrial and Commercial Finance Corporation.

(c) *The clearing banks.* In recent years the large joint stock banks have entered into the new issue business.

32. Role of the issuing house.

In **9** we saw that the issuing house either acts as principal or as agent to the company making the issue of securities. This distinction is essentially a legal one and does not affect their role as issuing house. Their functions are summarised as follows:

(a) They advise companies on the best method of issue, and

(b) what type of security to issue, and

(c) the issue price.

(d) They have a responsibility to the investing public. Consequently they make detailed investigations not only to meet the demanding legal and accounting requirements, but to guarantee as far as is possible the claims made in the prospectus and credentials, reputation and integrity of all persons concerned with the issue to avoid exploitation of the public. These investigations are carried out thoroughly (for the reputation of the issuing house is also involved) and will involve checks by issuing house staff who visit the company's premises to interview staff, agencies and possibly police enquiries.

(e) They devise the flotation timetable and act as co-ordinator of the many specialists engaged in the programme.

33. Expenses incurred in the flotation.

A typical extract from a prospectus to illustrate the various fees and expenses involved in an Offer for Sale is as follows:

"X Merchant Bankers has contracted to purchase 800,000 ordinary shares of 25p each at a price of 124p per share and to offer such shares for sale to the public [NOTE: at a price of 125p]. The company will pay the costs and expenses of and incidental to the increase in and reorganisation of the share capital and the application for quotation for and permission to deal in the issued Ordinary Shares, its accountancy and legal expenses, the stamp duty on the increase in the share capital, the cost of printing, advertising and circulating their Offer for Sale, the fees and expenses of the receiving bankers and the Registrars and a fee to X Merchant Bankers. The aggregate costs and expenses payable by the company in respect of the Offer for Sale are estimated to amount to £45,000. X Merchant Bankers will pay their own legal expenses, a fee to the Brokers and an underwriting commission of $1\frac{1}{4}$ per cent on the offer of each share."

34. Hypothetical timetable for a flotation of shares

(*i.e.*, original shareholders sell shares to the Issuing House).
Weeks
Commencing:

Monday 3rd June	1. Directors of company seeking a flotation of shares by Offer for Sale meet with Issuing House to decide on strategy and timing.
Monday 15th July	1. Solicitors, Brokers, Reporting Accountants appointed and instructed by Issuing House. 2. Solicitors begin drafting new Memorandum and Articles of Association to conform to the Stock Exchange Requirements.
Monday 22nd July	1. Meeting with company's joint stock bank or other organisation appointed Receiving Bankers. 2. Issuing House receives details of company's directors, management and staff. 3. Decision *re* extent of advertising of Prospectus in newspapers. 4. Application to Stock Exchange to make Offer for Sale of, say, 20 per cent of share capital.
Monday 29th July	1. Meetings of Directors, Reporting Accountants, Brokers, Solicitors, Issuing House to discuss the draft of the Accountants' full report. 2. Meetings to discuss narrative sections of the Prospectus, *i.e.* General and Legal sections. 3. Draft sent to printers.
Monday 5th August	1. All parties meet to discuss the first proof of the Prospectus. 2. Draft of Accountant's report for inclusion in Offer for Sale discussed. 3. Memorandum and Articles of Association proofed and discussed. 4. Second proof of Offer for Sale submitted to the Stock Exchange for comment.
Monday 12th August	1. Application form, letters of Allotment and letters of Acceptance proofed.

Weeks Commencing:

	2. Service agreements between company and executives completed and executed.
	3. Powers of Attorney obtained from each director authorising signature of issue documents on his behalf.
Monday 19th August	1. Full meetings to discuss second proof of Prospectus and Stock Exchange comment and Accountants prepare draft of current year's profit forecast and projection for following year.
Monday 2nd September	1. Accountants finalise current and following year's profit projections.
	2. Full meetings to consider third proof of Prospectus.
Monday 9th September	1. Book advertising space.
	2. Draft of Purchase Agreement between the Issuing House and the Shareholders presented.
	3. All necessary consents received, *i.e.* from Stock Exchange, Bank of England *re* exchange control and timing, and Bankers.
	4. Certificates of borrowings and facilities supplied by bank.
	5. Statement of company's adequacy of working capital and profits prepared by Auditors.
	6. Final proofs of all documents circulated to all parties.
Monday 16th September	1. Finalise all documents and fix the offer price of the shares for printing.
	2. Agree notes for City Editors for preliminary press release and announcement to employees.
	3. Bulk orders to printers.
	4. Extraordinary General Meeting of company to increase capital and adopt new Articles of Association.
	5. Board meeting to:
	(*a*) Capitalise reserves and allot shares.
	(*b*) Approve Offer for Sale.
	6. Purchase Agreement signed.

Weeks Commencing:

	7. Prospectus filed with Registrar of Companies.
	8. Printers commence delivery of documents.
	9. Brokers send underwriting letters to sub-underwriters.
	10. Press announcement and announcement to employees released.
Monday 23rd September	1. Offer for Sale published in newspapers.
	2. Submit documents to Quotations Dept. of Stock Exchange to support application for quotation.
Wednesday 25th September	1. Quotation granted by Stock Exchange.
Thursday 26th September	1. Application List opens and closes.
	2. Cheques paid in.
	3. If over-subscribed Issuing House decides on methods of allotment.
	4. If under-subscribed Broker informs underwriters of the short-fall and their commitments.
	5. Press announcement giving result of the Offer and basis of allotment.
Friday 4th October	1. The Issuing House posts Letters of Allotment.
Monday 7th October	1. Dealings commence.
	2. Receiving bank pays Issuing House the proceeds of the offer.
Monday 14th October	Last day for share splitting.
Wednesday 16th October	Last day for renunciation.
Monday 11th November	Share certificates available.

Responsibility for documents. There may be as many as fifty documents involved in an offer for sale issue. Table IX summarises the main documents and letters needed for the typical programme outlined above and indicates the responsibility of the parties engaged in the flotation.

TABLE IX. WHO IS RESPONSIBLE FOR FLOTATION DOCUMENTS

Letter/Document	Responsibility Company	Solicitors	Issuing House	Accountants	Registrars
Bank of England Timing Consent			×		
Surtax clearance				×	
Current year's accounts	×			×	
Service agreements		×			
Notice of E.G.M.		×			
Print of Resolutions		×			
New Memorandum and Articles		×	×		
Powers of Attorney		×			
Copies of contracts listed in Prospectus		×			
Accountants' Report				×	
Accountants' Statement of Adjustments				×	
Accountants' Consent				×	
Banks letter of consent	×				
Stock Exchange forms			×		
Bank certificates re company borrowings	×			×	
Statement of working capital	×			×	
Profit forecast	×			×	
Share Certificates					×
Share purchase agreement		×	×		
Offer for Sale			×		
Application forms			×		
Letter of Acceptance			×		
Press announcements			×		
Underwriting letters			×		
Statement re working capital for Stock Exchange			×		
Printed copies of Accountants' Report			×		
Authorisation of adverts			×		
Order of printing			×		
Distribution list			×		
Letter to Stock Exchange re splitting			×		
Letter of regret			×		

PROGRESS TEST 5

1. Compare and contrast the advantages of private and public companies. **(1–4)**

2. For what reasons do companies seek quotation? **(5)**

3. What are the prerequisites for a company seeking a Stock Exchange quotation? **(7)**

4. Describe the steps taken by a company leading up to an offer for sale. **(10–13)**

5. Describe the main features of an offer by tender. **(15–16)**

6. Compare placings and introductions as methods of making company securities available to investors. **(18–21)**

7. What are the pros and cons of a Rights Issue? **(22–27)**

8. Explain the following terms:

    (*a*) Issuing house.
    (*b*) Stagging.
    (*c*) Underwriting and sub-underwriting.
    (*d*) Convertible loan stock.
    (*e*) Application and allotment.
    (*f*) Bonus Issues. **(13–28)**

9. Describe the nature of Issuing houses and their role in floating new issues of shares. **(31–32)**

10. Draw up a typical timetable for a flotation of shares and indicate the responsibilities of the various parties concerned. **(34)**

CHAPTER VI

SHORT-TERM, EXPORT AND SPECIALISED FINANCE FOR INDUSTRY

SHORT-TERM FINANCE

1. Trade credit. It is an impossible task to measure this value accurately. Nevertheless, the Radcliffe Report 1959 indicated that the total amount of trade credit outstanding surpassed the total of bank credit. If this is true today (and there is no reason to think otherwise) trade credit exceeds £16,500m (1974). Little is known about its distribution pattern, but it is thought that it is relatively more important to small firms and fast-growing firms. The latter are likely to be net takers, as their need for working capital runs ahead of their resources. Larger firms on the other hand are perhaps able to economise on working capital, holding a smaller proportion to turnover.

2. Forms of trade credit. Credit terms, which vary between businesses, may be arranged as follows:

(*a*) They may be recommended by the industrial trade association.

(*b*) They may be a trade custom.

(*c*) They may be specially arranged by the parties. For example:

  (*i*) customers may advance loans to manufacturers to buy materials;

  (*ii*) customers may supply manufacturers with materials (to guarantee quality), paying for manufacturing costs with an allowance for material wastage (*i.e.* "free issue materials");

  (*iii*) customers may advance loans towards the costs of equipment.

3. Cost of trade credit. There are costs to firms giving and taking credit, as follows:

(*a*) Although invoices are usually submitted "terms net monthly," it may in practice be six weeks before settlement is made. This costs the creditor more than 1·5 per cent (if annual interest is taken as 8 per cent) in addition to the accounting and collection costs. There is evidence that firms now consider the opportunity cost of this credit, *i.e.* profitable alternative uses to which this money can be put, as judged from the growth of factoring services.

(*b*) Customers who take credit and thereby waive cash discounts forgo returns which for large-scale purchases may amount to substantial sums *per annum*.

For example, a customer who is offered a cash discount of 2·5 per cent if payment is made within seven days, or alternatively full payment at thirty days, is really paying interest of 40·6 per cent for this credit. This cost may be calculated by formula:

$$\text{Cost of credit} = \frac{\text{Percentage discount}}{100 - \text{Percentage discount}}$$
$$\times \frac{365}{\text{Final payment date} - \text{Period of discount}} \times 100$$
$$= \frac{2\cdot5}{97\cdot5} \times \frac{365}{23}$$
$$= 40\cdot6 \ \%$$

Clearly the customer should borrow to take advantage of the cash discount. However, one should remember that the gain to the customer is the loss of the supplier who is paying dearly to get payments in earlier.

4. Risks. Dependence on trade credit carries the following risks:

(*a*) Middlemen may find themselves in an impossible dilemma when placed between creditors, who withdraw or grant credit on less liberal terms, and their customers, who may also attempt to reduce their credit terms.

(*b*) As a result, customer goodwill is lost.

(*c*) Reliance on powerful creditors might result in a loss of independence.

5. Bank credit. British commercial banks do not generally advance long-term loans, which would conflict with their basic objectives of security and liquidity of funds. However, although theoretically repayable on demand, overdrafts are generally renewable by negotiation and constitute a flexible and a relatively cheap source of working capital since interest is only payable on money borrowed.

6. Rates of interest. The rates charged to a businessman will be influenced by the following factors:

(a) The current base rate, to which overdraft and loan rates are linked (Bank Base Rate plus 1½ to 3 per cent).

(b) The credit-worthiness of the borrower, which will depend on:

 (i) the records of profits;

 (ii) the relation of assets to liabilities;

 (iii) borrowers' integrity and commercial goodwill; and

 (iv) the quality of available collateral and securities.

7. Classification of bankers' advances. The importance of bank credit to the various sectors of the British economy is indicated in Table X.

TABLE X. CLASSIFICATION OF BANKERS' ADVANCES (FEBRUARY 1974)

	£m	(%)
Manufacturing sector	7,328	18·17
Extractive, agriculture and construction	3,221	7·98
Personal sector	4,009	9·94
Service sector	5,866	14·54
Financial institutions	7,031	17·43
Overseas	12,724	31·55
Total advances	40,179	

8. Bank bill finance. Bank bills of exchange are drawn on acceptance credit facilities granted by merchant banks to their customers, preferably against short-term self-liquidating transactions, which realise funds to meet the bills at maturity. They are termed "fine" bills in that their payment is guaranteed and are second only to Treasury bills for the lowest rate of discount when sold by the customer in the discount market. Thus they offer the businessman a relatively cheap and reliable source of short-term credit.

9. Cost of bank bills. The cost of this credit depends on the following factors:

(a) Current and expected short-term market rates of interest.

(b) The period of credit.

(c) The rate of commission charged by acceptance houses, which is determined by:

(i) the credit-worthiness of the borrower; and

(ii) the nature and quality of security.

10. Reasons for the revival of bill finance. Since 1959 when the Radcliffe Report observed an "irreversible shrinkage in the relative supply of commercial bills," there has been a marked increase in bill finance (£280m in 1960, £1,240m in 1970). This may be explained by the following factors:

(a) The abolition of the *ad valorem* stamp duty.

(b) Recurring credit squeezes, which reduced the availability of advances and loans, caused businessmen to seek alternative sources of finance.

(c) Acceptance credit terms were competitive with advances and loans in times of credit squeeze. However, the Bank of England's directive now limits this form of credit.

(d) The demand by discount houses for liquid securities to counter the decline in their holdings of Government bonds and Treasury bills (85 per cent of the total assets in 1958 to about 50 per cent in 1969). This decline was due to the following:

(i) Fewer bonds were held when interest rates were rising because of capital loss; instead shorter-term securities were preferred.

(ii) Treasury bill tenders were cut back from £3,480m in 1959–60 to £1,390m in 1968–9 because of budgetary surpluses and overseas funds which the balance of payments deficit provided.

(e) Trade expansion, particularly in those industries traditionally financed by bills of exchange.

11. Trade bills. This is a bill of exchange drawn by a trader on another in exchange for goods where the purchaser (acceptor) is granted a period of credit and makes payment on its maturity. However, should the creditor want immediate payment, then he discounts the bill. His success and the cost (discount) depends on the following factors:

(a) The general financial and commercial standing of both parties to the transaction.

(b) The nature of the transaction. There are no obstacles if the parties customarily finance their business by bills. However, banks may refuse to discount accommodation bills which are issued without valid consideration.

(c) The number of bills already in the discount market and particularly those bearing the acceptor's name. As a result of these factors, the differential on trade bills can be as low as 0·5 per cent and as high as 2 per cent a year.

12. Invoice discounting. Expanding companies often find that rising sales bring increased book debts. However, there are today a number of firms prepared to advance finance to alleviate the problem of insufficient liquidity which hinders further growth, by invoice discounting. Generally an invoice discounting facility is agreed for sound established traders who "offer" to sell to the specialist sales debts up to this limit and who guarantee the payment of any debts so bought. If the offer is accepted, then the trader receives a cheque for perhaps 75 per cent of the total amount and accepts a bill of exchange for the same amount as security for his guarantee. He then acts as the specialist's agent, collecting sales debts in the usual manner to honour the bill. The following advantages are claimed for the trader:

(a) The increased liquidity will mean that the trader can take advantage of cash discounts offered by suppliers which may exceed the overall cost of the facility, which is about 1 per cent per month.

(b) Greater credit terms can be extended to customers.

(c) More working capital is available for peak production periods in seasonal trades.

(d) Improved credit rating through prompter payments.

(e) Since the trader may use the facility at his option, it may be a more economical source of finance than fixed interest loans.

13. Factoring. Factoring, established in Britain in 1959, is similar to invoice discounting in that the specialist advances finance when it buys a trader's book debts, but in addition it may assume responsibility for the sales ledger and the credit risk. Naturally, the cost varies accordingly. The cost of the cash flow may be base rate plus 2 per cent, in addition to the service charge which will vary between 0·5 and 2 per cent on turnover, depending on:

(a) the size of the company;

(*b*) the amount of work (*i.e.* the number of invoices); and
(*c*) the degree of risk.

In 1974, the value of factoring amounted to £300m.

14. Advantages of factoring. The main advantages to a firm using the services of a factor may be summarised as follows:

(*a*) There are clerical and administrative savings, particularly for firms selling repetitively on credit, as follows:

(*i*) In effect the firm has one customer only, the factor. Even if the factor is "undisclosed" to the firm's customers, it is a simple matter for the firm to endorse cheques and pass them on.

(*ii*) The firm is no longer concerned with bad debt controls.

(*iii*) There are economies in management and staff salaries, since fewer supervisors and clerical workers are needed. Also there are corresponding savings in recruitment and training.

(*b*) There are also the following financial benefits:

(*i*) Capital locked up in sundry debtors' balances is available for use within the business, as all sales become in effect cash sales.

(*ii*) With this improved liquidity it can offer improved credit terms to its customers in order to increase orders.

(*iii*) It can take advantage of suppliers' cash discounts and make prompt payments.

(*iv*) This improves its credit rating.

(*v*) The turnover of stocks into cash is speeded up and this allows a larger turnover on the same investment.

(*vi*) Undisclosed factoring does not prejudice customer goodwill.

(*vii*) Since factoring is not borrowing, the company's balance sheet liquidity is not weakened nor its borrowing potential impaired.

These administrative and financial savings may be more than sufficient to cover the cost of the factoring service.

(*c*) The company is free to concentrate on the main jobs of producing and selling.

15. Financing of retail sales by H.P. Many retailers selling goods on hire purchase or rental basis use the services of the many specialists in this field, so as to maintain the liquidity of working capital. The retailer has a choice of either placing the customer with the H.P. company to draw up the agreement and arrange the payments of instalments direct, or using "block" discounting facilities where he sells his H.P. debts for an immediate payment of a high proportion of the value of H.P. sales. The retailer then collects the instalment in the normal way to repay the finance company. Today, H.P. financing has reached an enormous scale: £556m in 1958, £1,269m in 1968 and £2,451m in 1973.

16. Financing industry by H.P. This is an increasingly important source of medium-term finance for the purchase of capital goods, ranging from plant and equipment to commodities and vehicles and their insurance. Instalment credit extended by finance houses for industrial plant and equipment stood at £21m in 1958, £113m in 1967 and £347m in 1973 (Department of Trade estimates).

17. Types of H.P. agreement.

(a) *Ordinary H.P. agreement.* The seller invoices the goods to the H.P. company, which agrees with the customer on a charge to be added to the amount financed. This "balance of hire" is then repaid in equal instalments by the customer over, say, twenty-four months.

(b) *Machine life finance.* This recent innovation in the U.K. allows customers to purchase equipment over its anticipated working life. Once this is agreed, periodic payments are calculated by adding to the reducing balance a percentage finance charge which is linked to and slightly above base rate.

18. Advantages of H.P. agreements. Advocates of H.P. financing point out the following advantages:

(a) H.P. encourages firms to take a longer-term view of investment requirements, since they no longer have to buy only when they have sufficient funds for outright purchase. H.P. also avoids the problem of "bunching" of orders for the capital goods industry.

(b) It is the use of equipment which is important for profits and this is gained on payment of the first instalment.

(c) Since capital is not tied up immediately, it may find alternative profitable employment.

(d) The instalment charges are predetermined.

(e) Fixed instalments are advantageous in inflation.

(f) A variety of flexible H.P. agreements are available to suit the customer.

(g) Capital allowances and grants are retained by the users.

Legally, finance houses are entitled to re-possess goods if the terms of the agreement are broken. Consequently, they are generally reluctant to finance equipment in this way, when it becomes a fixture within a building, or it has restricted marketability, *e.g.* furnaces (where a secured loan is more suitable). Instead they favour identifiable goods with working lives exceeding the term of the agreement.

19. Leasing. The post-war practice of renting equipment from finance houses is now well established in the U.K. It has long been a method of equipping business offices, but latterly, with the development of complex and costly equipment which needs regular servicing, firms have taken advantage of leasing schemes. The parties negotiate a primary lease period of between three and seven years, according to the anticipated working life of the equipment, in which time the capital cost and service charges are recouped. Thereafter, for the indefinite secondary period, the lessee may continue to use the equipment at a nominal rental.

20. Differences between H.P. and leasing. Lease and H.P. financing have many advantages in common, although there are the following basic differences:

(*a*) Rentals are allowable against taxation.

(*b*) Unlike H.P. financing, it is the finance house which receives the investment grant payable for qualifying equipment, although it can pass on these benefits to the lessee by way of lower rental charges.

(*c*) The title never passes to the lessee, *i.e.* there is no option to purchase.

(*d*) Deposits are not required.

(*e*) Leasing agreements are not borrowings and so do not limit a company's borrowing powers.

(*f*) The lessee may use the equipment after the first payment.

THE FINANCE OF FOREIGN TRADE

21. Open account. The exporter treats the importer like any domestic customer, debiting his account for goods dispatched and receiving direct payments at agreed times upon the customer's receipt of the documents of title. This he does by:

(*a*) telegraphic transfers;

(*b*) mail transfers from the debtor's bank;

(*c*) personal cheques where exchange-control regulations permit; or

(*d*) banker's draft, drawn on the debtor's bank in favour of the creditor's bank or a correspondent bank.

These methods of settlement are also used for purchases without open account arrangements.

22. Bill of exchange. A bill of exchange is defined as "an unconditional order in writing addressed by one person to another, signed by the person giving it, requiring the person to whom it is addressed to pay on demand or at a fixed or determinable future time, a sum certain in money to, or to the order of, a specified person, or the bearer."

The exporter draws the bill on the importer who accepts its terms by signing it. A bill is to the advantage of both parties (and therefore figures prominently in foreign trade) for the following reasons:

(*a*) The exporter may realise cash by discounting it prior to maturity.

(*b*) The importer receives a term of credit. The transaction may be "self-liquidating," realising funds to meet the bill's payment.

23. Types of bills. They may be either:

(*a*) *documentary bills, i.e.* bills of lading indicating title to the goods are attached to the bill of exchange; or

(*b*) *clean bills.* Here documents are not attached but are sent direct to the purchaser. Naturally clean bills are used only when the purchaser's integrity is unquestioned.

24. Commercial credits. Here the importer arranges for his bank to draw up a letter of credit in favour of the exporter. The letter is sent to a correspondent bank in the exporter's country, who will, as agents, carry out its terms. A commercial credit may be either:

(*a*) a sight credit, where payment is immediate; or

(*b*) an acceptance credit, where payment is arranged through a bill of exchange drawn on the bank.

25. Forms of commercial credit.

(*a*) *A confirmed and irrevocable credit.* This guarantees payment to the exporter, since the terms of payment cannot be altered without the agreement of both parties. Furthermore such a bill will be honoured by the correspondent bank.

(b) *An unconfirmed and revocable credit*. This offers the exporter no such guarantee.

(c) *Revolving credits*. Here the importer specifies the maximum amount which may be drawn on his bank at any one time or may be drawn in any period by an exporter.

(d) *Transferable credits*. This prior arrangement with the importer allows the exporter to transfer part or all of the benefit of the credit to another party, usually his supplier.

26. Nature of risks. There are two types of risk facing exporters, as follows:

    (a) *Normal commercial risks:*
        (i) physical damage to the goods; or
        (ii) default of payment through insolvency of buyer, etc.
    (b) "*Political*" *risks:*
        (i) the introduction of exchange control prior to payment;
        (ii) import licensing changes; or
        (iii) local wars, etc.

27. Insurance cover. The normal commercial risks can be covered by insurance with commercial organisations (*e.g.* Trade Indemnity Co. Ltd.), and is sufficient for those transactions where the political risks are negligible. However, when full cover is required it is provided by the Government's Export Credits Guarantee Department. The reduction in risk makes firms more export-orientated and able to offer better credit terms. Even so the E.C.G.D. does not accept the whole risk but insists that the exporter carries a small share (5 to 15 per cent) in order:

    (a) to deter overtrading;
    (b) to encourage prudence; and
    (c) to encourage him to press for payment on default.

28. Types of E.C.G.D. policies.

    (a) *The comprehensive policy*. This is normally confined to goods sold for cash or on credit limited to six months. It provides cover either for the whole of the exporter's sales for a period of one or three years, or, in selected markets, for one year. The exporter is supplied with a confidential list of premium ratings for countries and remits monthly details of total export business with the appropriate premium, (average cost 24p *per* £100).

(*b*) *Investment cover.* This scheme has operated since 1972, whereby insurance cover is provided against political risks on overseas investment. The aim is to encourage private non-speculative investment in developing countries which will benefit both Britain and the receiving country. Currently, cover is provided for a maximum of fifteen years and a minimum of three years at a premium of 1 per cent of the insured sum.

(*c*) *The specific policy.* This applies to exports of large-scale capital goods. Cover is normally up to five years, a reasonable period of credit for expensive goods, and each premium is negotiated, because of each project's individuality.

(*d*) *The service policy.* This is available for the export of services on a comprehensive or specific policy basis.

29. Bank guarantees. The E.C.G.D. is used as guarantor for repayments to banks which have loaned to exporters for sales-credit purposes. First introduced in 1954 for contracts exceeding £250,000, it is now available for much smaller sums.

Today banks make advances against this security at preferential rates of interest: base rate $+ \frac{1}{2}$ per cent on business on up to two years' credit from shipment and at a fixed rate for business on two to three years' credit at 7 per cent (1973) and at a flexible rate determined by E.C.G.D. for business over five years.

30. Financial guarantees. Since 1961 the E.C.G.D. can guarantee loans made by British banks to overseas purchasers of high-value capital goods from Britain, as long as it can be shown that it will benefit the balance of payments, may lead to further orders, or will assist the exporting industry.

31. Value of E.C.G.D. business. The volume of business insured by E.C.G.D. has increased considerably: from £405m in 1952–3 to £976m in 1962–3 and £3,999m in 1972–3.

The reasons for E.C.G.D.'s continuous and steady growth can be explained by the following factors:

(*a*) Credit insurance has become more attractive with the extension of risks covered, lower premiums (average premium rate 58½p in 1954 and 24p in 1973) and higher percentage of losses paid out.

(*b*) Successful marketing by E.C.G.D.

(c) The buyers' market in world trade, which means that exporters need attractive credit terms to compete successfully.

(d) The availability of credit in times of credit squeeze.

SPECIALISED FINANCE

32. The Industrial and Commercial Finance Corporation. The Industrial and Commercial Finance Corporation was formed by the Bank of England and the Scottish and English commercial banks in 1945. The purpose of this commercial undertaking is to assist small- and medium-sized companies and "to provide credit and finance by means of loans or the subscription of loan or share capital or otherwise, for industrial and commercial businesses or enterprises in Great Britain." Finance from £5,000 to £500,000, to suit the requirements of the borrower, at competitive rates of interest, is available in the following variety of forms:

(a) Secured loans and debentures.

(b) Unsecured loans.

(c) Redeemable preference shares.

(d) Irredeemable preference shares.

(e) Ordinary shares.

(f) A plant purchase scheme, which enables customers to purchase plant and equipment by means of a hire purchase transaction over periods of up to five years.

(g) Leasing facilities, available for customers who wish to use new capital equipment without tying up finance in capital investment.

In addition, the I.C.F.C. operates an export and management advisory service, arranges issues and flotations and gives assistance on mergers through its subsidiary, Industrial Mergers Ltd.

33. Summary of I.C.F.C. assistance. Since its inception, the business of the I.C.F.C. has grown substantially. It has provided financial assistance of some £330m to more than 2,300 companies engaged in a wide range of activities throughout Great Britain (*see* table XI).

Furthermore, the continuing interest shown by the I.C.F.C. in the small- and medium-sized firm is indicated by the positively skewed frequency table, where amounts outstanding of £5,000 to £50,000 figure prominently.

34. The Agricultural Mortgage Corporation Ltd. This was
established in 1928 with the Bank of England and other banks
as its shareholders. Its objectives are to assist the farming industry by granting the following loans:

(a) Long-term loans on agricultural land and buildings.
(b) Loans for improvements to farms from funds. These are
derived from:

    (i) loans and grants from the Ministry of Agriculture,
Fisheries and Food; or
    (ii) issues of debentures on the open market at competitive
rates. The exceptionally high market rates of 1968–9 demanded very high coupons. Even so, 93 per cent of an issue
at 9½ per cent was left with underwriters and contributed to a
further increase in their loan rates to another all-time high
of 10·5 per cent. To date, its loan totals exceed £100m.

TABLE XI. EXAMPLES OF I.C.F.C. ASSISTANCE

*Classification of financial facilities by
amounts outstanding at 31st March 1968
and 1973*

Amount	Customers	
	1968	*1973*
Up to £10,000	386	493
£10,001–20,000	302	451
£20,001–50,000	419	596
	1,107	1,540
£50,001–100,000	289	371
£100,001–150,000	186	238
£150,001–200,000	64	85
£200,001 and over	42	47
	581	741

Source: I.C.F.C.

35. The Ship Mortgage Finance Co. Ltd. This was founded in
1951 with its share capital subscribed by the shipbuilding

industry, insurance companies and various finance companies. Its aim was to finance the construction of ships in British yards. It is managed by the I.C.F.C. Since its inception, it has contributed some £24m from its own funds and found participants for a further £17m. Its work is not entirely to finance. It uses its specialised knowledge to manage shipping lines owned by the I.C.F.C. and it acts on behalf of the Secretary of State for Industry in assessing the credit-worthiness of shipyards which have requested grants under the *Shipbuilding Industry Act* 1967.

36. The Finance Corporation for Industry Ltd. The F.C.I. was set up with Government encouragement in 1945 with 40 per cent of its capital held by insurance companies and 30 per cent each by the bank and investment trusts. Its object was the lending of £200,000 or more by secured or unsecured loans to businesses requiring urgent funds for re-equipment or development. Priority has been given where funds are otherwise unobtainable on reasonable terms and to projects deemed in the national interest, particularly in the mining, steel, chemical, electrical and textile industries. Since 1945 the F.C.I. has advanced some £300m to British industry and at March 1973 its outstanding loans stood at £62·4m.

37. The Technical Development Capital Ltd. The T.D.C., a commercial enterprise acquired by the I.C.F.C. in 1966, was set up in 1962 with shareholders from merchant banks and British and Commonwealth insurance companies. This followed the recommendation of the Radcliffe Report on the workings of the British monetary system for an institution to supply finance for the development of technical innovations. The T.D.C. was not intended to finance basic research like the National Research Development Corporation, but supplies risk capital for the later stages of development, production and marketing. It has no fixed method of financing, but negotiates terms on an individual basis. However, it expects a shareholding, in addition to any loan it makes, to compensate for the substantial financial risks, and since its object is to aid innovators, its policy is not to hold shares permanently, but to sell once the venture is established. Currently, it has investments of £90m in some 1,500 companies widely distributed throughout industry.

38. The Estate Duties Investment Trust Ltd. E.D.I.T.H. was formed in 1952 by insurance companies and investment trusts and is managed by the I.C.F.C. It went public in 1962. It is ready to acquire minority holdings in soundly-run private or small public companies without seeking to control management. The main benefits to the company's shareholders are as follows:

(a) Even though the market for their shares is restricted, they have access to funds.

(b) Company control is unaffected.

(c) Aged shareholders have liquid funds for payment of death duty, although capital gains tax liability may arise.

(d) Death duty liability is reduced if these funds are used:

(i) to purchase annuities;

(ii) for *inter-vivos* gifts; or

(iii) to acquire assets which carry a lower rate of duty, *e.g.* forestry land.

At March 1973 it had invested a total of £9·9m.

39. The National Research Development Corporation. The N.R.D.C. was set up in 1945 for "securing, where the public interest so requires, the development and exploitation of inventions resulting from public research and of any other invention which it appears to the corporation is not being exploited or sufficiently developed or exploited." In 1973, submissions totalled 2,175 of which 73 were accepted.

The N.R.D.C., which may borrow up to £50m for this purpose, should balance its revenue account in the long term. It will grant financial help if it is satisfied that:

(a) the project is technologically feasible;

(b) it stands a good chance of commerical success; and

(c) the company possesses adequate resources and management to exploit the invention.

A typical arrangement is where the N.R.D.C. agrees to buy part of the invoiced development costs and is repaid later by a levy on the sales of the product. The company may offset this against trading profits. Such assistance averages £3·4m annually and licence income totalled £5·6m in 1973 (£4·3m of which was foreign currency). Inventions earning significant revenue are Cephalasporin, dental cement, Rawcliffe electric motors, etc.

40. Other institutions.

(a) *The Charterhouse Group.* This important financial group will supply capital preferably on a large scale (£50,000 to £250,000), in return for equity and preference and loan stock. In addition it offers a comprehensive range of specialist financial services for industry.

(b) *The United Dominions Trust.*

(c) *Hambros* (merchant bank).

(d) *Bowmakers.*

PROGRESS TEST 6

1. Indicate the various sources of working capital available to a quoted company engaged in manufacturing activities. **(1–19)**

2. Compare and contrast Trade and Bank Credit as sources of working capital. **(1–6)**

3. The Radcliffe Report in 1959 observed "an irreversible shrinkage in the relative supply of commercial bills." Comment upon this observation in the light of subsequent experience. **(10)**

4. Explain the terms "invoice discounting" and "factoring" and the advantages of these services to the businessmen seeking funds. **(12–14)**

5. Compare and contrast hire purchase and leasing as methods of financing industry. **(16–20)**

6. What is meant by trading on open account? **(21)**

7. Outline the methods by which an exporter may be paid. **(21–25)**

8. Describe the main risks facing exporters and how these risks can be avoided. **(26–28)**

9. Describe the work of the E.C.G.D. **(26–31)**

10. Discuss the activities of the Industrial and Commercial Finance Corporation. **(32–33)**

11. Write notes on the following:

(a) The Estate Duties Investment Trust Ltd. **(38)**

(b) The Finance Corporation for Industry. **(36)**

(c) The National Research and Development Corporation. **(39)**

(d) The Agricultural Mortgage Corporation. **(34)**

12. What do you understand by the term "specialised finance for industry"? **(32–40)**

PART THREE

THE SEARCH FOR PROFITABILITY

CHAPTER VII

OBJECTIVES OF THE BUSINESS FIRM

PROFIT MAXIMISATION

1. Profit maximisation: the traditional objective. Alfred Marshall's *Principles of Economics*, 1890, a statement of contemporary economic theory, contained a convincing and impeccably-argued theory of the firm that explained the behaviour of firms operating in the highly competitive markets of the late 1800s. Furthermore, Marshall and contemporaries established plausible theories showing how monopolists behave; and subsequently to fill in the middle ground between these two extremes and thereby mirror the actual market situation the neo-classical economists (notably Robinson and Chamberlin) turned their attention to "imperfect competition" and "monopolistic competition." Throughout this extended development of micro-economic theory, one fundamental assumption subsisted, *i.e.* firms endeavour to maximise profits.

2. Perfect competition. In view of the prevalance of this profit-maximising goal in modern micro-economic theory, an objective which many writers on economics and corporate behaviour take for granted, it is surely relevant in an examination of firms' objectives to analyse the basis of this goal, its strengths and weaknesses and appropriateness to the modern business organisation as a prime motivating force. For this reason, let us first examine the classical theory of the firm in a competitive situation.

The theory of the firm in a perfectly competitive market predicts how a firm behaves and reacts to changes in market forces. This may be summarised by the following analysis and by reference to the supporting Figs. 3 and 4.

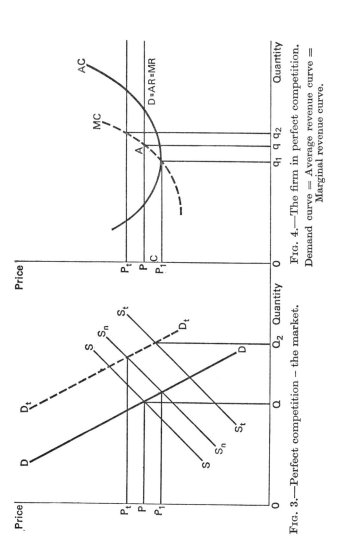

FIG. 3.—Perfect competition – the market.

FIG. 4.—The firm in perfect competition.
Demand curve = Average revenue curve =
Marginal revenue curve.

At the outset, the assumptions that are usually made for perfect competition must be stated. They are:

(a) The firm's objective is profit maximisation.
(b) Firms are free to enter the industry.
(c) All goods are homogeneous (*i.e.* no trade marks or branded goods).
(d) There is perfect knowledge regarding production methods.
(e) Consumers are rational and wish to maximise satisfaction.
(f) There are very many suppliers and buyers.

3. Determination of the market price. The very many buyers behave collectively in a manner characterised by the demand curve DD in Fig. 3. This means that they conform to the Law of Downward-Sloping Demand, preferring to buy smaller quantities of the product if the price is high and larger amounts if the price is low. Sellers' attitude towards price is summarised by the supply curve SS in Fig. 3. The Law of Upward-Sloping Supply states that they are prepared to supply larger amounts for higher prices.

Consequently, buyers and sellers interact in the market place to establish an equilibrium price (OP) where the quantity offered for sale exactly equals the amount buyers are prepared to purchase (OQ).

4. The firm—a price-taker. A careful examination of the assumptions in 2 reveals that the market price OP is the ruling selling price for the typical competitive firm (Fig. 4). Clearly, any attempt to sell above OP means it will fail to meet its fundamental objective of maximum profits because of assumptions (c) and (e) *above*. Moreover, any attempt to sell below OP is out of the question because it can sell its entire output at the ruling (higher) market price. Thus the firm has no choice regarding price: it must accept the ruling market price.

5. The optimum output. However, the profit-maximising firm can exercise choice in its output policy if not in its selling price. Furthermore, if it is to secure its goal it must first clearly understand its cost/production relationship and secondly, achieve a unique balance between its level and cost of production and its selling price. The first step in this process requires an appreciation of the relationship between average and marginal costs. The second step is to select the exact level of output/sales that maximises profits, given the selling price.

6. Average and marginal costs. The economist who is interested in the relationship between costs and output over the whole production range conventionally graphs U-shaped average and marginal cost curves to illustrate the influence of increasing and decreasing returns to a fixed factor of production. In other words, if extra variable factors, *e.g.* workers employed, with a fixed factor, *e.g.* factory, are employed, then variable costs rise less steeply than output because of the operation of the law of increasing returns; and eventually at high levels of operations the law of diminishing returns (*see* Fig. 5) causes variable costs to rise faster than output. Table XII illustrates a typical cost/output relationship based on hypothetical productivity figures over a company's range of output (see Fig. 6).

TABLE XII. COST/OUTPUT RELATIONSHIPS

Workers	Total output	Variable costs	Marginal costs	Average costs
1	10	£15		£1·50
			£1·00	
2	25	30		1·20
			0·75	
3	45	45		1·00
			0·50	
4	70	60		0·85
			0·75	
5	90	75		0·83
			1·00	
6	105	90		0·85
			1·50	
7	115	105		0·91

NOTES:
Variable costs consists of wages of £15 per worker. Marginal cost is the additional cost of one unit, *e.g.* the second worker adds 15 units to total output at an extra cost of £15. Therefore MC = £1 and since it is an average value corresponds to the 17·5 unit.

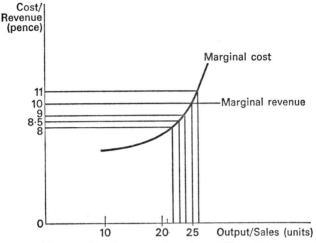

FIG. 5.—Maximum profits where MC = MR.

* By increasing output/sales, the *additional* profit is less and less, and total profits are maximised at 25 units; at 26 units the cost of the extra unit is 11p and therefore a loss of 1·0p is incurred. Consequently, profits are not maximised at output/sales below or in excess of MC = MR levels.

Output/Sales	MC	MR	Loss — or Gain +
22	8·0p	10p	2·0p+
23	8·5p	10p	1·5p+
24	9.0p	10p	1·0p+
25	10·0p	10p	—
26	11·0p	10p	1·0p−

7. Output that maximises profits. The concept of marginal analysis provides the answer: profits are maximised at that level of output/sales where the marginal cost (*i.e.* the incremental cost of producing/selling one extra unit) is equal to the marginal revenue (*i.e.* the incremental revenue of selling one extra unit) (*see* Fig. 5). Thus in the example shown on p. 89 the firm produces and sells Oq at a price of OP to realise the largest possible profit (CPAB in Fig. 4).

$$
\begin{aligned}
\text{Total revenue} &= \text{Average revenue} \times \text{output} \\
&= \text{OP} \times \text{Oq} \\
&= \text{OPAq}
\end{aligned}
$$

Total cost   = Average cost   × output
      = OC   × Oq
      = OCBq
Profit   = Total revenue   × total cost
      = OPAq   × OCBq
      = CPAB

8. The equilibrium state. However, newcomers are attracted by these excessive profits being earned by the industry (termed super-normal profits because they are the surplus above the minimum reward necessary to keep the resources in

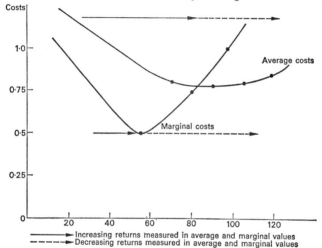

Increasing returns measured in average and marginal values
– – – – Decreasing returns measured in average and marginal values

Fig. 6.—Average and marginal costs.

their present employment) whose additional supplies eventually cause the market price to fall to a level where only normal profits are realised, OP, where supply is S_n–S_n. Consequently, the surplus profits are competed away, supply and market price are stabilised and firms are in a short-run equilibrium each producing Oq where marginal costs equal marginal revenue.

9. Monopoly. Monopoly is the extreme opposite of perfect competition in the range of possible market structure (*see* Fig. 7).

The assumptions for monopoly are:

  (*a*) The monopolist is the sole seller and acts rationally.
  (*b*) There are no substitutes for the monopolist's product.
  (*c*) The monopolist's objective is profit maximisation.

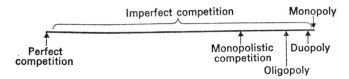

FIG. 7.—Degrees of competition.

Here the monopolist, faced with the downward-sloping market demand curve, has a choice of either setting price and allowing consumer demand to determine sales or placing any quantity on sale and charging what the market will bear. However, in order to meet the profit objective output/sales must be such that marginal cost = marginal revenue and is shown visually in Fig. 8, where output/sales are OQ and selling price is OP.

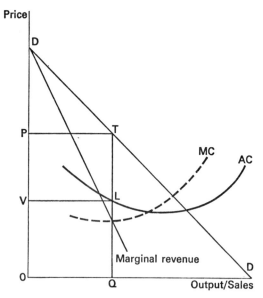

FIG. 8.—Equilibrium situation in monopoly.

Demand curve = average revenue.

Sales revenue $=$ OPTQ
Total costs $=$ OVLQ
Monopoly profit $=$ OPTQ $-$ OVLQ
    $=$ VPTL

No other price/output combination can secure a larger profit: the firm is achieving its profit objective and is in a short-term equilibrium situation.

10. Demise of profit-maximisation assumption. The foregoing analysis of the theory of the firm in perfect competition and monopoly has been included to give the reader an insight into the nature of classical micro-economic theory and to demonstrate its dependence on the profit-maximisation objective. Many people still unquestioningly regard this profit objective as the entrepreneur's motivating force; its proponents find it intellectually appealing and of practical value in that marginal analysis, in contrast to behavioural motivation theories, can be relied on to provide solutions in every situation; its logic is faultless, its underlying assumption of rational behaviour suggests that firms should act as hypothesised in the theory—indeed the amount of profit made by businesses, the conventional acid test of their managerial ability and performance—reinforces this view that firms should in practice try to maximise profits.

Nevertheless, this most powerful hypothesis of business motivation is severely criticised.

(a) It does not deal effectively with the *dynamic situation* for it is essentially a statement of general short-term equilibrium situations describing the *status quo* at one point in time. For instance, if as in Fig. 3, demand increases to Dt–Dt the temporary equilibrium is upset by a price rise of P–Pt. New firms are attracted into the industry (St–St) by the super-normal profits made by firms selling a quantity Oq_2 at a price of OPt (figs. 3 and 4) and the *status quo* is re-established where the industry and firm are in equilibrium once more at outputs of OQ_2 and Oq_1 respectively. However, the theory is incapable of predicting the longer-term equilibrium situation where the *status quo* is fundamentally upset, where, for instance, a firm or group of firms are prepared to discount short-term profits for stability of trade in order to guarantee maximum longer-term profits.

(b) There is no place in the theory for the *decision-maker*. However, firms are made up of individuals who may have personal business objectives and whose behaviour on occasion is certain to be different and perhaps incompatible with that predetermined by the theory of the firm.

OTHER OBJECTIVES OF THE BUSINESS FIRM

11. Objectives of technocrats. J. Galbraith in *The New Industrial State* hypothesised on the motivation of business behaviour by examination of the technostructure of the modern corporations which consisted of individuals who identified their own personal and pecuniary success with that of the corporation, *i.e.* "corporation men" who possessed powers of decision-making because of their specialised technical knowledge and skills necessary for the success of the corporation (*see* Chapter IV).

(*a*) Their first objective was to preserve the technostructure for self-interest by securing a minimum level of earnings for the corporation. Failure to do so would mean:

(*i*) The company going to the capital market for additional funds where lenders might impose limitations on managerial freedom.

(*ii*) Loss of office and power through shareholders' actions or take-overs.

(*b*) The next objective was corporate growth (with sufficient earnings to guarantee growth in rates of dividend for the shareholders and to finance investment projects) since this would increase the power and size of the technostructure.

(*c*) Technical innovation was pursued as a means to secure (*b*) and in its own right because it further increased the prospects of the technical managers.

(*d*) They strove to build up a sound corporate image.

Moreover, the justification for and power of the technostructure was further enhanced if their personal objectives of higher output and sales, innovation and corporate growth coincided with the goals of society.

12. Organisational objectives. Cyert and March in *A Behavioural Theory of the Firm* argued that corporations *per se* did not have objectives. Instead, business organisations are made up of persons with individual goals, *viz.* managers, staff, shareholders, creditors, suppliers, customers, etc. who by means of bargaining, established compromise objectives for a coalition of individual interests.

13. Formation of coalition objectives. Cyert and March

hypothesised also that coalition goals were fixed by the following processes:

(a) Individuals made *demands on the organisation* either in the form of monetary or policy commitments. For instance:

(i) Shareholders demanded monetary payments which if realised meant that they might adopt a passive role in further coalition bargaining.

(ii) Managers demanded and strove to secure monetary payments, plus authority and policy commitments.

(iii) Workers' goals were basically monetary.

Consequently, there was a trade-off between conflicting demands with the result that joint preference or compromise objectives emerged. Shareholders whose demands, expressed in dividend income or capital growth, were satisfied would leave management to pursue policy-making that achieved among other things managers' monetary and non-monetary aspirations. Workers would accept the organisational objectives but only for a price that satisfied their monetary demands.

(b) *Mutual control systems.* Coalition members needed a system to enforce the organisational objectives. Examples cited were:

(i) The *budget system* that controlled coalition members within the agreed plan.

(ii) *Allocation of functions.* Areas of responsibility and discretion of coalition members, if clearly defined, constrained members from pursuing their own self-interest.

(c) *Objective change through experience.* Coalition members would shift their attention to new or modified goals in the light of experience. Certainly the achievement of the individual and of others within his reference group caused a modification of current aspirations quantitatively and qualitatively, *e.g.* higher incomes or more stable dividend payments.

14. Economic goals. The size, composition and bargaining power of individuals within the coalition group resulted in economic objectives within the following areas:

(a) *Production.* Here the objective would be expressed in terms of:

(i) Stability of output.

(ii) Level of output.

The interpretation and relative emphasis placed on each depended on the demands and aspirations of the coalition members concerned with output.

(b) *Stocks.* Individuals concerned with stocks, *e.g.* stock controllers, accountants, salesmen and customers would pressurise for individual goals which through negotiations were reduced to compromise goals for:

(i) Level of stocks.

(ii) Range of stocks.

(c) *Sales.* The sales goal in unit or monetary terms summarised the objectives of individuals who were concerned with stability of production, earnings and employment and survival.

(d) *Market share.* Individuals interested in comparative performance or growth would demand market share goals.

(e) *Profit goals* were expressed in absolute terms or in relation to capital employed. A variety of individuals were interested in the former; shareholders demanded that they be sufficient to pay satisfactory dividends and that ploughed-back profits covered internal investment opportunities for future capital growth, and managers demanded that retained profits were adequate to finance the capital investment needed for corporate growth. Top managers might set profitability objectives to see how efficiently they had used shareholders' and total resources at their disposal in comparison with managers in other organisations.

15. Nature of shareholders' demands. The profit objective referred to above was the outcome of the various motives and the relative bargaining strengths of shareholder groups. Possible motives were as follows:

(a) *Maximum current dividends.* Certain shareholders wished to maximise dividend payments, *e.g.* persons living on investment income and company controllers who as "dividend strippers" exploited their position for maximum short-term gain.

(b) *Maximisation of share values.* There was a difference of opinion as to whether share prices were an increasing function of retained earnings or dividends. M. J. Gordon stated that higher dividends improved share values on the grounds that capital gains were less certain and more risky than immediate dividend expectations. Therefore, a company pursuing a policy of earning retention commanded a lower P/E ratio than one that maximised dividends. Friend and Puckett, on the other hand, argued that the value of ploughed-back profit was more significant. The controversy continues. However, there is one situation when earnings retentions contribute to capital gains.

The newly-established company at the innovative and subsequent growth stage of the life cycle of the firm is likely to be permanently short of funds. Shareholders in this situation are usually prepared to discount present income and reinvest earnings for the substantial gains that are anticipated in the subsequent maturity stage of the firm's life cycle. Thus, at this point in time, the prerequisite for success is additional funds which may be raised either externally or internally: however, additional funds raised outside will dilute the equity so that shareholders must share the anticipated gains, hence their preference for self-financing.

16. Objectives a management tool. In the preceding sections, we examined briefly various theories that have attempted to explain the principal goals of business firms and how they are selected. But whatever the selection process and choice of goal, objectives once decided on provide a valuable management tool.

(*a*) The goal provides management with a purpose and direction and pace of operations.

(*b*) Management can appraise their performance by comparison of actual performance with the standard.

17. Desirable characteristics of objectives. Objectives possessing the following characteristics provide a most valuable management tool.

(*a*) They must be quantified and measurable, *e.g.* to increase Return on Capital Employed (R.O.C.E.) from 10 per cent to 20 per cent.

(*b*) They must be qualified by a time-scale, *e.g.* to increase R.O.C.E. from 10 per cent to 20 per cent by December 31st 1975.

(*c*) They must be ends in themselves and not means, *e.g.* to secure good labour relations could be considered as a prerequisite for profits.

(*d*) They should be realistic and attainable, yet stretch management.

(*e*) They should be capable of revision.

(*f*) They should be communicable and communicated to all staff on whose shoulders implementation rests.

(*g*) They should be limited in number and reflect the compromise between coalition members' conflicting interests.

VISUAL REPRESENTATION OF ECONOMIC OBJECTIVES

18. Objectives and break-even analysis. A logical progression in an examination of company objectives is to consider the impact of selected goals on the company's operational

policy. Consequently, we shall select four of the most fre-
quently-quoted goals and show diagrammatically by means
of break-even analysis how the chosen goal influences corporate sales, costs and output. The objectives chosen for this
purpose are as follows:

(a) Maximisation of profits.
(b) Maximisation of sales volume.
(c) Maximisation of sales revenue.
(d) Maximisation of sales volume or revenue subject to a
profit constraint.

19. Total costs: the economist's viewpoint. The first step
in this exercise is the construction of a break-even model to
illustrate the typical behaviour of sales revenue and costs over
the company's entire range of activity. Let us start with costs.
Total costs are the sum of all costs incurred in an operation.
Therefore, if we classify costs under the heading of fixed costs
and variable costs, then we have the familiar equation

Fixed cost + Variable cost = Total costs.

Now of course we must quantify these costs and for this
purpose let us imagine that a company supplies the hypothetical cost/revenue data contained in Table XIII. From it,
we may graph the continuous total cost of production to see
how costs behave over the range of operations from zero
units to 115k units.

TABLE XIII.   TOTAL COST OF PRODUCTION

(i) Output k	(ii) Fixed cost k	(iii) Variable cost k	(iv) Total cost k	(v) Selling price	(vi) Total revenue k	(vii) Profit k
0	£100	£—	100		—	(£100)
10	£100	15	115	4·50	£45	(70)
25	£100	30	130	4·00	100	(30)
40	£100	45	145	3·75	150	5
70	£100	60	160	3·00	210	50
90	£100	75	175	2·28	206	31
105	£100	90	190	2·00	210	20
115	£100	105	205	1·64	189	16

Column (*ii*) states the value of fixed costs: the first element in the cost equation. Thus we see that fixed costs are constant at £100k and represent rent and rates, interest on loans,

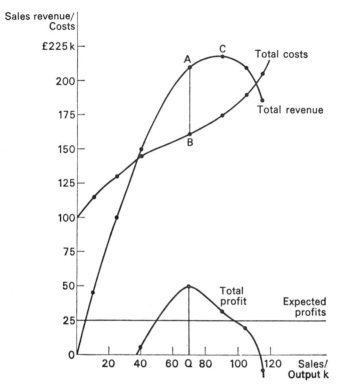

FIG. 9.—Break-even and company objectives.

management salaries and other costs that do not vary with output.

In contrast, variable costs (column (*iii*)) by definition change with the level of activity, *e.g.* wages of direct labour, materials and power, etc. However, they may not vary directly. In fact, at low levels of activity, variable costs probably rise less steeply than output as additional workers are taken on, because of the operation of the law of increasing returns and eventually at high levels of operations beyond optimum worker–capital combination the law of diminishing returns will cause variable costs to rise faster than output. The summation of these two costs (column (*iv*)) is the basis for the continuous non-linear total cost curve shown in Fig. 9.

20. Total revenue: the economist's viewpoint. Economic theory, supported by empirical studies, states that most firms are subject to the law of downward-sloping demand. This means that they are incapable of supplying an infinite quantity of any good at a fixed price. Inevitably there comes a point where at high sales volume suppliers wishing to extend sales further, encounter consumer resistance and/or reaction by competitors which forces them to reduce price. Naturally, this has an immediate and direct effect on sales revenue: it declines relative to sales volume when price cuts are made and falls absolutely if demand for the product is inelastic. The sales data in Table XIII is based on this assumption and is expressed as the non-linear sales revenue line graphed in Fig. 9.

21. Maximisation of profits goal. A basic tenet of economic theory is that profit maximisation (7) is achieved at a level of activity where marginal cost and marginal revenue are equal. This means in general terms that if at a certain level of activity the extra sales proceeds from the sale of an additional unit exceed the extra cost of producing and selling it, then total profits can be improved by producing and selling this marginal unit. If, however, the extra cost exceeds the extra revenue of an incremental unit of output, less total profit is made. The intermediate level of output and sales where no extra profits are possible and no losses are incurred, *i.e.* where marginal cost and revenue are equal, secures maximum profits.

Furthermore, it is a condition, if profits are to be maximised, that total sales revenue must exceed total costs by the greatest possible amount since:

Profit = Total sales revenue − Total costs

In Fig. 9, this occurs at a level of output/sales of OQ where AB is the longest possible vertical line between the total revenue and total cost curves.

Thus break-even analysis, based on the continuous total

sales revenue and cost lines that reflect the economist's view of cost/revenue/output behaviour, indicates that profits are realised when sales/output is in the range of activity 37k–114k units and that the profit maximiser's goal is realised at 70k units where:

(a) The vertical distance between these curves is maximised (£50) and where

(b) marginal cost must equal marginal revenue and where

(c) the slope of the total revenue curve equals the slope of the total cost curve.

The profit maximiser's selling price will be

$$OA \div OQ,$$

i.e.

$$£210k \div 70k = £3·00$$

which is confirmed by examining the appropriate selling price for 70k units.

22. Maximisation of sales volume goal. This assumed objective is only realised when sales/output are at the highest level possible, and in this example is achieved at 114 units where the company breaks even. Its selling price will be

$$£197·5k \div 114 = £1·73.$$

Sales/output activity beyond this level, although desirable, is unrealistic because losses are incurred because total costs exceed revenues. Nevertheless, although the higher break-even level of operations satisfies the assumed goal, it is doubtful whether it is no more than a very short-run equilibrium, for although no losses are incurred, neither are any profits made. It is obviously an unhealthy situation for survival but may be qualified at a later stage in this analysis to represent a realistic and variable long-term objective by building in a profit constraint on the grounds that many companies do actually pursue the highest possible sales figures as long as they are making satisfactory profits.

23. Maximisation of sales revenue goal. This assumed goal is achieved at 90 units where the total revenue curve is at its highest point C, (in the economist's terminology, where marginal revenue is zero). Here the selling price is

£216k ÷ 90k = £2·40 per unit.

24. Maximisation of sales with a profit constraint. We assumed in **18** (*b*) and (*c*) that the sole objective was maximisation of sales in unit and revenue terms. However, more realistic goals (which are intuitively satisfying and supported by several studies) are likely to include a prescribed level of profit which checks the firm's ability to pursue sales *ad infinitrum*. For example, management may require a £25k profit in order to satisfy the demand of shareholders and to provide internal funds for new investment. In this case:

   (*a*) The sales volume-maximising firm will produce and sell less than before, *i.e.* 98k units at a selling price of £2·17 (£213·5k ÷ 98k).

   (*b*) The sales revenue-maximising firm will wish to produce and sell 90k units. In fact, the inclusion of a profit constraint of £25k is quite compatible with revenue maximisation and will not effect the the sales revenue-maximiser's policy, since 90k units already realise profits of £31k.

In this example, the sales volume-maximiser who is subject to this profit constraint is forced to cut back sales from 114k to 98k units and raise prices from £1·73 to £2·17. Furthermore, this illustrates a typical compromise demanded by a coalition of members representing the sales and profit interests referred to by Cyert and March (*see* **12**). Thus shareholders are presumably satisfied with the profit of £25k, leaving managers to sell as much as they can to maximise their satisfactions.

PROGRESS TEST 7

   1. Compare and contrast the theory of perfect competition and the theory of monopoly. **(1–9)**

   2. Critically analyse the "profit-maximisation" objective. **(10)**

   3. "Organisations *per se* do not have objectives." Discuss. **(11–12)**

   4. Describe the process whereby coalition objectives are formed. **(13–15)**

   5. Explain the principal goals of business firms and how they are selected. **(1–16)**

   6. "Objectives to be useful must be qualified and quantified." Discuss. **(17)**

   7. Explain by means of break-even graphs how the selection of objectives affect company operations. **(18–24)**

CHAPTER VIII

THE CHOICE OF FINANCE FOR COMPANIES

TYPES OF CAPITAL

1. Classification of company capital. The capital of a joint stock company can be summarised as follows:

(a) *Share capital.* This consists of variants of preference shares and ordinary shares.

(b) *Loan capital.* This consists of loans, debentures and mortgages.

2. Ordinary shares. These equities issued to individuals subscribing towards a company's share capital confer on shareholders a residual claim to dividends and repayment of capital in the event of liquidation after all prior charges have been met. Normally they carry voting rights by way of compensation.

Since the demise of the owner-manager (who traditionally performed the entrepreneurial functions of risk-bearing, decision-making and co-ordinating factors of production) and the development of large-scale industry, it has become more difficult to identify the entrepreneur. One may regard the ordinary shareholders of joint stock companies (the typical business unit) as the entrepreneurs of the twentieth century, since they perform the main entrepreneurial functions of risk-bearing for profit. Despite apathy on their part, which has led in some cases to a divorce between ownership and control, in theory they exercise control by voting on boards and delegating authority to managers who perform the other entrepreneurial functions of decision-making and factor-co-ordination.

3. Risk and control. The "golden rule of capitalism" (*i.e.* "where the risk lies, there the control lies also") described a situation where, as in sole proprietorship, the risk-taker and business controller were one. However, today this rule needs to be modified in view of the divorce between ownership and control which has occurred with the development of the joint stock company.

4. Causes of this divorce. The factors responsible for this situation, where the board of directors in effect controls business affairs, are as follows:

(a) The usual provision in articles of association making directors fully responsible for management.

(b) The unwillingness of shareholders to dismiss the board in order to overrule decisions.

(c) Diversity of shareholdings, which hinders unanimity in policy and action.

(d) The apathy of shareholders while dividends are maintained.

(e) The reluctance of institutional shareholders to "act as a public watchdog" and to set an example by intervening and criticising boards when necessary.

(f) The difficulties involved in attending shareholders' meetings.

(g) The clash of interests between controllers and shareholders.

5. The interests of shareholders. The following conditions serve the interests of shareholders:

(a) Their company earns for them at least long-term normal profits appropriate to the degree of risk in that trade.

(b) Dividends are maximised to give shareholders the choice of reinvesting most profitably. Undistributed profits are regarded by some as a source of cheap funds for management. On the other hand sufficient profits should be retained to secure long-run growth objectives.

(c) Shares are freely marketable so that investments may be realised.

6. Interests of controllers. The following conditions serve the interests of controllers:

(a) The "corporation man" identifies himself with the company and may plough back a high proportion of his earnings for capitalisation since corporate success brings personal success by way of increased authority, status, prestige and remuneration.

(b) They have a duty to shareholders and pursue policies which serve their interests. However, they may be tempted through self-interest to:

(i) favour other companies in which they have financial interests with advantageous contracts;

(*ii*) use inside information (*e.g.* for profitable transactions in the company's shares, directly or indirectly); or

(*iii*) selfishly advise shareholders on a certain course of action in a take-over situation.

It must be emphasised that these are temptations only. It would be wrong to conclude that directors generally abandon the interests of shareholders by benefiting personally from the opportunities which their privileged position affords.

7. Deferred shares. Deferred ordinary shares rank after ordinary shares in profit-sharing and are sometimes issued to companies' promoters and underwriters with various voting rights.

8. Preference shares. These shares carry the prior right to a fixed dividend (a fixed percentage of the nominal value) from profits and to preferential payments before ordinary shareholders in the event of winding-up (if the articles allow). They may be:

(*a*) *cumulative* (*i.e.* shareholders receive full payment of dividends in arrears before any other shareholders are paid);

(*b*) *non-cumulative* (*i.e.* shareholders receive a yearly dividend when sufficient profits are available);

(*c*) *participating* (*i.e.* shareholders receive a fixed dividend and participate in surplus profits with ordinary shareholders); or

(*d*) *redeemable* (*i.e.* shareholders may redeem their shares for cash at or before a date specified at the time of issue).

9. Debentures. A debenture security is a written acknowledgment of a debt incurred by a joint stock company. It provides for repayment of the debt with a fixed interest, usually twice-yearly. A debenture may be one of the following kinds:

(*a*) A simple "unsecured" or "naked" debenture, so called because the holder has no lien or pledge on any assets of the company and ranks after secured creditors for payment in the event of winding-up.

(*b*) A debenture having a "fixed" charge on specified assets, *e.g.* property. Stockholders are entitled to interest and repayment of the loan out of the sale of these assets should it be necessary.

(*c*) A debenture having a "floating" or general charge on the company's unpledged assets.

10. Convertible debentures and loan stock. Such issues may be made when a company needs to raise capital when rates of interest are high. Investors are induced to subscribe for these securities (which carry a lower coupon and are generally unsecured) by the option which allows them to convert their stock on predetermined dates and turns into the company's ordinary shares. Success is assured if the investors feel that corporate success and inflation are certain to lift the price of the share above the conversion price. On the other hand they offer some security by way of fixed interest even if things go ill with the company. Reactions of shareholders will be favourable for the following reasons:

(*a*) Prior charges on earnings are less than for normal debentures.

(*b*) Equity holders enjoy the benefits of high gearing when earnings are large in relation to these fixed interest charges.

(*c*) Equity is not immediately diluted.

(*d*) Assets are not generally pledged, so that borrowing powers are unrestricted.

11. Mortgages. A mortgage is similar to a debenture in that it is a loan secured by assets of the borrower, but it differs in that it is a debt to a single lender, the mortgagee. The provision of mortgages is especially well known in the private sector, but it is also a valuable source of long-term capital for commercial undertakings. Insurance companies, pension funds and finance companies are the main mortgagees, although limited funds are available from solicitors and building societies. Organisations like the Ship Mortgage Finance Company and the Agricultural Mortgage Corporation make special-purpose loans.

GEARING

12. Capital gearing. The gearing ratio or coefficient indicates the relative proportions of the types of capital employed in a company. For example, a company is said to be "highly geared" if the proportion of fixed income capital is large in relation to the total. The gearing ratio can be measured by:

(*a*) the proportion of total debt interest and preference share dividends to total ordinary share dividends;

(b) the percentage,

$$\frac{Long\text{-}term\ loans\ and\ Preference\ shares}{Ordinary\ shareholders'\ funds} \times 100;$$

(c) the percentage,

$$\frac{Long\text{-}term\ loans}{Capital\ employed} \times 100.$$

13. Determinants of the gearing ratio. The ratio varies between firms and industries and is influenced by the following factors:

(a) The borrowing powers in a company's articles of association.

(b) The existence of charges on the company's assets.

(c) The attitude of shareholders towards control. They may resist attempts to diffuse their equity holding and prefer "debt" capital as a source of new finance.

(d) The relative costs of raising debt and share capital.

(e) The level of anticipated profits in relation to the fixed interest charges on debt capital.

14. Effect of gearing on profits. A simple example illustrates the effect of different gearing ratios on company dividends. Let us assume there are two equally capitalised companies but with different capital structures: A is low-geared (1 : 4) and B is high-geared (7 : 3). Profits in each case for 1971, 1972 and 1973 are £9,000, £7,000 and £4,000 respectively. Company A has a share capital of 20,000 at £1, preference at 5 per cent, 80,000 ordinary at £1. Company B has a share capital of 70,000 at £1, preference at 5 per cent, 30,000 ordinary at £1.

	1971		1972		1973	
Company	A	B	A	B	A	B
Total profits for distribution	£9,000		£7,000		£4,000	
Total dividends for 5 per cent preference shares	1,000	3,500	1,000	3,500	1,000	3,500
Dividends for ordinary shares	8,000	5,500	6,000	3,500	3,000	500
Dividend percentage	10	18·3	7·5	11·6	3·7	1·6

Thus if one ignores taxation and profit retention one sees that the high gearing in company B produces higher dividends at higher profits and lower dividends at lower profit levels, in contrast to company A. This has important implications for companies and shareholders.

15. Advantages of gearing.

(a) When profits are high in relation to total fixed interest charges, the ordinary shareholders in a highly-geared company benefit immediately from additional dividends, or in the future from the earnings generated by the retained profits.

(b) It enables a company to increase its capital without dilution of equity and shareholders' control.

16. Disadvantages of gearing.

(a) High gearing is disadvantageous to equity holders when profits are falling since they receive disproportionately less by way of dividends.

(b) The company is committed to long-term fixed-interest payments which could cause cash flow problems.

(c) If gearing is affected by debentures, then charges may be placed on company assets.

(d) Once assets are pledged, further gearing may be accomplished only by offering higher yields to lenders to compensate for the lack of security.

(e) Gearing demands that management produce sufficient profits to pay interests and dividends and meanwhile establish a sinking fund for the redemption of debentures.

(f) Companies whose incomes fluctuate (perhaps their products are elastic in demand) will find it difficult to maintain satisfactory dividend rates and share prices.

(g) Investors will be reluctant to subscribe new capital.

17. Vote-gearing.
The concept of gearing may be used also to indicate the degree of control exercised by ordinary shareholders.

(a) For example, the vote-gearing of a company with issued capital of 100,000 £1 ordinary shares (with full voting rights) and 50,000 £1 preference shares, plus 20,000 £1 debentures (without voting rights) is:

$$\frac{\text{Total capital}}{\text{Total voting capital}} = \frac{£100,000 + £50,000 + £20,000}{£100,000} = 1 \cdot 7$$

Here ordinary shareholders control capital 1·7 times their own nominal capital.

(b) However, vote-gearing of ordinary shareholders is tempered if similar voting rights are given to the preference share-holders, *i.e.*

$$\frac{£100,000 + £50,000 + £20,000}{£100,000 + £50,000} = 1 \cdot 1$$

18. The choice of finance. A company in need of additional finance has a wide choice, its final option being influenced by the following considerations:

(*a*) The *relative cost* of borrowing by different methods:

(*i*) The "cost of capital" is the interest which has to be offered on debentures, the dividends on preference shares and yields on ordinary shares to attract investors' capital. Obviously the opportunity cost of capital is relevant, but in addition it is influenced by the investors' attitudes towards risk, reward and control offered by various securities. For instance, lenders will demand higher rewards on ordinary shares and unsecured loan stock than on preference shares or secured debentures, to compensate for the higher risks. But they will demand less if they confer control with its attendant advantages.

(*ii*) The administrative costs involved in raising the capital.

(*b*) The *term of the finance.* Projects which mean that expenditure will not be recouped in the short term suggest long-term finance, which is generally more expensive. However, in times of high interest rates, a company should consider financing a long-term project by redeemable securities and by short-term borrowing when there is a good chance that it can be re-financed later when rates are lower.

(*c*) The *effects of taxation, e.g.* loan interest is allowable against profits (unlike dividends) in the assessment of corporation tax.

(*d*) The *value and nature of corporate assets* available as security.

(*e*) The nature of *conditions imposed by lenders* on a company's freedom of action, *e.g.* restrictions on future borrowing ability if assets are pledged.

(*f*) The company's *ability to earn a sufficient cash flow* to pay fixed charges and repay loans, *e.g.* redeemable debentures.

(*g*) The company's *existing capital structure* and the effect of new borrowing on capital and vote-gearing.

(*h*) *Market conditions, e.g.* a severe "credit squeeze" may make it impossible to obtain short-term bank finance, or the capital market may already be "saturated" with new issues.

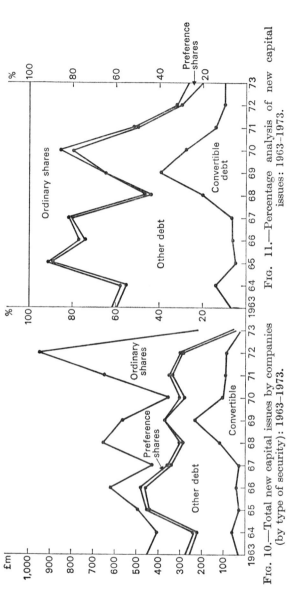

Fig. 10.—Total new capital issues by companies (by type of security): 1963–1973.

Fig. 11.—Percentage analysis of new capital issues: 1963–1973.

19. Recent trends in capital gearing. The Annual Abstract of Statistics and the Midland Bank's statistics on total new issues by companies (by type of security) (*see* Table XV) highlight the increasing dependence by companies on borrowed funds. The average percentage of dept capital to total new capital raised by companies over the period 1954–62 was 37·6. Table XIV and Figs. 10 and 11 show a dramatic increase in borrowings after 1965, in particular in 1965 and 1970, when the percentages were 90·3 and 82·0 respectively, and although there has been a revival in equity financing since 1971 companies generally still rely heavily on borrowed funds. Whether one measures capital gearing in terms of long-term debt to capital employed or includes preference share capital in the numerator the trend is the same, *i.e.* a higher percentage of fixed-interest and dividend capital to total funds (*See* Table XIV).

TABLE XIV. CAPITAL GEARING IN QUOTED COMPANIES

Year	(i) Equity funds (£m)	(ii) Preference shares (£m)	(iii) Long-term debt (£m)	(iv) Capital employed (£m)	(v) Gearing factor (%)	(vi) Long-term debt as % of capital employed	(vii) Long-term debt + preference shares as % of capital employed
1964	12,907	1,042	2,276	17,516	25·7	12·9	18·9
1965	14,050	1,028	2,622	18,985	25·9	13·8	19·2
1966	14,466	924	3,158	19,872	28·2	15·9	20·5
1967	14,386	837	3,635	20,323	31·0	17·8	22·0
1968	15,323	734	4,150	21,049	31·8	19·7	23·2
1969	15,850	606	4,355	21,745	31·3	20·0	22·8
1970	16,238	533	4,767	22,454	32·6	21·2	23·6
1971	17,571	514	5,250	24,428	32·8	21·5	23·6

Source: Annual Abstract of Statistics, H.M.S.O.

NOTE:
Column (v) = (ii) + (iii) ÷ (i).
Column (iv) = Total net assets.

Furthermore, one can regard overdrafts as long-term sources of capital on the grounds that although theoretically repayable on demand, most companies operate on a permanent overdraft basis. Thus if these funds are included the gearing factors are increased significantly in view of the substantial overdrafts and loans, and support the view that companies and shareholders recognise the benefits of "trading on the equity," and the advantages of debt financing in an inflationary situation.

DEBT AND EQUITY FINANCE

20. Effect of corporation tax. This tax, introduced in 1965, replaced the system of income and profits tax on company profits, and has changed industry's method of raising new capital in the following ways:

(a) Equity, traditionally employed, was replaced by loan capital.
(b) Issues of preference shares virtually disappeared.

The impact of this tax may be seen in Table XV. Preference and ordinary capital as a percentage of total new issues fell from 2·6 and 40·8 in 1964, to 0·6 and 9·0 respectively in 1965. Loan capital rose sharply from 56·5 to 90·3. 1968, however, saw a widening "reverse yield gap" between equities and loan stock, which meant it was no longer cheaper to raise money by loan stock, hence the revival of equity financing.

21. Slump in capital issues 1973. In 1973 new company issues fell by 78 per cent, *i.e.* from the all-time high figure of £970·8m in 1972 to £210·5m (actually only £133·8m in 1963 prices) for the following reasons.

(a) The low level of capital investment meant that companies did not need to raise additional finance.
(b) High profit levels in 1972–3, and dividend restraint contributed to a substantial source of internal funds.
(c) Bank credit was readily available.
(d) The introduction of V.A.T. contributed about £800m to companies' liquid assets.
(e) The decline in share values on the Stock Exchange and rise in interest rates in 1973 meant that companies making new issues would not realise the high premiums of 1972 and would have to offer very high coupons to guarantee successful issues.

In summary, the sufficiency of internal funds and bank over-drafts to finance new investment and an unattractive capital market were responsible for the sharp decline in new capital issues.

TABLE XV. TOTAL NEW CAPITAL ISSUES BY COMPANIES (BY TYPE OF SECURITY)

	Loan capital				Share capital				
	Con-vertible (£m)	Other (£m)	Total (£m)	% of total	Pref-erence (£m)	% of total	Ordi-nary (£m)	% of total	Total (£m)
1964	60·2	173·8	234·0	56·5	10·7	2·6	168·9	40·8	413·6
1965	28·1	426·5	454·6	90·3	3·2	0·6	45·5	9·0	503·4
1967	29·7	313·8	343·5	81·5	5·7	1·4	72·6	17·2	421·9
1968	128·3	181·3	309·5	45·8	3·1	0·5	363·7	53·8	676·4
1969	231·7	165·7	397·4	67·1	—	—	195·0	32·9	592·4
1970	101·3	211·6	312·9	82·0	17·2	4·5	51·9	13·6	382·0
1971	96·7	273·4	370·1	53·4	12·8	1·8	310·4	44·8	693·3
1972	96·4	213·6	310·0	31·9	10·9	1·1	649·9	66·9	970·8
1973	21·6	21·3	42·9	70·4	14·0	6·7	153·6	73	210·5

(Based on Midland Bank figures for new money raised by the issue of market-able company securities.)

22. Effect of corporation tax on company financing. The method of corporation tax assessment makes it cheaper for a company to service loan capital than to pay dividends on equal amounts of equity.

(a) Corporation tax is assessed on profits after interest charges, but not ordinary and preference dividends, have been deducted.

(b) Ordinary and preference dividends, which were charged net of tax to the company, are now charged gross.

If corporation tax is assumed to be 40 per cent, it costs a company just as much to pay a 6 per cent dividend as it does to pay interest on a 10 per cent debenture. For example see table on top of next page.

Thus to retain the same profits, Company B can afford to pay total dividends of £6,000, equivalent to 6 per cent against 10 per cent for debentures by Company A.

Another example illustrates the effect that gearing has on earnings *per* share. Here the comparison is between a wholly

Company A: 100,000 £1 debentures at 10 per cent		Company B: 100,000 £1 ordinary and preference shares	
Company profits	£50,000	Company profits	£50,000
Debenture interest	10,000	Corporation tax	20,000
	40,000		30,000
Corporation tax 40%	16,000	Dividend	6,000
Profits retained	£24,000	Profits retained	£24,000

equity-financed company and one which has a gearing ratio of 1 : 1. Profits of £50,000 are assumed and corporation tax and debenture interest are taken to be 40 per cent and 10 per cent respectively.

	Company A	Company B
Ordinary shares	£100,000	£50,000
Debentures @ 10%	—	50,000
Capital employed	100,000	100,000
Profits	50,000	50,000
less Debenture interest	—	5,000
Profits before tax	50,000	45,000
less Corporation tax 40%	20,000	18,000
Profits available for shareholders	30,000	27,000
Earnings per share	30p	54p

Clearly both companies are equally efficient in terms of profitability; both realised a R.O.C.E. of 50 per cent. However, Company B having earned a 50 per cent return on its borrowed funds which cost only 10 per cent to service, retains the surplus earnings for the benefit of the shareholders so that £27,000, although a smaller absolute profit than A's, is spread among only half the number of ordinary shares. Consequently earnings per share amount to 54p compared with 30p for Company A.

23. Effect of gearing on profitability. The above advantages of gearing on the ordinary shareholders' earnings *per* share may also be expressed in a slightly different way in terms of return on investment. For instance, the 50 per cent R.O.C.E. for Company B in the previous example lifts the Return on Investment (R.O.I.) to 54 per cent because it is trading on the equity

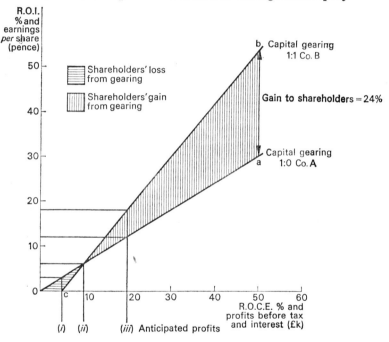

Fig. 12.—Relationships between R.O.C.E. and R.O.I., profits before tax and interest and earnings *per* share for given capital gearing structures.

(*i.e.* £27,000 ÷ £50,000 share capital × 100). In fact, at the profit level of £50,000 shareholders receive the substantial benefit of an extra 24 per cent return over the shareholders in Company A whose R.O.I. figure is 30 per cent. This information is plotted in Fig. 12 (points a and b). A third plotting is O where for a R.O.C.E. of zero the wholly equity-financed company's R.O.I. would also be nought: the fourth

BFM—E

point is C that shows that a R.O.C.E. of 5 per cent must be earned by the geared company B to cover its interest charge of £5,000, thus leaving the ordinary shareholder with a zero R.O.I. Then by joining these points we establish two lines that indicate the relationship between R.O.C.E. and R.O.I. for the two companies with their very different capital structures.

This visual representation of gearing confirms the conclusions drawn in (14) that gearing operates against shareholders' interests when profits are very low but is beneficial when profits are high. In fact, when the R.O.C.E. is less than 10 per cent gearing actually reduces the R.O.I. return; consequently whole-equity financing is preferable. However, when the R.O.C.E. exceeds 10 per cent a degree of gearing is desirable.

These important principles of financial management may be summarised as follows:

> (a) An equity-financed capital structure is recommended if the anticipated R.O.C.E. is inadequate to service the cost of borrowing.
> (b) A degree of capital gearing is recommended when the R.O.C.E. exceeds the cost of borrowing.
> (c) When the R.O.C.E. exceeds this break-even point, then the higher the gearing the higher the return to the shareholders.

24. Forecasting R.O.I. and earnings per share. The principle underlying Fig. 12 may be usefully extended into the areas of financial forecasting. For example, it provides the financial accountant with a simple method (once he has drawn in the company's appropriate gearing line) of translating targeted or anticipated R.O.C.E. figures for the company into the appropriate R.O.I. values. Furthermore, by considering only the numerators of the percentages on the two axes, i.e. profits before tax and interest on the horizontal axis and profits available to the ordinary shareholders expressed as earnings per share on the vertical axis, we can forecast the earnings per share for any given level of profits. Thus if profits so defined are (i) £5k for both companies A's shareholders earn 3p per share, B's earn zero pence per share; with profits of (ii) £10k A and B's shareholders earn 6p per share; and with profits of (iii) £20k A's shareholders earn 12p and B's earn 18p per share. This analysis shows clearly that if anticipated profits are greater than £10k (the real cost of servicing the debt since the company must earn £10k before tax to leave £6k after deduction of 40 per cent corporation tax) then a geared capital structure is in the interest of shareholders in that earnings *per* share are improved.

25. Advantages of issuing loan capital.

(*a*) The effect of corporation tax made it cheaper for a company to service its debts than to make dividends on equal amounts of equity.

(*b*) It encourages higher gearing, which is to the advantage of equity holders, while long-term corporate earnings exceed debt interest.

(*c*) Long-term capital may be raised without dilution of ordinary shareholders' holdings and control.

26. Limitations to debt financing.

(*a*) Every company has a maximum equity to debt capital ratio. Beyond this point:

(*i*) the burden of debt interest and perhaps sinking fund provisions becomes unacceptable;

(*ii*) the risk of default increases; and

(*iii*) future borrowing is restricted.

(*b*) Companies' articles of association limit their borrowing capacities.

(*c*) Companies have to offer higher coupons in order to attract investment funds if the supply of debt securities in the market is increasing. This reduces the cost advantage of debt over equity capital.

(*d*) Rising share prices reduce yields and thereby the cost of making Rights Issues *vis-à-vis* loan stock. Since 1966 the "reverse yield gap" has widened to such an extent that after 1968 it was cheaper to raise capital by way of equity issues.

(*e*) Potential lenders are disinclined to advance funds when they feel that their money is at risk. Therefore companies with above industry average debt ratios and times interest earned ratios may be unable to attract additional debt capital.

(*f*) Investors may find debt securities unacceptable in continuing inflation. However, companies may overcome this reluctance by offering convertible loan stock.

27. Demise of preference shares. As Table XV reveals, preference shares form a negligible part of new capital issues. Indeed they have not been generally popular, since in their usual form they are unsecured, possess no voting rights to influence company policy and, unlike ordinary shares, do not partake in the success of the company. They are less attractive too from the viewpoint of companies, since their dividends are not allowable for corporation tax and are therefore costly.

CONVERTIBLE DEBT V. OTHER DEBT ISSUES

28. Significance of convertible debt. New convertible debt and loan stock securities (*see* **10**) have ranged between 5 per cent and 40 per cent of total issues in the London capital market over the period 1963–73 (*see* Figs. 10 and 11). In 1973 they represented some £21·6m or 10 per cent of total new funds.

29. Why issue convertibles? Company financial managers may decide to issue convertibles in preference to straight debentures or loan stock, for the following reasons:

(*a*) Lenders of funds may require the added inducement of *potential capital gains* over and above the guaranteed interest payment to persuade them to advance funds. In effect, the lender receives a minimum-risk security that offers a hedge against inflation and deflation, *i.e.* capital gains and a minimum floor value determined by the coupon.

(*b*) The company can normally offer convertibles at *lower coupons* than straight debt securities. Consequently, the company can minimise the burden of interest charges until the conversion date which may be set at the outset to coincide with the anticipated fall in market interest rates. Alternatively, they may provide cheap short-term finance, say, during the development and growth stage of the product life cycle when the company is generally short of funds.

(*c*) The company may use convertibles as a *delaying tactic for issuing new shares*. For instance, if the current market share price is depressed but expected to improve, then the company may issue convertibles with the option to convert later into equities. Consequently, the company may gain a premium by floating shares at the higher price.

(*d*) The low risk associated with convertible investment means that the company can demand a redemption premium payment. Consequently, the conversion price is increased and since fewer shares are issued at conversion equity is less diluted compared with a straight equity issue.

30. The price of convertibles. The determination of the price of convertibles is complicated by their hybrid nature, *i.e.* their ordinary shares and fixed-interest security characteristics. For example, a company may decide when market interest rates are 12 per cent to issue convertibles for £1·00 each earning 10 per cent *p.a.* convertible at four years into three ordinary shares. Consequently, the conversion price is:

$$\frac{\text{Issue value of convertible}}{\text{No. of shares receivable}} = \frac{100}{3} = 33\text{p/share.}$$

(*i*) *Situation 1.* If the share price is 33p prior to conversion then the convertible's price will also be 33p per share, the value at which it is freely converted.

(*ii*) *Situation 2.* If the share price declines to, say, 11p ordinary shareholders will have incurred a capital loss of 66 per cent. By contrast, convertible bond holders will have lost only 17 per cent because of the straight debt value of 27·5p, *i.e.*

$$\text{Bond price} = \frac{\text{Bond interest rate}}{\text{Market interest rate}} \times \text{Bond issue price}$$
$$= \frac{10}{12} \times 33\text{p}$$
$$= 27\cdot5\text{p}$$

In fact the price is likely to be higher than 27·5p because of the lower risks of holding convertibles in comparison with equities and straight debt securities.

(*iii*) *Situation 3.* If the share price is expected to increase over the four years by 5 per cent *per annum* from an original value of 33p, then the conversion value can be forecast as follows:

Value at end of
Year 1 = Initial conversion price × (1 + Share growth rate)
= 33p × (1·05)
= 34·6p

2 = 33p × (1·05)^2
= 36·4p

3 = 33p (1·05)^3
= 38·2p

4 = 33p × (1·05)^4
= 40·1p

31. Convertibles and earnings per share. In (14) we considered the effect of capital gearing expressed as the ratio of preference share capital to equity capital and concluded that at high level of net profits a higher ratio benefited ordinary shareholders in terms of higher earnings *per* share and thereby dividends available for the equity. The result would be similar instead we had substituted debenture or loan stock and in fact more beneficial to the equity than preference capital because of the further advantages of tax shielding illustrated in (23). Let us now summarise this analysis by comparing the relative advantages of equity and debt financing in the forms of debentures and convertibles using as a criterion maximisation of earnings *per* share (E.P.S.).

Imagine that a company requires additional capital of £1m which may be raised by issuing 1,000,000 ordinary shares at 100p bringing total issued shares to 3,000,000. Alternatively, it may issue £1m worth of debentures at 12 per cent *p.a.* or convertibles to the same value paying 10 per cent *p.a.* convertible into 600k ordinary shares. If corporation tax is taken to be 50 per cent and anticipated profits £800k the effect on E.P.S. is as follows:

	(i) Equity	(ii) Debentures	(iii) Convertibles (undiluted)	(iv) Convertibles (diluted)
Net profit before interest	800,000	800,000	800,000	800,000
less Interest	—	120,000	100,000	—
Net profit after interest	800,000	680,000	700,000	800,000
less Tax at 50%	400,000	340,000	350,000	400,000
Earnings available for equity	400,000	340,000	350,000	400,000
No. of shares	3,000,000	2,000,000	2,000,000	2,600,000
E.P.S.	13·3p	17p	17·5p	15·4p

Conclusions:

$$(i) \text{ Conversion price} = \frac{\text{Issue value of convertible}}{\text{No. of shares receivable}}$$

$$= \frac{100}{\cdot 6}$$

$$= 166p$$

(*ii*) Since the conversion price is significantly above the proposed equity issue price, there must be some doubt whether the company can raise the market price by the required amount before the option date, particularly if it is close at hand. Perhaps the equity issues market is depressed at this point in time and hence the interest in convertibles, which delays the issuing of new shares until perhaps a bullish market exists. Alternatively, if the market capitalises this company's earnings at 12–13 times then the company can afford to convert on the basis of its diluted E.P.S. of 15·4p.

(*iii*) As one would expect with this very high profit situation, debt financing scores heavily over equity financing and confirms our earlier conclusions about the benefit of trading on the equity. Moreover, convertibles undiluted perform more satisfactorily than straight debentures than if fully diluted (*i.e.* after conversion since the anticipated profits are now shared among 2,600,000 shares).

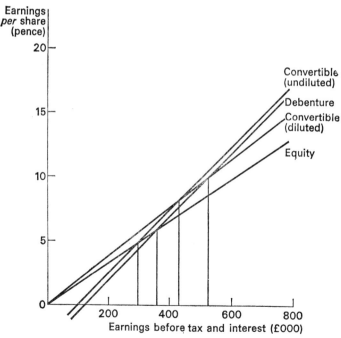

Fig. 13.—Comparative sources of finance and E.P.S.

(iv) Convertibles are preferential to ordinary share finance while profits available for equity remain above £100k (or £300k before tax and interest); below this level of profits, the interest charge of £100k works against the interest of shareholders.

32. Convertibles v. straight debt. The above example shows that if the company objective is to maximise E.P.S. then convertibles may score over straight debt while earnings are undiluted because of the lower coupon.

Furthermore, it provides the company with greater flexibility over straight debt issues, allowing them either to postpone equity issues or to redeem the debt for cash or to convert into equity or possibly to raise additional straight debt either in the interim, since the bond holders are subordinated creditors, or upon redemption if bond holders are unwilling to take up their option and require cash redemption.

33. Choice of finance and E.P.S. The level of anticipated profits will naturally influence the choice of finance. The reason, of course, is gearing, which is explained in principle in (**14**) but for a wider comparison of financing possibilities we must consider Fig. 13. It is based on the data contained in (**31**), and by assuming different profit levels (before tax and interest) examines the effect of the choice of finance on E.P.S. values.

(a) If anticipated profits are £200k then the methods of financing ranked in order of preference that maximises E.P.S. are:

(i) Convertible (fully diluted)	: E.P.S.	3·8p
(ii) Equity	:	3·3p
(iii) Convertible (undiluted)	:	2·5p
(iv) Debenture	:	2·0p

(b) If anticipated profits are £300k:

(i) Convertible (fully diluted)	:	5·76p
(ii) Convertible (undiluted) }break-even	:	5·0p
(iii) Equity		
(iv) Debenture	:	4·5p

(c) If anticipated profits are £365k:

(i) Convertible (fully diluted)	:	7·0p
(ii) Convertible (undiluted)	:	6·6p
(iii) Equity }break-even	:	6·1p
(iv) Debenture		

(*d*) If anticipated profits are £430k:

(*i*) Convertible (undiluted) ⎫ break-even	:	8·2p
(*ii*) Convertible (diluted) ⎭		
(*iii*) Debenture	:	7·75p
(*iv*) Equity	:	7·2p

(*e*) If anticipated profits are £520k:

(*i*) Convertible (undiluted)	:	10·5p
(*ii*) Debenture ⎫ break-even	:	10·0p
(*iii*) Convertible (diluted) ⎭		
(*iv*) Equity	:	8·6p

(*f*) If anticipated profits are £800k:

(*i*) Convertible (undiluted)	:	17·5p
(*ii*) Debenture	:	17·0p
(*iii*) Convertible (diluted)	:	15·4p
(*iv*) Equity	:	13·3p

34. Choice of finance and capital requirements. Different conclusions as to the optimum financing method, however, are drawn if the objective is to maximise capital receipts. In this case, the key determining factor is the present and anticipated market value of the ordinary shares.

(*a*) If the current market value is low, then the order of preference is:

(*i*) *Straight debt, e.g.* debentures. This could be redeemed and replaced by equity when the share price has recovered, subject of course to the company's attitude to risk and its borrowing capacity.

(*ii*) *Convertibles.* Presumably a high interest rate would have to be offered because of the small capital gains anticipated by investors.

(*iii*) *Ordinary shares.* An equity issue would raise only limited amounts for this company's shares in the depressed market.

(*b*) If the current market value is high, then the order of preference is:

(*i*) Ordinary shares
(*ii*) Convertibles
(*iii*) Straight debt

DETERMINING THE LEVEL OF GEARING

35. General determinants of the gearing ratio. In (**13**) we noted the main determinants of a company's gearing ratio, *i.e.* its borrowing ability, the level of anticipated profits in relation to the interest charges on debt capital, the relative costs of raising debt and equity funds and shareholders' attitude towards control. These general influences now serve as a basis for a more comprehensive examination of a company's capital structure and its gearing factor.

36. Borrowing capacity. The first two factors mentioned above are closely related. The first, borrowing ability, is subject to a constraint contained in the company's articles of association and by the attitudes of company officials and shareholders towards borrowing. In other words, the company promoters who originally framed the articles and defined the limits and the managers who determine and implement the financial policy must assess the risks inherent in borrowing:

(a) Loans have to be repaid.
(b) Loans have to be serviced.

Thus a decision to borrow places on managers an obligation to generate sufficient earnings to service and redeem the debt. However, success cannot be guaranteed: management is faced with the ever-present possibility that cash holdings may be insufficient to meet these continuing commitments and repayment of the capital. In this event, default on interest payments has serious repercussions for managers and shareholders in that creditors can legally take control and petition for the winding up of the company for repayment of their debt: the former loses the benefits that control affords and the latter loses perhaps part or all of their investment.

What then determines a company's borrowing policy? It is suggested that a decision to borrow and the degree of borrowing is a compromise decided by the size and composition of the coalition members within the company who, as individuals, possess different attitudes to risk, ranging from the optimistic risk-takers to the pessimistic risk-averters.

The second factor influencing the company's borrowing capacity is management's view of the level of anticipated profits in relation to the interest charges on the debt capital. Clearly, risk of default on debt servicing, with its attendant detriment to coalition member's interests, is minimised where earnings are expected to remain stable and well above the fixed-interest payments. Thus the company's past record of earnings and the anticipated earnings cover on a proposed loan, *i.e.* the expected margin of safety, may cause coalition members to qualify their attitudes towards the risk inherent in a borrowing decision.

37. The lender's attitude. So far, we have not mentioned the attitude of the other party in the transaction, *i.e.* the lender of the finance. He too is concerned with minimising risk, and tends to:

(*a*) *Diversify his lending* so that he hasn't got all of his eggs in one basket.

(*b*) *Advance money at a price.* This means that:

(*i*) He will stipulate a price or rate of interest that is a satisfactory trade-off between the anticipated return on his investment with the company's quantity and quality of expected future earnings.

(*ii*) He will set a price that is a trade-off between the return on the investment and the probability that the capital will be repaid.

38. Quantifying the lender's expectations. Let us imagine that X Ltd. approaches Advance Ltd. with a view to obtaining two loans, *i.e.* £100,000 secured and £100,000 unsecured. X Ltd. provides the following data:

	Balance sheet of X Ltd. £k		*Break-up value of assets*	
Fixed assets				
Land and Buildings	450		500	
Plant and machinery	200		100	
Total		650		600
Current assets				
Raw materials	25		25	
W.I.P.	75		25	
Stocks of finished goods	100		33	
Debtors	150		135	
Cash	50		50	
Total	400		268	
less Current liabilities (unsecured creditors)	100	300	100	168
Net assets		950		768

financed by:
Equity   550
Debenture 8% (secured
  on land and build-
  ings)   400   950

Advance Ltd. will consider the following:

(a) *Earnings cover*. If X Ltd. has a good record of stable profits and forecasts annual earnings before tax and interest of £80k for the duration of the loans then Advance Ltd. can determine with the help of the balance sheet information the terms of the loans.

(i) Loans ranked in order of repayment on winding up	(ii) Annual cost of servicing loans	(iii) Available earnings before tax and interest	(iv) Earnings cover $(iii) \div (ii)$
10% Debenture £400k	£40k	£80k($-$£40k)	2·0
12% Secured loan £100k	£12k	£40k($-$£12k)	3·3
15% Unsecured loan £100k	£15k	£28k	1·8

Advance Ltd. should start by applying the opportunity cost rates, *i.e.* 12 per cent and 15 per cent for secured and unsecured loans respectively, which means a satisfactory margin of safety for the secured loan (earnings cover 3·3 times). However, the 1·8 times earning cover for the unsecured loan is rather low, as is the 2·0 times cover for the debenture, and Advance should decide whether their loans become callable if earnings cover falls to a predetermined level.

The next step is to trade-off between the interest rates and the risk of default, *i.e.* to raise the rate to compensate for the slim margin of safety (although this will necessarily reduce the earnings cover further). Thus, if $\frac{1}{2}$ per cent is added to each loan we have:

(i)	(ii)	(iii)	(iv)
10% Debenture £400k	£40k	£80k	2·0
12$\frac{1}{2}$% Secured loan £100k	£12·5k	£40k	3·2
15$\frac{1}{2}$% Unsecured loan £100k	£15·5k	£27·5k	1·7

Advance Ltd. should next consider the security of the investment, *i.e.* asset cover.

(b) *Asset cover.* Advance Ltd. should next compare X Ltd.'s assets valued on a going concern basis with realistic market values on the break-up value (*see* balance sheet for X Ltd. *above*).

Land and buildings valued at £450k in the balance sheet provide the security for the debenture holder. However, its market value may be currently £500k, in which case there is a surplus of assets of £100k available for other creditors. The asset cover for the debenture holder is:

$$\frac{\text{Value of secured asset at break-up value}}{\text{Amount of the loan}} = \frac{£500k}{£400k}$$

$$1 \cdot 25 \text{times}$$

The asset cover for the secured loan of £100k on a break-up valuation is the total of fixed and current assets less the prior claim of the debenture, *i.e.*

£600k + £268k − £400k = £468k ÷ £100k = 4·68 times

(assuming that there are no preferential creditors, *e.g.* tax, wages and salaries owing).

The asset cover for the unsecured loan is

£368k ÷ £100k = 3·68 times.

Advance Ltd. might consider the asset cover to be satisfactory and confirm the interest rates of 12½ per cent and 15½ per cent, with the proviso that the loans become callable if earnings cover falls below a minimum level, on the grounds that the low overall earnings cover, *i.e.* only 1·17 times (*i.e.* £80k÷£68k total annual interest charge) puts the interest receipts at risk.

39. Shareholders' attitudes to control. Another factor influencing a company's gearing ratio is the attitude of shareholders towards control. If they are unwilling to dilute the equity and thereby weaken their control, they will borrow additional funds when required and pay the higher interest premiums demanded by lenders as compensation for the inevitable deterioration in earnings or asset cover.

40. Relative costs of raising finance. This is another consideration influencing capital gearing which has been discussed earlier. In summary, the financial planner will compare:

(a) The net proceeds of equity/debt issues in relation to capital requirements.

(*b*) The Tax treatment of dividends and interest payments to establish the true cost of shares and debt capital financing.

(*c*) The coupon rate that the company must offer, which depends on:

(*i*) The company's potential earning capacity.

(*ii*) The opportunity cost of capital at the time of issue.

(*iii*) The asset cover.

41. Summary. Financial planners attempting to fashion a satisfactory capital structure should proceed in the following manner:

(*a*) Determine the economic objectives of the coalition, *e.g.* maximisation of E.P.S. either for dividends or retention, dilution or extension of control by shareholders. Naturally, these objectives will be tempered by attitudes to risk.

(*b*) The determination of the broad long-term financial policy to secure these objectives and in particular the selection of a target gearing ratio which the company could reasonably support, bearing in mind the anticipated earnings.

(*c*) A consideration of the alternative methods of debt financing available to the company.

(*d*) Selection of the financing method that fulfils the financial policy requirements.

42. Short-term deviations. Of course, things do not always proceed to plan. Financial policy goals and the long-term target gearing level may have to be set aside for short-term considerations, *e.g.* immediate cash flow problems which must be resolved if the company is to survive. For example, British Leyland's accounts revealed a severe crisis experienced in 1970 when, because of rising costs and industrial action, profits attributable to shareholders slumped to £6m. The short-fall in cash flow was met by borrowing, so that the gearing percentage that stood at 43 per cent of shareholders' funds in 1968 more than doubled to 96·5 per cent in 1970. In fact, total borrowing rose from £102·5m to £227·7m over the two years. However, the situation improved in 1971 with the result that the gearing percentage steadily regained a more respectable level (although still high historically) to 88·8 per cent and 81·0 per cent in 1971 and 1972 respectively.

The above example illustrates the use of gearing for overcoming short-term cash flow problems, subject of course to the constraint imposed by the company's borrowing capacity.

PROGRESS TEST 8

1. Compare the main features of ordinary shares, preference shares and debentures. (1–2,–7–9)

2. What do you understand by "the divorce between ownership and control in modern joint stock companies"? What are the causes of this divorce? (3–6)

3. Compare and contrast the interests of shareholders and company controllers. (5–6)

4. Compare debentures, convertible loan stock and mortgages as sources of long-term capital for industry. (9–11)

5. What do you understand by "capital gearing"? Outline the pros and cons of a high gearing ratio. (12–16)

6. Indicate the main considerations which affect a company's choice of capital to finance a long-term project. (18)

7. What has been the effect of corporation tax on the choice of company finance? (20–22)

8. Consider the pros and cons of loan capital as a means of long-term company finance. (22–26)

9. Compare the effects on earnings *per* share if finance is raised by ordinary shares, debentures and convertibles. (28–35)

10. Explain how the gearing level is determined with specific reference to the company's borrowing policy and the attitude of lenders. (35–42)

CHAPTER IX

PRINCIPLES OF INVESTMENT

THE CHOICE OF INVESTMENT

1. Investment objectives. In theory, the ideal investment is one which offers perfect security, maximum income and perfect liquidity. However, in practice there is no such ideal investment, for these objectives are basically contradictory: liquidity and income, and income and security generally vary inversely. The investor is forced therefore to compromise and choose investments with the specific features which best suit his circumstances.

Age, anticipated future earned and unearned incomes, attitude towards risk, liquidity preference and tax liability are important considerations influencing the individual's investment choice. For example, a person who does not pay standard rate income tax would lose by investing in building societies, since no tax refund is possible. The investors' attitudes towards future interest rates and economic conditions are relevant too to the investment decision. Generally the following rules hold:

(*a*) Liquid securities are preferred if high interest rates are anticipated.

(*b*) Illiquid securities are preferred if low interest rates are anticipated.

(*c*) Equities are preferable if economic expansion is anticipated.

(*d*) Fixed-interest securities are preferable if depression is anticipated.

(*e*) Equities, particularly foreign securities, are preferable if devaluation is threatened.

(*f*) Equities are preferable in moderate inflation.

(*g*) A balance between cash, equities and bonds is advisable if no change is expected in interest rates and economic conditions.

(*h*) Cash is preferable in times of economic and financial uncertainty.

132

2. Types of investment. The investor may choose between the following three broad categories of investments:

(a) Fixed-capital investments, which guarantee security and high liquidity, although this must be sacrificed for high returns (see 3).

(b) Fixed-income investments, which guarantee a certain annual income but less security of capital (see 4).

(c) Investments which guarantee neither capital nor income but which may produce above-average returns (see 9).

3. Fixed-capital investments. There are several types of competitive deposits which afford the investor security of capital (albeit in money terms in inflation) with a high degree of liquidity. They are, at April, 1974, as follows:

(a) Commercial bank "time" deposits, which pay $9\frac{1}{2}$ per cent.

(b) Building society deposits, which pay 11 per cent.

(c) Finance company deposits, which pay 13 per cent.

(d) British Government Savings Bonds, which pay $9\frac{1}{2}$ per cent.

(e) National Savings Certificates, which pay $9\frac{1}{4}$ per cent.

(f) Post Office and Trustee Savings Banks, which pay $4\frac{1}{2}$ per cent and 6 per cent.

(g) Local authority loans, which pay $14\frac{1}{2}$ per cent.

4. Fixed-income investments. There are many fixed-income securities available to the investor. They are as follows:

(a) British Government stocks (gilt-edged).

(b) British corporation and county stocks.

(c) Public board stocks.

(d) Commonwealth Government stocks.

(e) Commonwealth municipal stocks.

(f) Foreign Government stocks.

(g) Industrial loan stocks.

(h) Preference shares.

5. Categories of fixed-income stocks. Fixed-income stocks fall into two groups:

(a) Irredeemable or undated securities, issued in the form of industrial loan stock, certain preference shares and gilt-edged stock on the understanding that the capital will not be repaid.

(b) Redeemable or dated securities which will be repaid on

predetermined dates and terms. They fall into the following three categories:

   (*i*) Short-term, with lives up to five years.
   (*ii*) Medium-term, with lives over five and under fifteen years.
   (*iii*) Long-term, with lives over fifteen years

6. Fluctuations in capital values. Changes in interest rates are certain to affect the capital value of fixed-interest stocks. For example, the Government (in the Dalton "cheap money era") offered Consols at $2\frac{1}{2}$ per cent, guaranteeing an annual interest of £2·50 on a £100 investment. When, however, investors attempt to realise this investment later when market rates are, say, 5 per cent, they find that prospective purchasers will not pay £100 but only £50, which at $2\frac{1}{2}$ per cent (on £100 nominal value) yields the market rate of return of 5 per cent. The price of $2\frac{1}{2}$ per cent Treasury stock (£15·5 at Aug. 1974) indicates the size of possible capital losses under inflation for this type of investment, especially when it is so low that it is less than its yield (£15·8)!

   Table XVI clearly shows that generally speaking the average coupon on government stock has remained below market rates of interest because their nominal values have always been in excess of market values since 1962.

TABLE XVI. MARKET AND NOMINAL VALUES OF QUOTED
GOVERNMENT SECURITIES (£m)

	1962	*1963*	*1964*	*1965*	*1966*	*1967*
Nominal values	18,588	19,828	20,027	19,648	19,771	21,706
Market values	14,251	16,306	16,257	15,202	15,220	17,720
Ratio[1]	1·76	1·82	1·81	1·77	1·76	1·81

	1968	*1969*	*1970*	*1971*	*1972*	
Nominal values	21,928	20,881	21,569	22,533	25,019	
Market values	17,089	14,739	16,041	17,108	20,679	
Ratio[1]	1·77	1·70	1·74	1·75	1·82	

Source: Annual Abstract of Statistics, H.M.S.O.

[1] Unity would indicate that the average coupon rate on Government securities is in line with market rates.

7. The yields of stocks. The prospective purchaser of gilt-edged stocks will compare the return, or "yield," of the investment with its opportunity cost, *i.e.* what it could earn elsewhere at current interest rates. Two yields may be calculated, as follows:

(*a*) *Flat yield.* This is the annual return on the investment. It is appropriate for irredeemable stocks. Suppose $2\frac{1}{2}$ per cent undated Consols are quoted at £30. Then:

$$\text{Flat yield} = \frac{\text{Coupon rate}}{\text{Market price}} \times £100$$
$$= \frac{2\frac{1}{2}}{£30} \times £100$$
$$= £8\cdot30\%$$

(*b*) *Redemption yield.* The true return on dated stocks must include the rate of interest and any capital gain which results from differences between their cost and redemption price. Suppose $5\frac{1}{4}$ per cent Conversion Bonds redeemable at par in 1978 are quoted at £84 in 1973. Then:

$$\text{Flat yield} = \frac{5\frac{1}{4}}{£84} \times £100$$
$$= £6\cdot25\%$$

In addition, the investor will make a capital gain of £16 over six years since the bond is redeemable for £100 in 1978. Capital gain may be expressed as an annual yield for the period. In practice this is found in actuarial tables, which allow for compounding, but it may be estimated as follows:

$$\frac{\text{Capital gain}}{\text{Years to redemption}} = \frac{£16}{6}$$
$$= £2\cdot60$$
$$\text{Redemption yield} = \text{flat yield } £6\cdot25 + £2\cdot60$$
$$= £8\cdot85$$

8. Factors determining yields. The general level of yields on stocks is determined by a complex of factors:

(*a*) *The bank rate and the corresponding level of interest rates.* A change in interest rates will affect security prices and yields as follows:

(*i*) A fall in interest rates brings about a rise in the price of fixed-interest securities and a fall in yields.

(*ii*) A rise in interest rates has the opposite effect.

(b) *The borrower's financial standing.* The Government offers absolute security for its debts so that yields on gilt-edged are the finest in the market and establish a standard for other yields. Since the standing of other borrowers is lower, investors expect higher yields. This difference is known as the "yield differential" or "yield gap," which at April 1974 was as follows:

Type of security	Gross yield (%)
20-year Government stocks	13·4
20-year industrial debentures	15·9

(c) *Duration of the loan.* The element of risk increases with the duration of the loan so that, *ceteris paribus*, investors expect higher yields on long-term bonds than for short, by way of compensation. However, in reality other things are not equal, for there are other considerations which affect the outcome, not least the investors' expectations about the direction of future interest rates. Ideally one should buy long when rates are highest and short when they are lowest. However, in practice expectations regarding these trends will differ between individuals. Their decisions to switch between securities will cause distortions in the general pattern of yields between short-, medium- and long-term stocks, with short-term rates even exceeding long-term rates if lower interest rates are expected.

(d) *The general economic outlook.* A bullish outlook for industry or the prospect of inflation and high rates of interest will cause investors to switch to equities to depress the prices of gilts and to raise their yields.

(e) *Political events.* Prices and yields are also influenced by political events, *e.g.* changes of government, industrial unrest, publication of trade figures, international crises or any events likely to effect business confidence.

9. Variable income and capital investments. Ordinary shares are known as risk capital because neither income nor capital is guaranteed. Companies pay shareholders an income or dividend, expressed as a percentage of its ordinary shares' nominal value, the size of which depends finally on its trading profits. These may, of course, vary considerably and in bad years shareholders may receive nothing. The price of shares tends to fluctuate as well, according to the forces of supply and demand, so that investors are liable to capital gains or losses.

10. Methods of investment. An investor wishing to take up equities may do so in the following ways:

(a) *Direct investment.* He may take up shares in a company or from issuing houses when new issues are available, or he may buy existing shares through a stockbroker.

(b) *Investment intermediaries.* Instead he may rely on the expertise of professional managers of investment or unit trusts to select a portfolio of shares which are expected to produce above-average returns.

INVESTMENT INTERMEDIARIES

11. Investment trust. An investment trust is a limited company which uses the capital subscribed by its shareholders to build up a portfolio of securities for income and long-term capital growth. Despite its name, which dates from last century, it is not a trust in the legal sense: its directors are not trustees, nor are its shareholders beneficiaries and the normal director-shareholder relationship exists.

12. Organisation. Since the ordinary share capital of these companies is fixed at any time and increases are made by Rights Issues to existing shareholders, their shares tend to be tightly held, although supplies of quoted shares are normally available on the Stock Exchange at prices reflecting supply and demand and not necessarily the current market value of their securities in their portfolios. However, this share capital represents only one source of funds available for investment. There is also borrowed money, undistributed profits, investment income and any capital gains on the sale of shares in its portfolio.

13. Advantages of investment trusts. Generally speaking, the investment trust offers investors several advantages, as follows:

(a) Diversification of investment. An investment trust can minimise the risk of unstable income and capital associated with equity investments by building up a portfolio spread between companies, industries and countries. Thus it may average its yields in a way which is beyond the resources of individual investors. North American stocks figure prominently in most portfolios. Most have performed well since the war (share prices have risen by over 500 per cent since 1949) and some have made sensational gains, *e.g.* I.B.M., Avon, Polaroid and Xerox, where $1,000 invested in 1954 was worth $283,000 in 1968.

The difficulty with the $ investment premium (as high as 50 per cent) and the tax liability on overseas investment income, stresses the need for professional management to follow the market closely, to identify smaller companies that might emulate these performances and to minimise cost.

(*b*) Professional management. If investment is regarded as a science rather than an art, then professional management, using investment analysis to make efficient security and portfolio selections, may be expected to predict returns and risks more accurately than non-specialists.

(*c*) An investment trust can select investments which have different dividend dates to produce a steady flow of income for distribution or reinvestment.

(*d*) An investment trust can realise economies in brokerage and administration charges through bulk buying and the selling of shares.

(*e*) Shareholders may benefit from an investment trust's high gearing factor. Long-term finance, raised through issues of preference shares and debentures at keen rates of fixed interest, because of the trust's high-class security, forms a good proportion of total capital. This may be used to buy securities earning a higher rate of return. This net income is available either for distribution or reinvestment. However, this satisfactory situation exists only while average returns exceed the fixed-interest charges. If returns are insufficient, then dividends can fall considerably, although trusts have built up large reserves to ensure stability of dividends. The discount on highly-geared investment trusts' ordinary share prices (*i.e.* the difference between market price and the higher break-up value) which is general except for those with particularly impressive dividend records or under bullish market conditions when premiums may be established), reflects the doubts of investors that gearing may act against them.

(*f*) The financial strength of an investment trust with unified management secures privileged market dealings and an influence over companies in which it has shares which outmatches individual or unorganised shareholders.

(*g*) An investment trust secures the privileges which membership of merchant banks' sub-underwriters and placing lists afford.

14. Unit trust. A unit trust is an association of investors, established by a trust deed approved by the Department of Trade, who employ professional management to build up a portfolio of securities for income and capital appreciation.

15. Organisation. Most trusts have a banker or insurance company as trustee, to register and hold investments and to see that the terms of the trust are observed, and a professional management company for the selection of securities and overall investment policy.

Unit trusts were first introduced into the U.K. from the United States in the 1930s as "fixed" trusts, which meant that investments were limited to a definite selection of securities listed in the trust deeds. Later "flexible" trusts were adopted, allowing managers to switch to securities showing greater promise of income and capital growth.

Blocks of shares bought by the managers are sold to the public in the form of sub-units at a price based on the current asset value per unit, plus expenses covering stamp duty, brokers' commission and an initial service charge. Units are re-purchased by the managers at the current asset value *per* unit less expenses, should the investor wish to sell. Since new block issues of units are available from time to time, unit trusts are said to be "open-ended" (no fixed capital) in comparison with the "close-ended" investment trusts.

16. Portfolios. Although a small number of trusts cater for certain types of investors (*e.g.* pensions funds, family trusts, and "off-shore" funds for the investor interested in $ securities), the majority are designed to attract the savings of the small investor, although there is a noticeable trend towards the trust aimed at the relatively rich. Some specialise in certain types of investments (*e.g.* insurance companies, banks, investment trusts and North American securities), but most have portfolios containing a spread of equities in industrial, commercial and financial fields. In addition trusts offer the investor a choice of units, providing for the following factors:

(*a*) High income yield.
(*b*) Capital growth.
(*c*) A combination of (*a*) and (*b*).

17. Development of unit trusts. The last decade has witnessed an impressive increase in the number and type of trusts and also in their financial growth (*see* Table XVII). The reasons for this are as follows:

(*a*) Successful advertising of block issues in national media, backed up by comprehensive marketing facilities, *e.g.* "over the counter" sales and sales by instalment credit.

(*b*) Continuing inflation since the war and the outstanding success of certain trusts has focused attention on equity invest-

TABLE XVII. MARKET VALUE OF UNIT TRUST AND
INVESTMENT TRUST ASSETS (£m)

	Unit trusts	*Investment Trusts*
1961	222	2,269
1962	257	2,334
1963	350	2,817
1964	406	2,887
1965	500	3,119
1966	553	3,033
1967	787	4,013
1968	1,349	5,583
1969	1,344	4,902
1970	1,316	4,469
1971	1,910	5,758

Source: *Annual Abstract of Statistics*, H.M.S.O.

ment as a means of combating it. Unit trusts have benefited from this "cult of equity."

(*c*) The introduction of trusts which cater for all types of investors.

(*d*) The introduction of schemes which link regular purchases of units with life insurance to secure for investors tax relief on the whole of the savings.

(*e*) The willingness of trusts to sell units in small amounts to attract small savers.

(*f*) The ease with which units can be bought and sold.

(*g*) Investors benefit from lower initial and annual charges for larger-scale transactions, *e.g.* £1,000 plus.

(h) The ability to expand supply to match demand for the units. "Open-end" trusts merely have to add to their holdings of securities and issue more unit certificates.

18. Criticisms of unit trusts. Two criticisms of unit trusts are as follows:

(a) Some are fairly expensive.

(b) Managers are responsible to the Department of Trade and not to the unit holders, who bear risk. Unfortunately this widens the divorce between ownership and control.

19. Insurance companies. The business of insurance companies is the underwriting of risk. There are about 550 companies in Great Britain and they are of two kinds:

(a) General business (including fire, motor, accident and marine).

(b) Life assurance (a very important source of savings).

20. Liabilities and choice of investment. Insurance companies' liabilities from these two types of business are quite different. General business constitutes short-term liabilities by way of claims during the life of the policy, which is generally one year. Life assurance liabilities, on the other hand, are considerably longer term, perhaps forty to fifty years. One may expect insurance companies, therefore, to distribute their assets in a way which matches their liabilities, in order:

(a) to keep those funds providing general business cover in secure short-term liquid assets; or

(b) to invest life assurance premiums in less liquid securities, which may be expected to achieve income and capital appreciation in the long run.

21. Distribution of assets. This latter objective suggests that a life office's investment policy should be equity-orientated; even so recent years have seen a marked shift to equities. Today equity-linked life policies are available to the public, representing some 15 per cent of total new life premium income. The reasons for this trend are as follows:

(a) Inflation, which has reduced the purchasing power of the pound by 4 to 20 per cent *per annum*, has caused investors to shun the fixed-sum policy. Instead, "with profits" policies are demanded. This has caused investment managers to turn to equities and property which offer opportunities for income and capital growth.

(b) Competition for the available funds of the small saver from other insurance companies and unit trusts has spurred managers to produce good records of profit bonuses.

(c) The need to provide a rate of growth in shareholders' dividends comparable with other companies.

The result is likely to be a rapidly rising demand for equities in the future.

22. Trends in net investment. The decision to shift a greater proportion of funds into equities is not immutable. On occasions when a fall in the price of equities seemed likely, insurance companies have been quick to reduce their purchases of equities for the guaranteed returns of fixed-interest debenture stock, which are as high as 16 per cent. 1965 was such an occasion. The Department of Trade figures for insurance companies' net investment—the difference between total acquisition and realised investments (*see* Table XVIII)—shows

TABLE XVIII. NET INVESTMENTS BY INSURANCE
COMPANIES (£m)

		Total	Debentures	Preference shares	Ordinary shares	Property
Net acquisitions	1970	972	94·0	−2·0	261·5	197·5
	1971	1,230	115·0	−4·5	265·3	198·1
	1972	1,618	166·0	2·8	679·9	131·1
	1973	1,666	62·9	10·4	356·7	306·8

how these funds totalling £1,666m in 1973 are spread between debentures, preference shares, ordinary shares and property. Institutions generally have been attracted by the good security, immediate yields and growth potential of land values and rents in inflation, especially since good equities have been in short supply. Nevertheless, a clear trend has been established over recent years, so that today insurance companies place a greater part of their funds in equities and property at the expense of gilts.

23. Role of insurance companies in the capital market. The relative importance of insurance companies as large-scale investors in the capital market and as a medium for marshalling the resources of small savers is indicated by the magnitude of their total assets spread between different classes of securities and the volume of new premiums channelled into the market each year. This need to find suitable outlets for these funds, which exceeded £857m in 1970, has caused them to enter the new issues market as underwriters and as members of issuing houses' placing lists.

24. Pension funds: definition. Pension or superannuation funds are trusts set up to provide employees of private industry, local and central government with pensions on retirement. Pensions are taken out of contributions paid in by employers and employees throughout their working lives. These contributions are invested by the funds' trustees, who have wide powers of action to select securities which will secure incomes for pensioners.

25. Pension funds' investment objectives. Actuaries calculate the size of contributions needed to provide a scale of pensions which is acceptable at the expected level of prices on the basis that invested funds earn a compounded interest of, say, 10 per cent. However, the trustees' investment policy is to exceed this minimum return, for the contributions and calculated rate of appreciation may eventually prove insufficient to provide acceptable pensions in times of inflation.

26. Pension funds as investors. Pensions funds, like insurance companies, need to match their investments with their liabilities, which are in the main long term. Consequently they look to high-yielding but safe long-term investments. A large proportion of their assets are held in the form of Government stocks and increasing amounts of property and equities, which can best realise capital appreciation. Only a very small proportion need to be kept in liquid form, since short-term liabilities of current pensions and repayments to employees leaving the pension scheme are more than covered by current contributions. Thus pension funds may be described as permanent net investors. They provide, indirectly through insurance companies, which administer many private schemes, and directly in the case of self-administered funds, a reliable and expanding source of long-term finance for the capital market. While only part of this is used as venture capital, purchase of existing securities releases funds which may take up new issues.

Table XIX shows the growth in market values of the pension funds' assets held in public, private and local authority schemes.

27. Institutional investors. The financial institutions play a vital role in the capital market, bringing the savings of individuals to companies. They do this both directly, in their capacity as underwriters and mortgagees, etc., and indirectly when they purchase existing securities and thereby release funds for reinvestment in risk ventures. An examination of their balance sheets reveals an impressive financial involvement.

TABLE XIX. MARKET VALUES OF PENSION FUNDS' ASSETS (£m)

	Public sector schemes total	Local authority schemes total	Private sector schemes total	Total assets
1961	777	612	NA	—
1962	852	667	2,440	3,959
1963	1,027	727	2,883	4,637
1964	1,071	791	2,985	4,847
1965	1,145	NA	3,293	—
1966	1,182	838	3,365	5,385
1967	1,434	907	3,879	6,220
1968	1,746	1,086	4,648	7,480
1969	1,699	1,220	4,468	7,387
1970	1,846	1,246	4,673	7,765
1971	2,523	1,317	6,120	9,960
1972				

Source: *Annual Abstract of Statistics*, H.M.S.O.

From this, another advantage follows. Financial institutions tend to exert a stabilising influence on the market, for they are unlikely to engage in short-term switching of investments, although they influence it by their disposition of investment incomes.

28. Disadvantages of institutional investment.

(*a*) Some observers view with alarm the increasing participation of institutional investment in British industry, on the grounds that security of investors' capital, their principal concern, conflicts with risk-taking. Their considerable corporate holdings are sufficient perhaps to moderate management's dynamic policies.

(*b*) Institutions have been taken to task for failing to use their influence to "prod companies on efficiency." Only rarely have they taken a positive line, as when they forced the abandonment on the "Second Premiere Investment Trust."

MEASURING THE PERFORMANCE OF INVESTMENTS

29. Selection of investments. A useful criterion by which the investor may measure the performance of the equities he selects is the additional return they realise in the long term over that which could be earned on fixed-interest stocks. This profit he regards as his reward for risk. Naturally, it cannot be assured at the outset, but there are a number of indicators which the would-be investor may use in investment decision-making.

However, it is advisable to explain the tax system, which has changed with effect from 6th April 1973, before examining the fundamentals of investment:

(*a*) Before 1965, company profits paid *income tax and profits tax*. The balance was paid as dividends on which income tax had already been paid.

(*b*) After 1965, company profits paid *corporation tax*. The balance was paid as dividends after deducting income tax for the Revenue from the gross dividend. Thus, the cost to a company paying a dividend was the gross instead of the net amount.

(*c*) Since 1973, we have the *imputation system*, whereby companies no longer account to the Revenue for the income tax on dividends paid to shareholders. They pay advance corporation tax (ACT) of $_7$ of the cash dividends but can offset this against the mainstream of corporation tax in the accounting period in which the dividends were paid.

Now returning to the problem of investment: the criteria for judging shares are summarised as follows:

(*i*) Quality of earnings, meaning the amount and reliability of profits. Basically, three standards are employed to measure quality of earnings and how the market judges the company's performance in this respect; dividend yield, dividend cover and price/earnings ratio.

(*ii*) Asset backing of the shares, indicating the value of assets that are attributable to shareholders.

(*iii*) Cash flow, and

(*iv*) Liquidity ratios which indicate the ability of the company to survive when trade is bad.

(*v*) Institutional backing, on the grounds that the institutions in the forms of pension funds, banks, etc. are unlikely to embarrass the company by short-term switching of shares, but will take a longer-term view of investment.

(*a*) *Dividend yield.* This refers to the current year's dividend and, if used as a measure of future yield, assumes that rates of dividend remain unchanged. Its usefulness, therefore, is limited, although it does give the investor a standard for comparisons between similar investments:

Company X has issued 3,000,000 shares at 33·3p = £1,000,000
Post-tax profit   =   500,000
Dividend paid   =   420,000
Dividend *per* share   =   14·0p

Thus the shareholder who has bought shares for, say, 110p receives a dividend of 14p *per* share with a tax credit of 6p (*i.e.* $\frac{3}{7}$ which he can offset against his tax liability. If he has no tax liability, it is refunded. Thus in effect his "gross" dividend is 20p.

$$\text{Dividend yield} = \frac{\text{Dividend } per \text{ share}}{\text{Market price}} \times 100$$
$$= \frac{20\text{p}}{110\text{p}} \times 100$$
$$= 18\cdot2\ \%$$

(*b*) *Cover for income.* This indicates the number of times dividends are covered by earnings. Naturally, a higher cover is preferred. Similarly, higher dividends and therefore higher dividend yields are preferred but naturally not be at the expense of cover. At June 1974, the industry average was 2·75 .

$$\text{Cover for income} = \frac{\text{Post-tax profits available for distribution}}{\text{Dividend}}$$
$$= \frac{£500,000}{£420,000}$$
$$= 1\cdot2$$

(*c*) *Earnings yield.* This is a better pointer to the value of an investment, since it indicates the true return on the investment (*i.e.* total earnings for shareholders) whether it is distributed in full or not.

$$\text{Earnings yield} = \frac{\text{Earnings } per \text{ share} \times 100}{\text{Market price}}$$

$$= \frac{£500,000 \times 100}{£3,000,000 \times 1\cdot10}$$

$$= 15\cdot15\%$$

(d) *Price/earnings ratio.* This is the most commonly used indicator of a share's performance.

$$\text{P/E} = \frac{\text{Market valuation of shares}}{\text{Total earnings}}$$

$$= \frac{100}{\text{Earnings yield }\%}$$

where earnings yield % $= \dfrac{\text{Earnings } per \text{ share} \times 100}{\text{Price } per \text{ share}}$

So that if the earnings yield is $15\cdot15\%$, then:

$$\text{P/E} = \frac{100}{15\cdot15} = 6\cdot6$$

or

$$= \frac{110\text{p} \times 3,000,000}{500,000}$$

$$= 6\cdot6$$

Alternatively, if a company's share price is £1·00 and available earnings are 10p *per* share then the P/E ratio is 10:1 or 10. Thus the share price of £1·00 represents ten times the last annual earnings, or, put another way, the investor will recoup his capital outlay in ten years if earnings are unchanged. Expressed in yet a different way, he must pay £10 to buy company post-tax profits of £1. Generally, the higher the P/E ratio the greater the expectations of growth by investors.

It is quite possible for P/E and dividend yield to move in opposite directions, where for instance a company making less earnings in fact raised its dividend payments. Consequently, the dividend yield would rise but investors would probably mark down price on the grounds of the lower dividend cover.

30. Comparison of yields. Having examined the meaning and basis of calculation of yields for fixed-income securities and equities, we are now in a position to compare these relative returns and explain the significance of movements in the yield differential.

At the outset, one should remember that the yield attributed to a security represents the state of mind of investors towards the immediate and anticipated rewards in relation to the inherent risk. Furthermore, this investment opinion, while cognisant of the underlying facts, is susceptible to shifts in investment fashion and is exaggerated by feelings of optimism and pessimism: indeed the opinion may be so extreme as to be irrational, so that yields become excessively high or low in relation to the real underlying situation.

Nevertheless, one important principle of investment is that investors generally expect a higher yield to compensate for higher risk. For instance in April 1974 with a prospect of recession and a gloomy outlook for capital investment generally, investors' opinion established yields of 17·73 per cent for equities in companies producing capital goods compared with 15·76 per cent for the less risky non-durable consumer goods sector.

Another principle is that opinion takes account of current and anticipated rates of inflation and interest rates. Thus before 1959 when inflation and rates of interest were contained at moderate levels, investors required a 2 per cent premium for holding ordinary shares over gilts in order to compensate for the extra risk (*i.e.* the yield gap). However, with higher interest rates and inflation, investors saw the capital values of these gilts and their real income whittled away: in contrast, dividends on equities showed greater promise so that the situation was reversed with investors demanding higher returns for gilts than for equities, *i.e.* a reverse yield gap was established.

31. The reverse yield gap. The recent trends in the reverse yield gap measured in terms of dividend can be seen from the following:

TABLE XX. TRENDS IN THE REVERSE YIELD GAP

Date	*Dividend yield gap*
1972 May	5·8
November	5·1
1973 May	6·5
November	7·3
1974 May	8·2

Based on the percentage dividend yields of 496 equities forming the *Financial Times* Industrial Group and the yield on 2½% consols.

The size of the reverse dividend gap at May 1972 (when the *Financial Times* Index stood at its all-time high) clearly reflects the willingness of investors to accept a lower yield on equities in return for the prospect of the higher dividends necessary to keep abreast of inflation. Subsequently, the relaxation of dividend restraint with higher company profits caused the gap to widen further; at May 1974, purchasers of equities anticipated an 8·2 per cent increase in their income from industrial companies.

However, while this dividend yield gap reflects the dividend growth prospects, it is the earnings yield gap that more accurately reflects the risks of investing in equities. The dramatic fall in share values, the prospect of 20 per cent inflation and recession caused investors to reappraise the risks of holding equities: accordingly, the earnings yield was adjusted upwards and in summer of 1974 a significant positive earnings yield gap appeared to reflect this risk differential (*i.e.* earnings yield on industrial equities compared with the yield on consols).

32. Factors determining the P/E ratio. If P/E comparisons are to be meaningful indicators of the relative values of company shares, then earnings must always be measured on a consistent basis. Therefore non-recurring items which affect company profits (*e.g.* revenue from the sale of a fixed asset or the writing off of a capital loss) must be discounted.

The factors that determine a company's P/E ratio are as follows:

(*a*) The value of earnings attributable to each share. The company's dividend policy is also relevant since many investors still cling to dividend yield when valuing shares.

(*b*) The P/E ratio of similar companies which are in direct competition for the funds of the investor.

(*c*) The prospects of the company.

(*d*) The prospects of the industry in which the company lies.

(*e*) The size of the company:

(*i*) Small companies have good growth records.

(*ii*) Large companies have stable dividend policies.

(*f*) The net asset value *per* share.

(*g*) The prospects of a take-over bid for the company.

33. Capital gains. Investors correctly consider this appreciation as their reward for risk-bearing, part of which may be regarded as an aggregation of deferred income, especially if past dividends have failed at least to maintain the returns of alternative safer investments. Looked at in this way, the imposition of a capital gains tax seems equitable so long as capital losses may be offset against gains. However, the introduction of capital gains taxation raised the problem of determining the correct rate. Since tax liability arises only when investments are realised, the effect of too high a rate is to make capital less mobile in its search for profitable investment, to the disadvantage of industry and the national interest.

34. Factors affecting share prices. The more extreme fluctuations of share prices cannot be explained solely in terms of economic realities. They are more likely to be caused by the following factors:

(a) Investors' response to developments which may affect the fortunes of particular companies, e.g. merger proposals.

(b) Investors' response to "bullish" and "bearish" markets:

(i) Fears or hopes of budgetary measures.

(ii) Easy or tight monetary measures.

(iii) Publication of balance of payment figures, e.g. The Financial Times Index fell 16·8 points on 14th May 1969 through the nervous selling as a result of the publication of poor trade figures and fears of stringent economic measures.

(iv) Political and economic conditions abroad.

(c) Speculation, which tends to aggravate share movements, e.g. in 1969 Poseidon shares rocketed from 37p each to £120 in a matter of a few months.

(d) Levels of interest rates and yield differentials between stocks and shares.

35. Performance of equities. *The Financial Times* Industrial Ordinary Share Index, *The Financial Times* Actuaries Share Index and the Moodies Index are the most commonly quoted share indices which indicate to the investor the movements of share prices on the Stock Exchange. Generally, they show a clear upward trend over the past three decades, although they are not without periodic down-turns or plateaux, e.g. 1932, 1940, 1949, 1952, 1958, 1961, 1966, 1969 and 1974. In contrast there have been periods of high growth-rates in 1932–6, 1942–6 and 1952–5, and times when share values have appreciated at exceptionally high rates. For example, in

1957–8 they doubled, in the nine months following devaluation (1967) they increased by 30 per cent, and by 44 per cent in 1968, rising from £28,554m to £41,201m. The overall growth in share prices is indicated by *The Financial Times* Industrial Ordinary Share Index, whose base in 1935 was 100, and which reached its all-time high figure of 543 in May 1972.

36. "Beating the index." If a share "beats the index" it means that its market price has risen more than the average for a group of similar shares or that its price has fallen less. Thus it suggests a better than average performance. *The Financial Times*, in association with the Institute of Actuaries in London and the Faculty of Actuaries in Edinburgh, publishes a comprehensive set of daily share-price indices with other information useful for investment analysis, *e.g.* P/E ratios, earnings and dividend yields for the following industries:

(*a*) Capital goods industries and for each of the ten sub-sections, *e.g.* aircraft, building materials, etc. (a total of 181 stocks).

(*b*) Consumer durables industries and for each of the five sub-sections, *e.g.* electricals, household goods, etc. (a total of 59 stocks).

(*c*) Consumer non-durables industries and for each of the ten sub-sections, *e.g.* breweries, food manufacturing, etc. (a total of 164 stocks).

(*d*) Other groups, *e.g.* chemicals, oils, shipping and miscellaneous (a total of 96 stocks).

From these the 500 share index is compiled. Also it publishes a financial group share price index with indices for each of the nine sub-sections, which range from banks to property (a total of 100 stocks).

The 500 share index and the financial group combine to form an all-share index (651 stocks).

In addition, indices are given for commodity share groups ranging from rubbers to tins (a total of fifty-five stocks) and fixed-interest securities, *i.e.* $2\frac{1}{2}$ per cent Consols, six twenty-year Government stocks, fifteen twenty-year redeemable debentures and twenty five-year preference stocks.

Thus the performance of any shipping company's shares may be compared directly with the *Financial Times* Actuaries

Shipping Share Index. If it is superior the share is said to have "beaten the index."

37. Equities become less attractive. The steady flow of investment funds into equities, which characterised the previous twenty years ("the cult of equities"), was checked in 1969 when their yields became so much lower than for first-class debentures and gilt-edged securities. In June 1974, *The Financial Times* Actuaries Share Index dividend yield stood at 7·2 per cent and Government stocks redemption yield at over 13·2 per cent, creating a "reverse yield gap" of some 6 per cent. Investors became disenchanted with equities for the following reasons:

(*a*) There were no signs of lower interest rates to stimulate equity prices; a substantial capital growth is needed to compensate for this low yield.

(*b*) The lower level of take-over activity in 1969 reduced the chances of higher share prices.

(*c*) Initially share prices might rise enough to cover inflation, say 4½ per cent per annum, but the gross redemption yield on gilts does this without the risks inherent in equity investment.

38. "Collapse of the stock market." In October 1974 share prices reached a sixteen-year low. The *Financial Times* index fell dramatically in 1974, in fact proportionally more than the notorious financial collapse in the stock market of 1929–32 and stood below 200 in the autumn of 1974.

39. Causes of the collapse. There were a variety of factors contributing to the collapse in 1974. They can be summarised as follows:

(*a*) *Dividend restraint.* Phase Three controls under the anti-inflationary measures prevented companies from increasing dividends beyond 5 per cent. In effect, shares were regarded as "fixed-interest" investments but which failed to pay sufficient dividends to cover the rate of inflation. Consequently, investors marked down share prices.

(*b*) The *reverse yield gap* widened to 6 per cent and caused investment switching between shares and fixed-interest securities. Furthermore, the prospect of lower rates of interest accelerated this trend as investors contemplated capital gains.

(*c*) *Political and economic uncertainty:*

    (*i*) Possibility of a general election.

    (*ii*) Possibility of further nationalisation.

(*iii*) Fear of deflationary measures to remedy the worsening balance of payment deficit caused by the petrol crisis.

(*d*) *High interest rates.* Short-term interest rates in the region of 15–16 per cent meant that companies were forced to cut back on borrowings employed in the areas of working capital. This meant cash flow problems.

(*e*) *Falling land property values* caused problems in the banking and property markets. The collapse of companies operating in these markets caused a cash crisis for many more as investors withdrew their supplies of cash.

40. Market value of quoted shares. Table XXI and Fig. 14 show the market value of company ordinary shares quoted on the Stock Exchange. The trend over the period 1962–74

TABLE XXI. SECURITIES QUOTED ON THE STOCK EXCHANGE

(£m valued at March)						
	1962	*1963*	*1964*	*1965*	*1966*	*1967*
Ordinary shares	29,845	32,204	35,917	51,425	52,358	53,150
Ordinary share price index	—	106·3	113·4	106·7	107·6	114·9
Total of all securities	50,224	55,309	59,841	75,155	78,164	82,033

(£m valued at March)				
	1968	*1969*	*1970*	*1971*	*1972*
Ordinary shares	73,872	102,937	89,598	89,652	112,701
Ordinary share price index	162·4	160·5	142·2	168·1	207·48
Total of all securities	103,331	131,679	120,040	120,504	149,531

clearly brings out the short-term cyclical nature of financial investment with the alternating bull and bear periods which are superimposed on the longer-term period of capital appreciation ("cult of the equity") which culminated in the collapse of 1974. An ordinary share price index based on 500 shares which is the most sensitive and accurate indicator of movements in ordinary share prices across the broad range of industry and commerce, is included for comparison, and to a degree qualifies the growth in ordinary share market values which are of course absolute figures and include the values of new securities brought on to the Exchange.

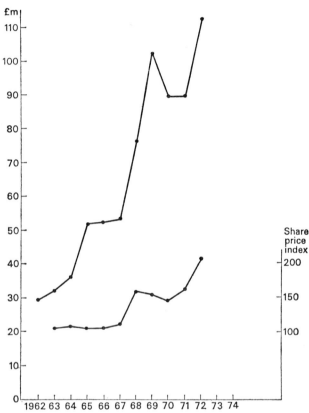

FIG. 14.—Market values of quoted ordinary shares.
Source: Annual Abstract of Statistics, H.M.S.O.

PROGRESS TEST 9

1. "The investor chooses investments with specific or compromising features which best suit his circumstances." Discuss. **(1)**

2. What are the main features of "fixed-capital investments"? Give five examples. (3)

3. What are the main features of "fixed-income investments"? Give five examples. (4–5)

4. Give an example to show how one can calculate:

    (a) the flat yield of an investment;

    (b) the redemption yield of an investment. (7)

5. Explain the various factors which determine the yield on investments. (8)

6. What are the main features of "variable income and capital investments"? (9)

7. Describe the organisation of investment trusts and their advantages as an investment medium for the investor. (11–13)

8. Define a unit trust and describe the advantages and disadvantages as an investment medium for the small investor. (14–18)

9. Outline the main assets of insurance companies, their distribution and the reasons for such a distribution. (19–23)

10. Describe a pension fund, its objectives and the success of such funds as investment media. (24–26)

11. "Many observers view with alarm the increasing participation of institutional investors in the economy." Discuss. (27–28)

12. Explain the following terms:

    (a) Dividend yield.

    (b) Cover.

    (c) Earnings yield.

    (d) P/E ratio.

    (e) Reverse yield gap. (29–32)

13. Outline the factors which affect share prices. (34)

14. How may the investor assess the performance of his equities? (35)

15. What do you understand by "beating the index"? (36)

16. "1968 saw the end of the 'cult of equity.'" Comment. (37–40)

CHAPTER X

MEASURING COMPANY PERFORMANCE

INTERPRETATION OF COMPANY ANNUAL REPORTS

1. Meaning of "Company Annual Reports." Company Annual Reports refer to the company's Trading and Profit and Loss Account and the Balance Sheet (*see* Fig. 15). The former provides an historic assessment of the company's trading position, *i.e.* a "true and fair view" of the profit or loss for the financial year; the latter gives a "true and fair view" of the company's financial position at the time of the statement.

These qualities (true and fair) demanded of financial statements by the Companies Acts are unfortunately undefined, but are interpreted to mean that the auditor applies generally accepted accounting principles and judgment so that the statements reflect "reality and objectivity." In other words, there is a duty on the part of the accountant preparing these accounts to interpret all company transactions as objectively as possible, conforming to the generally accepted accounting standards and applying any special accountancy conventions customarily used in that industry or trade. On the other hand, "reality" calls for the reporting of transactions that are genuinely different or unusual.

Details set out in these reports laid before the company in annual general meeting and thereafter possibly published in the financial press and lodged in Companies House are carefully analysed by interested parties for a variety of reasons.

2. Persons interested in company annual reports.

(*a*) *Management.* Managers naturally wish to compare their performance over the past year with selected market and profitability objectives and with performance of competitors. Possibly management has set corporate objectives in terms of market share, growth in sales value or units and/or a return on investment, and although there are several sources of information that identify the company's comparative performance in these areas, annual company reports provide a reliable and inexpensive method. Hence senior managers and accountants await the publication of rival company's annual reports with keen interest.

(b) *Ordinary shareholders.*

(i) Short-term income maximisers look for distribution of earnings, *i.e.* the amount of dividend declared.

(ii) Those who take a longer-term view are more interested in profit retention for future growth in earnings and capital appreciation.

(iii) Prospective shareholders examine the company's profitability, earning potential and risk *vis-à-vis* alternative investments.

(c) *Preference shareholders.* These look for stable profits at a level that provides adequate dividend cover.

(d) *Debenture holders.* These as individuals, banks or finance companies, keep a close watch on the level of current and future earnings, dividend payments, company borrowings and the underlying valuation of assets that cover their debt.

(e) *Creditors and bankers.* They ascertain the value of prior charges on company property, since they rely on sufficiency of available assets to provide security for their claims.

(f) *Offerors or asset-strippers.* These are interested in the company's earning potential or the possibility of acquiring assets at a discount, *i.e.* buying the shares at below their real value.

(g) *Financial analysts, investment advisers and speculators* on the stock exchange. They compare the balance sheet valuation of the company's shares with the Stock Exchange valuation and the yield in relation to opportunity cost (*i.e.* the yield in comparison with the yield of alternative investments).

(h) *Trade unions.* Unions compare the trends of directors' and shareholders' earnings with union members' wages.

3. Criteria for examination. In summary, these observers are motivated to analyse the published accounts on one or more of the following grounds.

1. Profitability.
2. Activity.
3. Solvency.
4. Gearing and capital structure.
5. Ownership and control.

TABLE XXII. SELECTED CRITERIA FOR

Source of information	Profits/Profitability	Activity
Register of Charges		
Register of Shareholders' Interests		
Memorandum and Articles of Association		
Trading and Profit and Loss Account	1. Gross profit 2. Net profit after tax	1. Sales revenue
Balance Sheet and Notes	1. Change in Revenue Reserve and 2. Interim and final dividends declared	1. Movements in assets

Ratio Analysis
(Selected)

Profits/Profitability

1. R.O.C.E. =
$$\frac{\text{N.P. before tax and interest}}{\text{Total assets}}$$

2. $\dfrac{\text{Trading profit}}{\text{Net capital employed}}$

3. R.O.I. =
$$\frac{\text{Net profit after tax}}{\text{Share + Reserves capital}}$$

4. Margins on Sales
$$\text{Gross} = \frac{\text{Gross profit}}{\text{Sales}}$$

$$\text{Net} \quad \frac{\text{Net profit}}{\text{Sales}}$$

Activity

1. $\dfrac{\text{Sales}}{\text{Stocks}}$

2. $\dfrac{\text{Sales}}{\text{Debtors}}$

3. $\dfrac{\text{Sales}}{\text{Current assets}}$

4. $\dfrac{\text{Sales}}{\text{Fixed assets}}$

5. $\dfrac{\text{Sales}}{\text{Total assets}}$

6. $\dfrac{\text{Sales}}{\text{Total employees}}$

EXAMINATION OF COMPANY ACCOUNTS

Solvency	*Gearing and capital structure*	*Ownership and control*
1. Value of assets not charged		1. % of company assets charged and nature of charges
		1. Shareholders with 10% or more of class of voting share capital
1. Company borrowing powers	1. Debentures and preference shares and redemption dates	1. Voting rights of classes of capital
1. Capital uncalled 2. Value of net assets (especially property) 3. Estimate of contingent liabilities	1. Equity capital 2. Preference and "loan" capital and annual charges	1. Authorised and issued share capital and classes of share capital
1. Current ratio = $\dfrac{\text{Current assets}}{\text{Current liabilities}}$	1. Debt Ratio = $\dfrac{\text{Total debt}}{\text{Total assets}}$	1. Vote-gearing = $\dfrac{\text{Total capital}}{\text{Total voting capital}}$
2. Quick Ratio = $\dfrac{\text{Liquid assets}}{\text{Current liabilities}}$	2. Times Interest Earned = $\dfrac{\text{Profit before tax and interest}}{\text{Interest charges}}$	
3. $\dfrac{\text{Liquid assets + o.d. facility}}{\text{Current liabilities}}$	3. $\dfrac{\text{Net worth}}{\text{Fixed assets}}$	
4. Average collection period = $\dfrac{\text{Debtors}}{\text{Average daily sales}}$ 5. Average payment period	4. Gearing factor = $\dfrac{\text{Fixed- "interest" capital}}{\text{Ordinary shares}}$	

4. Sources of information. The balance sheet with notes to the balance sheet, and the profit and loss account, are the main sources of information because companies are under a statutory duty to publish annually, and include details specified in the Companies Acts, *e.g.* sales revenue, profit, the company's valuation of its investments, value of fixed and current assets, depreciation provided, authorised and issued share capital, payments to directors, the total of long-term loans made to the company and the interest payable, etc.

Additional information that enables observers to assess company performance in terms of the above criteria is found in the following:

(a) *The Directors' Report.* This is attached to the balance sheet and contains details of the principal activities and any significant changes that have taken place and the dividend the directors are recommending, with a report on the company's state of affairs for the benefit of the shareholders. Naturally, trade secrets or details that could be damaging are not reported. Furthermore, it must contain, *inter alia*:

(*i*) Details of new share and loan capital issues.

(*ii*) Group turnover and profits before tax.

(*iii*) Names of directors.

(*iv*) The number of shares or debentures of the group owned by each director.

(*v*) The number of employees and their aggregate annual remuneration.

(b) *The Register of charges.* This register is kept at the company's registered office and contains details of all charges on the company's property. It is freely available for inspection by shareholders and creditors and to others for a modest fee.

(c) *The Register of Shareholders' Interests.* This records the names and addresses of shareholders of the company and their number of shares. In addition it contains an index of shareholders' names who have an interest in 10 per cent or more of the shares of any class of capital which carry voting rights. The register is freely available for inspection and in conjunction with the Register of Directors' Interests provides a clue to the true owners of the company.

(b) *Memorandum and Articles of Association.* The former states the constitution of the company and defines its powers and objects while the latter contains the rules on how company affairs are to be conducted, the rights of members and duties and powers of directors.

CRITERIA FOR EXAMINATION OF COMPANY ACCOUNTS: PROFITABILITY

5. Introduction. In this section, we consider the five selected criteria for examination of company accounts listed in (3), namely Profitability, Activity, Solvency, Gearing and Capital Structure, and finally Ownership and Control in relation to the sources of information outlined in (4). The whole relationship can be visualised in the matrix found in Table XXII.

Figure 15, the balance sheet and summarised profit and loss account of the Auto Co. Ltd. are used to illustrate how company accounts may be interpreted using our selected criteria.

6. Gross and Net Profit. In order to assess the performance of the Auto Co. Ltd. in terms of profitability we note from the matrix in Table XXII that the first source of information on this subject is the trading and profit and loss account. This account indicates the 1974 gross profit and net profit post-tax figure to be £45,000 and £16,000 respectively. However, these figures mean little by themselves; if we compare them with the respective figures for the previous year (£40,000 and £14,000) they become more meaningful. In fact we see that in the year to 31st March 1974 Auto Co. has been more profitable than in the preceding year. However, this may be due to one of several reasons unconnected with the efficiency of the company. For example, general inflation, sales of old stocks made from low-cost materials may be the reason. In order to assess and interpret company performance more accurately, and on a comparable basis we rely on a ratio, expressing one figure in terms of another. The matrix indicates the main ones we will use.

(a) *Change in revenue reserve.* The balance sheet shows that the company has retained an additional £4,000 after payment of dividends.

(b) *The dividend.* The balance sheet note states that the directors propose a dividend of 11 per cent or 11p *per* share. By itself, this figure is not very meaningful; an investor receiving the 11p share will calculate its yield or return in relation to this investment and compare this with alternative investments.

Assume that the current share price is £2·00

$$\text{Dividend yield} = \frac{\text{Dividend paid}}{\text{Share price}} \times 100$$

$$= \frac{11p}{200p} \times 100$$

$$= 5\cdot5\% \quad \text{(or } 7\cdot8\% \text{ with imputed tax credit added)}$$

The Auto Co. Ltd.
Balance Sheet as at 31st March 1974

		1973			1974
Fixed Assets					
Land and Buildings		£60,000		£60,000	
Plant and Machinery		25,000		20,000	
TOTAL FIXED ASSETS			£85,000		£80,000
Current Assets					
Inventories		40,000		46,000	
Trade debtors		52,000		65,000	
Bank and cash balances		5,000		2,000	
TOTAL CURRENT ASSETS		£97,000		£113,000	
Less current liabilities					
Trade creditors	£27,000			£29,000	
Taxation including					
Corporation tax payable					
1st Jan next year	8,000			10,000	
Dividend payable	10,000			11,000	
Bank overdraft	2,000			3,000	
TOTAL CURRENT LIABILITIES		£47,000		£53,000	
NET CURRENT ASSETS			£50,000		£60,000
TOTAL NET ASSETS			135,000		140,000
Representing:					
Issued Capital					
100,000 £1 ordinary shares		£100,000		£100,000	
10,000 £1 preference shares					
at 10%		10,000		10,000	
Reserves		14,000		18,000	
AUTO SHAREHOLDERS INTEREST		£124,000		£128,000	
Loan capital 10% debentures		10,000		10,000	
Deferred taxation		1,000		2,000	
		£135,000		£140,000	

Signed .... Directors
....

NOTES:
Contingent liability. The contractors who built the plant have brought an action against The Auto Co. Ltd. which together with a claim by the Architects could involve liability amounting to £25,000.
The directors recommend a dividend to the ordinary shareholders of 11%.
Preference dividend amounted to £1,000.

(a) Balance Sheet as at 31st March 1974.

Profit and Loss Account for 52 weeks ended 31st March 1974

		1973		1974
Company Sales		£230,000		£245,000
Gross Profit		40,000		45.000
Net profit before tax		28,000		32,000
is arrived at after charging				
Depreciation	£5,000		£5,000	
Directors' remuneration	2,000		2,000	
Auditors' remuneration	1,000		1,000	
Interest payable				
Bank overdraft	100		150	
Long-term loans	1,000		1,000	
Less taxation:				
Corporation Tax		£14,000		£16,000
Net Profit after tax		14,000		16,000
Preference dividend 10%		1,000		1,000
Net Profit attributable to				
ordinary shares		13,000		15,000
ordinary dividends		10,000		11,000
Undistributed profit for the period		£3,000		£4,000
Earnings *per* ordinary share before tax		27p		31p
Earnings *per* ordinary share after tax		13p		15p

(*b*) Profit and Loss Account.

Fig. 15.—Published Accounts: The Auto Co. Ltd.

If the average yield for this industry is 7 per cent then present and prospective investors will naturally become disenchanted with the current dividend policy of Auto Co. Ltd., and in consequence the share price of £2·00 will be marked down.

To say that a company makes a profit of, say, £16,000 in 1974 does not really tell us very much about the performance of the company. It may employ £100,000 capital or £1,000,000 capital to generate this profit. Therefore to assess performance in terms of profitability, we must relate profits to capital employed.

7. Return on capital employed.

$$\text{R.O.C.E.} = \frac{\text{Net profit before tax and interest}}{\text{Gross capital employed (total assets)}} \times 100$$

The profit and loss account for the year ended 31st March 1974 shows the pre-tax profit figure to be £32,000. However, this is after charging interest on the debenture and so £1,000 must be added back, making the numerator in the above fraction £33,000. The reasons for using the profit figure before tax and interest on long-term borrowings are as follows:

(a) *Company tax liability varies* according to **Finance Act** requirements. Unfortunately Finance Acts are beyond the control of managers, and consequently it is useful to use the profit figure that does reflect the internal operating performance of management, *i.e.* pre-tax profit. Nevertheless, there is a case for taking the post-tax figure, on the grounds that tax minimisation is a responsibility of management (who therefore should employ tax specialists to avoid taxation): it is the post-tax profit figure that reflects their performance in this area.

(b) Interest is added back to the profit figure because we want to measure the total return (*i.e.* profit plus interest payments) resulting from the employment of the total sources of finance whether it be share or loan capital. Clearly interest payments are part of the return on borrowed funds.

If we apply the above formula, then

$$\text{R.O.C.E.} = \frac{£33,000}{£193,000} \times 100$$
$$= 17 \cdot 1\%$$

The percentage for the previous year is 15.9, showing a significant improvement in management's performance in its use of total assets.

Alternatively R.O.C.E. is measured by the fraction:

$$\frac{\text{Net profit before tax and interest[1]}}{\text{Net capital employed (net assets)[2]}}$$

[1] The pre-taxation trading profit should be established from the profit and loss account and adjusted as follows:

(a) Debenture loan interest should be included.
(b) Investment income and subsidiary company dividends should be excluded.
(c) Capital gains should be excluded, *e.g.* profit on the sale of an asset.
(d) Notional depreciation on the revalued assets should be excluded.

[2] Net assets should be ascertained from the latest balance sheet and adjusted as follows:

(a) Asset values should be based on current replacement values.
(b) Intangible items, *e.g.* goodwill, should be excluded.
(c) Fictitious assets should be excluded, *e.g.* preliminary expenses.

(*d*) Trade investments and,
(*e*) Investments in subsidiaries should be excluded if the object is to measure the parent company's real profitability.
(*f*) Non-trading loans by the company should be excluded, *e.g.* loans to directors.
(*g*) Long-term loan capital and deferred liabilities should be included.

Only the denominator is different, and includes only the longer-term funds employed in the business, consisting of shareholders' funds and borrowed funds. Thus short-term liabilities such as creditors are excluded, since they are used for short periods only before they are paid and replaced by different funds. However, a business that effectively uses short-term funds such as trade creditors and bank overdrafts as long-term sources could regard these funds as semi-permanent and include them in the denominator when calculating R.O.C.E.

Thus the R.O.C.E. percentages measured in this way for 1973 and 1974 are 21·5 and 23·5 respectively and compare very favourably with the average figures for some 2,000 quoted companies in the U.K. over the period 1961–71 (*see* Table XXIII).

TABLE XXIII(A). PROFITABILITY TRENDS IN QUOTED U.K. COMPANIES ENGAGED IN MANUFACTURING, DISTRIBUTION, CONSTRUCTION AND MISCELLANEOUS SERVICES (1961–1971)

	Total net assets (£m)	Earnings before tax and interest (£m)	Earnings after tax (£m)	R.O.C.E. (%)
1961	14,221	1,883	932	13·2
1962	15,140	1,834	850	12·1
1963	16,122	2,092	1,039	12·9
1964	17,087	2,404	1,177	14·0
1965	18,985	2,524	1,453	13·2
1966	19,872	2,373	974	11·9
1967	20,323	2,697	1,514	13·3
1968	21,049	3,111	1,674	14·7
1969	21,745	3,123	1,621	14·4
1970	22,454	3,063	1,681	13·6
1971	24,430	3,796	2,647	15·5

Source: Annual Abstract of Statistics, H.M.S.O.

8. Return on investment. This measures the return on the proprietors' investment in the company, being their total share capital plus the reserve that they indirectly own. Naturally they are interested in the profits available for distribution, *i.e.* the post-tax profit figure.

$$\text{R.O.I.} = \frac{\text{Profits after tax}}{\text{Total share capital plus reserves}} \times 100$$

TABLE XXIII(B). RATIO OF DEBTORS TO CAPITAL EMPLOYED

	Debtors (£m)	Capital employed (£)	Debtors/capital employed
1964	5147	17,087	0·30
1965	5695	18,985	0·29
1966	6167	19,872	0·31
1967	6622	20,323	0·32
1968	7500	21,049	0·35
1969	8362	21,745	0·38
1970	8948	22,454	0·39
1971	8759	24,430	0·36

In this case, the post-tax profit figure accruing to the shareholders in 1974 is £16,000, *i.e.*

$$= \frac{£16,000}{£128,000} \times 100$$

$= 12·5\%$: again an improvement over the preceding year's figure of 11·2%

It is possible to develop the concept of R.O.I. further, and to calculate the return on the investment contributed by each class of proprietor.

(a)   Return on proprietors' equity investment.

$$= \frac{\text{Net profit accruing to ordinary shareholders}}{\text{Ordinary share capital} + \text{reserves}}$$

$$= 1974 \frac{£16,000 - £1,000 \text{ preference dividend}}{£118,000}$$

$$= 12·7\%$$

(b) Return on proprietors' preference investment.

$$= \frac{\text{Net profit accruing to the preference shareholders}}{\text{Preference share capital}}$$

$$= 1974 \; \frac{£1,000}{£10,000}$$

$$= 10\%$$

In this case, the return on preference capital is that stipulated in the terms under which these shares are issued. However, their R.O.I. could be less than 10 per cent if net profits are inadequate to cover their dividend. Alternatively it could be greater than 10 per cent if the shares are participating preference, which entitle them to their fixed dividend plus an extra dividend out of remaining profits when the ordinary shareholders are paid.

9. Margins on sales. These measure the mark-up on cost of sales and therefore the degree of protection to profits arising from inflationary trends in costs. The first ratio—Gross profits to Sales—measures the efficiency of management in converting materials into sales.

$$\frac{\text{Gross profit}}{\text{Sales}} \times 100$$

$$= 1974 \; \frac{£45,000}{£245,000} \times 100$$

$$= 18 \cdot 4\% \; : 1973 = 17 \cdot 4\%$$

Naturally the highest possible profit mark-up is preferred, but the limiting factor will always be customers' reactions and competitors' marketing policies if sales prices are raised in an attempt to increase the margin.

The second margin relates Net profit to Sales, i.e. it is the income remaining after charging all indirect expenses and is an excellent indication of the efficiency of management in controlling such costs.

$$= \frac{\text{Net profit}}{\text{Sales}} \times 100$$

$$= 1974 \; \frac{£32,000}{£245,000}$$

$$= 13 \cdot 1\% \; : 1973 = 12 \cdot 1\%$$

ACTIVITY

10. Activity. Company accounts contain information that indicates the activity level, or more specifically how effectively the company uses its resources.

11. Sales revenue. The figure found in the trading and profit and loss account indicates how successful the company has been in generating income. In isolation, it is of limited value although the trend in sales revenue can be established when comparisons are made with previous years' figures.

12. Movements in assets. Changes in the value of assets should be inspected and any significant movements in items noted and the cause discovered. For example, stocks may have risen disproportionally to other assets, with the result that too much working capital is tied up. However, caution is needed, for on the other hand the company could have adopted different distribution arrangements, *e.g.* direct selling, which requires higher stock levels because the company is itself performing the wholesale function; or it could be in the process of building up stocks of a new product or model in anticipation of its launch. Similarly, the cause of higher debtor figures should be investigated and credit control tightened if the cause is non-payment by debtors rather than a deliberate policy of credit extension by the organisation.

13. Turnover of capital employed. The activity ratios (*see* matrix in Table XXII) are the best measures to show how effective the organisation has been in using the resources under its control. They relate the various asset items to the sales revenue figure, measuring the appropriate asset turnover, *i.e.* how many times an asset item has been turned over to generate the sales revenue figure. Naturally the higher the turnover the greater the efficiency in using these scarce resources.

14. Stock turnover. This is calculated as follows:

$$\text{Stock turnover} = \frac{\text{Sales revenue}}{\text{Stocks}}$$

and in the case of the Auto Co. Ltd, is:

$$= \frac{\text{£245,000}}{\text{£46,000}}$$

$$= 5 \cdot 3 \text{ for 1974} \quad \text{and} \quad 5 \cdot 7 \text{ for 1973.}$$

The lower turnover figure reveals that the company was less successful in 1974 in utilising its stocks. Expressed in a slightly different way, this means that 18·8p worth of stock was needed to generate £1 worth of sales $\left(i.e. \ \dfrac{\text{£46,000}}{\text{£245,000}} \right)$ and only 17·4p in 1973.

There are two points worth mentioning. First, there is a case for averaging the stock figure for use as the denominator (*i.e.* opening stocks + closing stocks ÷ 2) because stocks are measured at one point in time whereas the sales revenue accrues over the financial period. Seasonality of sales or an expanding or contracting sales trend add weight for the use of adjusted stock figures. Secondly, "cost of sales" figures could be employed as numerator, which would then make sales directly comparable with stock values which are measured at cost. This overcomes a possible objection of comparing stocks valued at cost with sales revenue, which may produce unreliable or misleading results if the percentage mark-up is changed.

Thus, in this example, the stock turnover (*i.e.* how quickly stocks are converted into sales) can be calculated as follows:

$$\text{Stock turnover} = \frac{\text{Cost of sales}}{\text{Average stock of goods held}}$$

$$= \frac{\text{£200,000}}{(\text{£40,000} + \text{£46,000}) \div 2}$$

$$= 4 \cdot 6 \text{ times in the year}$$

Naturally a high turnover figure means that there is less risk to the company if there is a fall in the market price of the goods.

15. Debtors' turnover. This measures the number of times that debtors' balances are turned over to secure the sales revenue.

$$\text{Debtors' turnover} = \frac{\text{Sales revenue}}{\text{Debtors}}$$

$$= 1974 \; \frac{\pounds245,000}{\pounds65,000} = 3\cdot8$$

$$= 1973 \; \frac{\pounds230,000}{\pounds52,000} = 4\cdot4$$

However, a convenient method of measuring the effectiveness of debtors' control is to calculate the time it takes on average for debtors to pay for their purchases which can then be compared with the period of credit allowed to debtors. Thus sales revenue is divided by the number of calendar days in the year and this sales *per* day figure in turn divided into the debtors' total.

Sales *per* day

$$= 1974 \; \frac{\pounds245,000}{365} = \pounds671 \qquad 1973 \; \frac{\pounds230,000}{365} = \pounds630$$

Average collection period

$$= \frac{\text{Debtors}}{\text{Sales } per \text{ day}}$$

$$= 1974 \; \frac{\pounds65,000}{\pounds671} = 97 \text{ days} \quad 1973 \; \frac{\pounds52,000}{\pounds630} = 83 \text{ days}$$

These calculations reveal that the debtor position has deteriorated since 1973. Debtors are receiving an additional sales value of £671 every day but are paying more slowly than the previous year, *i.e.* it takes on average 97 days to collect the cash compared with 83 days in 1973.

16. Current-asset turnover. This ratio of sales revenue to total current assets measures how effective management is in controlling the more liquid assets.

Current-asset turnover

$$= \frac{\text{Sales revenue}}{\text{Current assets}}$$

$$= 1974 \; \frac{\pounds245,000}{\pounds113,000} = 2\cdot2 \quad 1973 \; \frac{\pounds230,000}{\pounds97,000} = 2\cdot4$$

17. Fixed-asset turnover. Fixed assets are basically long-term investments authorised in the past on the basis of capital appraisal in one form or another. Consequently, the room for manoeuvre in controlling fixed assets at any point in time is severely restricted by their very nature. Suffice it to say that the fixed-asset turnover ratio, while measuring the company's efficiency in the use of long-term capital resources, tells us more about the efficiency of the capital investment appraisal decisions that authorised such expenditure. Thus the fixed-asset activity ratio measures the turnover of all capital assets including land, building, plant and machinery, furniture and fittings, motor vehicles, etc., although for a detailed analysis the turnover of each category of fixed asset could be calculated.

Fixed-asset turnover

$$= \frac{\text{Sales revenue}}{\text{Fixed assets}}$$

$$= 1974 \, \frac{£245,000}{£80,000} = 3 \cdot 1 \qquad 1973 \, \frac{£230,000}{£85,000} = 2 \cdot 7$$

18. Total asset turnover. This measures the efficiency of utilising all capital employed within the organisation, and is calculated as follows:

Total asset turnover

$$= \frac{\text{Sales revenue}}{\text{Total assets}}$$

$$= 1974 \, \frac{£245,000}{£193,000} = 1 \cdot 27 \qquad 1973 \, \frac{£230,000}{£182,000} = 1 \cdot 26$$

These activity ratios reveal that 1974 was a slight improvement on 1973, and that the company had generated a larger volume of sales revenue from its total investment of assets.

SOLVENCY

19. Solvency. Solvency means the ability of the company to pay its debts.

Assuming that the assets of Auto Co. Ltd. shown in Fig. 15 are realistically valued, then the company is clearly solvent, *i.e.* if all assets are sold then the proceeds are more than sufficient to meet the claims of the debenture holders and creditors.

Liquidity is a closely-related concept that measures the

ability of the company to find cash to meet maturing obligations. Nevertheless, it is quite possible for a company to fail if it cannot raise sufficient cash funds to meet immediate debts, even though it is solvent in that total assets (when realised) match total debts.

20. Value of assets not charged. Land has for long been regarded as suitable collateral for borrowing, since it tends to appreciate and thereby offers the creditor a high degree of safety. Therefore a comparison between a company's fixed assets, particularly land and the Register of Charges, will reveal what assets are free of liens or charges of creditors and available if required as collateral for further borrowing.

21. The company's borrowing powers. These powers and borrowing limits are set out in the Memorandum and Articles of Association.

(*a*) Company borrowing ability is further restricted by the terms of the debenture deed. In order to protect debenture holders, the borrowing limits are often set very low in terms of today's rate of inflation, which may lead to conflict between the interests of the debenture trustees, who desire adequate security of the debt, and the company which desires additional liquidity. Alternatively, debenture holders may be induced to waive borrowing restrictions in return for above-average returns.

Moreover, debenture deeds frequently impose further restrictions, *e.g.* preventing scrip issues and substitution of securities which can conflict with management's financial strategy.

(*b*) Preference shareholders may have the right to block increases in borrowing powers. Here, the solution may be to buy out these shares, as when George Sandeman, the port, sherry and brandy company, offered to buy out its 426,016 3½ per cent preference shares in July 1974.

(*c*) Debenture trustees will look critically at dividend cover and could argue that a distribution out of reserve jeopardises their security.

22. The authorised capital. In the case of Auto Co. Ltd., the authorised share capital is 150,000 £1 shares, of which 100,000 have been issued. This means that the company could issue a further 50,000 shares should it require additional capital.

23. Value of net current assets. The net current assets figure is the difference between total current assets and total current liabilities. Thus the figures for 1974 and 1973 in our example are £60,000 (£113,000 − £53,000) and £50,000 (£97,000 − £47,000) respectively. This shows the margin of safety between the company's assets and those debts coming up for repayment and is one of the most important measures of solvency and the ability of the company to continue trading.

24. Estimates of contingent liabilities. This liability becomes payable upon the happening of an event, *e.g.* a court decision goes against the company, at which time liquid funds must be found to settle the liability. An example is found in the balance sheet of Auto Co. Ltd.

25. Current ratio. The current ratio is the conventional measure that shows whether a company can meet its short-term liabilities out of the assets that are realised into cash within the same time-scale.

Current ratio

$$= \frac{\text{Current assets}}{\text{Current liabilities}}$$

$$= 1974 \frac{£113,000}{£53,000} = 2 \cdot 13 \qquad 1973 \frac{£97,000}{£47,000} = 2.06$$

These ratios show that the Auto Co. Ltd. had a higher margin of safety in 1974 to deal with any fluctuations that might occur in cash flow.

The informed manager who fears that sales turnover is increasing too quickly in relation to working capital, *i.e.* overtrading could be occurring, can confirm this by calculating the current ratio and the ratio of creditors to debtors. If the latter figure is increasing while the former is falling, then there is indication of overtrading, the shortage of cash forcing the organisation to finance trade through credit and loans. The consequences are serious, and could, if credit became tight, affect the security of the shareholders' investment, employees' wages, and creditors' debts and therefore demand immediate investigation to identify the cause and remedial measures.

26. Quick ratio or "Acid Test." This ratio of liquidity is similar to the current ratio except that stocks, the least liquid of current assets, are eliminated from the numerator.

Thus the quick ratio tests the ability of the company to pay off its immediate debts out of its most liquid assets and is more useful than the current ratio for general comparisons between companies since it ignores stocks which in practice may be valued by a variety of methods.

Quick ratio

$$= \frac{\text{Current assets—Stocks}}{\text{Current liabilities}}$$

$$= 1974 \, \frac{£67,000}{£53,000} = 1 \cdot 26 \qquad\qquad 1973 \, \frac{£57,000}{£47,000} = 1 \cdot 21$$

27. Average collection period. This has already been calculated as 97 days in 1974 compared with 83 days in 1973. Obviously these figures should be compared with the terms of sales and a policy of tight credit control implemented if the average collection period is significantly longer than the credit terms.

GEARING AND CAPITAL STRUCTURE

28. Gearing and capital structure. Creditors and shareholders have a conflict of interest, and consequently have different views on the ideal capital structure. Creditors firstly require some degree of security and prefer that shareholders have a substantial stake in the company's total capital. Shareholders on the other hand may prefer to control the company through a small share capital and raise additional capital by means of non-voting debenture and loan capital to take advantage of capital gearing. This means that if the company can earn 18 per cent on capital when interest rates are 10 per cent, it pays the shareholders to finance additional capital through loans and to retain "8 per cent profit" for themselves.

29. Redemption dates. If a company has already issued fixed-interest or dividend securities then its room for manoeuvre is obviously more limited than one that has relied exclusively on ordinary share capital. However, if these securities have been issued with a fairly wide time span, then the company may redeem and replace with lower interest rates when market rates are lower. Information regarding these redemption dates and classes of share and loan capital is contained in the Memorandum and Articles and balance sheet.

30. Debt ratio. The debt ratio measures the proportion of total funds contributed by creditors. The conflict of interest already referred to implies that creditors prefer a low ratio and shareholders a high figure. A low figure will cushion the creditor against losses in the event of winding-up, while a high debt ratio benefits the owners in terms of gearing and control.

Debt ratio

$$= \frac{\text{Total debt}}{\text{Total assets}} \quad \begin{array}{l}(i.e. \text{ current} + \text{ deferred liabilities} + \text{ long-}\\ \text{term loans})\end{array}$$

$$= 1974 \, \frac{\pounds 65,000}{\pounds 193,000} = 34\% \quad 1973 \, \frac{\pounds 58,000}{\pounds 182,000} = 32\%$$

Thus we see that in Auto Co. Ltd. the creditors have little to fear on the above score. Generally they will not want their debt to exceed the total investments of shareholders; in fact, their debt is very safely covered.

A related measurement of the degree of protection afforded to a lender by an asset is the asset cover, *i.e.* the number of times the asset covers the loan. Thus if in an example the debenture of £10,000 is secured on the land and building valued at £60,000, then the cover is 6, which appears to be safe, especially so if the land is undervalued.

31. Interest cover. This shows the extent to which earnings can fall and still cover fixed-interest charges. Naturally a high margin of safety is preferred. A low interest cover figure could be serious because a bad trading period resulting in non-payment of interest could result in the creditors petitioning for winding-up and the repayment of their debts.

$$\text{Interest cover} = \frac{\text{Profit before tax and interest}}{\text{Interest charge}}$$

$$= 1974 \, \frac{\pounds 32,000}{\pounds 1,000} = 32 \quad 1973 \, \frac{\pounds 28,000}{\pounds 1,000} = 28$$

Thus interest payments are well covered in both years.

32. Net worth: Fixed assets. Shareholders should have a substantial contribution of the total capital employed. It is considered desirable for them to contribute funds that finance all fixed assets and a proportion of current assets.

$$\frac{\text{Net worth}}{\text{Fixed assets}} = 1974 \ \frac{£128,000}{£80,000} = 1\cdot60 \quad 1973 \ \frac{£124,000}{£85,000} = 1\cdot45$$

Thus shareholders have contributed the whole of fixed assets and part of current assets.

33. Gearing factor. This factor measures the relative proportion of the type of capital employed in a company.

$$\text{Gearing factor} = \frac{\text{Loan capital and preference share capital}}{\text{Ordinary share capital}}$$

$$= 1974 \ \frac{£20,000}{£118,000} = 16\cdot9\% \quad 1973 = 17\cdot5\%$$

Thus in both years preference shareholders and debenture holders have contributed a small proportion of funds in comparison with ordinary shareholders.

Chapter VIII provides a detailed analysis of gearing, and in particular shows how borrowed funds may be employed for the benefit of ordinary shareholders. However, there is a limit to which a company is able or is prepared to use gearing to boost returns for the equity.

(*a*) Risk may be the deciding factor, especially when company profits are volatile. Shareholders may feel that the risk of bankruptcy which might result from a default on debt interest payment becomes unacceptable at higher levels of gearing.

(*b*) Creditors may be reluctant to advance additional funds on the grounds that they and not the shareholders are bearing the risk. Clearly lenders of funds will compare the company's gearing ratio with the average for industry generally and ideally with the ratio for that particular trade, to establish whether it is over-borrowing (*see* Table XIV).

OWNERSHIP AND CONTROL

34. Ownership. The final criterion for examining and interpreting company accounts is ownership.

35. Secured creditors. If the proportion of secured assets is small in relation to total assets, then ownership is unaffected.

However, as the proportion increases the company's freedom of action is reduced so that secured creditors may become ineffective controllers.

36. Shareholders' interests. The Register of Shareholders' Interests records those shareholders holding 10 per cent or more of share capital. A significant holding of a class share capital possession voting rights gives the shareholder a degree of influence and perhaps control in company affairs. Examination of the voting rights of the classes of share capital can be revealing, *e.g.* preference shares may have no voting rights except if dividends are in arrears.

37. Vote gearing.

(*a*) For example, the vote-gearing of Auto Co. Ltd., with issued capital of 100,000 £1 ordinary shares (with full voting rights) and 10,000 £1 preference shares, plus 10,000 £1 debentures (without voting rights) is:

$$\frac{\text{Total capital}}{\text{Total voting capital}} = \frac{£100,000 + 10,000 + 10,000}{£100,000} = 1·2$$

Here, ordinary shareholders control capital 1·2 times their own nominal capital.

(*b*) However, vote-gearing of ordinary shareholders is tempered if similar voting rights are given to the preference shareholders:

$$\frac{£100,000 + 10,000 + 10,000}{£100,000 + 10,000} = 1·09$$

USE OF RATIOS

38. Value of ratios. We have already established that absolute figures can be misleading when assessing company performance; ratios, however, enable us to summarize and clarify information and throw up inter-relationships. Five general rules apply in the use of ratios:

(*a*) Compilation should be speedy.

(*b*) Compilation is costly and only those ratios of direct application should be compiled. However, as staff become conversant with their construction and application, ratio analysis may be developed further.

(*c*) Ratios should be presented in the most appropriate manner for the organisation.

(*d*) Ratios do not give financial control, but pinpoint areas for investigation.

(*e*) Ratios should not be used in isolation, *e.g.* if sales increase by 6 per cent per year and profits by 3 per cent, this apparently satisfactory situation is proved otherwise if this is achieved by the injection of a larger amount of capital. Therefore, ratios become more meaningful when compared with others. Comparison may be made within the organisation, and is described as Trend Analysis, or with other firms in the industry or industry generally. This latter form of comparison is termed Comparative Analysis.

Throughout this chapter, we have concentrated on trend analysis to assess the performance of Auto Co. Ltd., *i.e.* direct comparisons between 1974 and 1973 to establish whether the Auto Co. Ltd.'s performance is improving or deteriorating. The remainder of the chapter will deal with comparative analysis.

39. Comparative analysis. There are a number of sources of ratio statistics available to companies. Trade associations and the Centre for Inter-Firm Comparisons among others supply subscribers with detailed ratios indicating the range of performance of constituent firms, with often a comment on the subscribers' strengths and weaknesses. Statistics within the following areas are of considerable value for companies wishing to compare their performance with other companies.

(*a*) Return on assets.

(*b*) Profit on sales.

(*c*) Sales to capital employed on operating assets, showing how much capital is "tied up" to achieve these sales.

(*d*) Stocks and sales. This shows how many weeks of stocks are carried to maintain current sales. Naturally the length of the manufacturing cycle and material supply delivery situation are considerations in setting stock levels, but as a general rule industry will aim to have approximately two months' stocks.

(*e*) Debtors to sales. The average length of time for customers to pay invoices is six weeks. If this figure is exceeded, then it represents tied-up funds that cannot be used unless invoice discounting facilities are used.

(*f*) Current assets to current liabilities. The generally accepted rule of thumb ratio is 2 : 1. However, this should be interpreted with caution, since much depends on the characteristics of the industry, *e.g.* normal seasonality of trade may require excessive stock levels with obvious deteriorations in the ratio.

(g) Quick assets to current liabilities. The Acid Test's generally accepted norm is 1 : 1.

(h) Advertising costs to sales.

(i) Production costs to sales. If this increases then the profit margin must deteriorate, and the cause should be investigated.

(j) Administration cost to sales.

(k) Distribution costs to sales.

40. Use of investment ratios. In the post-war period, a number of investment ratios have been used as the yardsticks of investment performance.

(a) Dividend and earning yields in the 1950s.

(b) Price/earnings ratio after the introduction of corporation tax in 1965. This means that if a company's share price is £1·00 and post-corporation tax earnings are £0·10, *per* share, then the P/E ratio is 10 : 1 or 10. Thus the share price £1·00 represents ten times the last annual earnings or, put another way, the investor will recoup his capital investment in ten years, if earnings are unchanged.

Companies with good prospects of high future earnings command a higher P/E and offer the investor a better hedge against inflation.

(c) In the 1970s the rate of inflation overtook the anticipated rate of earnings and with the added confusion of the imputation system of corporation tax in 1973, investors' attention turned to the following:

(i) *Liquidity ratios.* The very high cost of money meant that companies should be self-financing as far as possible. Alternatively, trade credit should be used when cheaper than loans. Consequently, the current and quick ratios and stocks to creditors ratio became more widely used.

(ii) *Dividend and earning yields.* With the very high yields on fixed-interest stock (15 per cent in May 1974) attention once more reverted to comparative yields on equities.

41. Window dressing. Whilst the published accounts represent the state of affairs of the company when they are drawn up, the reader should be aware that the company might carry out window-dressing operations to show its position in the best possible light. These operations might include the following:

(a) Paying off overdrafts with money borrowed from subsidiaries.

(b) Borrowing long-term money which is then maintained in liquid form.

(c) Pressing debtors for cash at the end of the financial year.

It is argued that these measures do not materially change the company's balance sheet and are perhaps endorsed by management in order to present the information in the best possible light. However, measures that do alter the real financial position, *e.g.* revaluation of stocks, unwarranted changes in bad debt provisions, capitalisation of expenditure and manipulation of inter-company transactions that are contrary to best accounting practice, are inexcusable and may be fraudulent.

PROGRESS TEST 10

1. (a) What is the purpose of the balance sheet? **(1)**

   (b) Who is interested in its contents? **(2)**

2. Describe the main indicators (contained in company reports) of company performance, in terms of the following:

   (a) Profitability. **(6–9)**

   (b) Activity. **(10–18)**

   (c) Solvency. **(19–27)**

   (d) Gearing and capital structure. **(28–33)**

   (e) Ownership and control. **(34–37)**

3. Examine the meanings of profit and profitability. **(6–7)**

4. State three ways of measuring profitability. **(7–8)**

5. Distinguish between comparative and trend analysis. **(38–40)**

6. Examine and analyse the published accounts of Triumph Electro-Mechanical Ltd. contained in Fig. 25 and comment on its overall efficiency and financial position with specific reference to profitability, activity, solvency, gearing and capital structure. **(1–40)**

Balance sheet P.P. Refrigeration Ltd.

	1973	1974		1973	1974
Share capital	£1,250	£1,250	Fixed assets (net)	£21,346	£27,316
Capital reserve	5,500	5,500	Current assets		
Revenue reserve	13,485	22,124	Stock and W.I.P.	13,458	24,911
	24,885	36,429	Debtors	90,248	116,669
Deferred taxation	4,650	7,545	Cash	11	250
Current liabilities					
Creditors	66,031	97,545			
Unexpired maintenance	5,206	4,835			
Liability on guarantees	3,352	4,125			
Balance due on H.P.	3,100	7,268			
Overdraft	15,345	2,111			
Tax payable	1,448	3,750			
Loans from directors	5,696	13,093			
	125,063	169,146		125,063	169,146
Sales revenue	304,576	386,717			
Gross profit	81,393	100,569			
Net profit before tax	11,375	15,294			
Taxation	4,605	5,333			

7. Critically appraise the performance of the P.P. Refrigeration Co.

CHAPTER XI

CONTROLLING PROFITABILITY

HOW TO IMPROVE PROFITABILITY

1. Profitability. Company profits are expressed in pounds: profitability is the relationship (expressed as a percentage) between this profit figure and the capital used to generate these profits and is a more useful indicator of how efficiently management is using total company funds.

$$\text{Profitability} = \frac{\text{Profits}}{\text{Assets}} \times 100$$

This is the product of two separate ratios: profit margin and asset turnover:

$$(i) \text{ Profit margin } \% \quad \times \quad (ii) \text{ Asset turnover}$$
$$\frac{\text{Profits}}{\text{Sales}} \times 100 \quad \times \quad \frac{\text{Sales}}{\text{Assets}}$$

Thus, if profitability is measured by R.O.C.E. (*see* Chapter X) and sales revenue is £2,000, profits before interest and tax are £100 and total assets are £1,000 then the whole relationship between ratios (*i*) and (*ii*) can be visualised from the following:

$$\frac{\text{Profit before tax and interest}}{\text{Sales}} = \frac{£100}{£2000} \times 100 \times \frac{\text{Sales}}{\text{Assets}} \frac{£2000}{£1000}$$
$$= 5\% \times 2$$
$$= 10\%$$

Furthermore, the sales values cancel out so that we are left with the profitability formula (R.O.C.E.):

$$\frac{\text{Profit before tax and interest}}{\text{Assets}} = \frac{£100}{£1000}$$
$$= 10\%$$

2. Ways to improve profitability. A closer examination of the above relationship reveals that profitability can be im-

182

proved either by increasing the numerator (profits) or reducing the denominator (assets). Consequently, management has four variables under its influence or control that directly affect company profitability. They are:

1. Price.
2. Cost.
3. Sales volume.
4. Assets.

(a) *Increase selling price.* If price is raised while costs remain unchanged or rise proportionally less than the price increase, then the profit margin is obviously increased. However, in practice there is a real danger of reaction by customers who may turn to alternative suppliers; ideally, management should predetermine the elasticity or responsiveness of demand to price changes before taking any action in this respect.

(b) *Reduce costs.* The problems and uncertainties of (a) may be overcome by approaching profit from the viewpoint of costs. In comparison with selling price, costs are more predictable and more easily controlled by managers, so that a more positive way of improving profit margins is to cut costs rather than to increase price. This is clearly seen in the following example:

profit		sales price	−	cost of sales
£10	=	£100	−	£90
£15	=	£100	−	£85

A comprehensive cost-reduction exercise covering the areas of purchasing, production, selling and distribution administration and research and development could well produce significant savings in costs, and consequently a corresponding improvement in profit and the profit margin.

(c) *Increase sales volume.* Thirdly, profitability can be increased by generating a higher sales turnover from the same value of assets, *i.e.* a better utilisation of assets.

(d) *Reduce capital employed.* Finally, it may be possible to reduce capital employed in the business. Then if sales are maintained from a smaller value of capital employed, then the more efficient utilisation of assets raises the asset turnover figure and directly contributes to a higher profitability percentage.

3. Example of profitability analysis. Consider the following information supplied by a small manufacturing company for the year 1972.

	1972
Profit	£2,700
Sales revenue	37,000
Production costs of sales	27,380
Establishment costs	1,000
Administration costs	4,000
General expenses	1,924
Assets	
Motor van	1,000
Plant and equipment	3,000
Land	10,000
Stock and work-in-progress	3,000
Debtors	4,000
Cash	1,000

This data can now be analysed by means of ratios (*see* Fig. 16 for a worked example of simple profitability analysis).

The left-hand side of Figure 16 deals with the costs/sales percentages. Since profits are 7·3 per cent of sales, costs must be 92·7 per cent of sales which are further analysed as follows: production costs 74 per cent, establishment 2·7 per cent, administration 10·8 per cent and general costs 5·2 per cent.

The right-hand side deals with asset turnover. However, this is more clearly visualised if $\frac{\text{Sales revenue}}{\text{Assets}}$ fractions are reversed so that $\frac{\text{motor van}}{\text{Sales}} = 0\cdot27$, which means that 0·27p worth of investment in a motor van is required to generate £1 of sales revenue. Similarly, 8·1p of plant, 27·02p of land and in total 37·88p of fixed assets is needed to produce £1's worth of sales revenue. The corresponding figure for total current assets is 21·61p.

However, the corresponding ratios for 1973 (figures in brackets) reveals that the R.O.C.E. is down to 7·6 per cent (the product of a lower profit margin of 3·8 per cent and a slightly higher asset turnover of 2·0) and clearly show the usefulness of ratios as a control technique. Obviously higher costs have caused the deterioration in the profit margin. In particular, production costs/sales has increased from 74 per cent to 76·3 per cent so that if we assume that the 1972 ratios are the norm or standard for the organisation, management

$$R.O.C.E. = \frac{£2,700}{£22,000} \times 100$$
$$= 12.2\% \ (7.6\%)$$

$$Profit \ margin = \frac{£2,700}{£37,000} \times 100 \quad \times$$
$$= 7.3\% \ (3.8\%) \quad \times$$

$$Asset \ turnover = \frac{£37,000}{£22,000}$$
$$= 1.68 \ (2.0)$$

Profit = Sales − Cost
7.3% = 100% − 92.7% (96.2%)

Now turn the fraction upside down

$$\frac{Production \ costs}{Sales} = \frac{£27,380}{£37,000} \times 100 = 74.0\% \ (76.6\%)$$

$$\frac{Establishment \ costs}{Sales} = \frac{£1,000}{£37,000} \times 100 = 2.7\% \ (2.6\%)$$

$$\frac{Administration \ costs}{Sales} = \frac{£4,000}{£37,000} \times 100 = 10.8\% \ (11.9\%)$$

$$\frac{General \ costs}{Sales} = \frac{£1,924}{£37,000} \times 100 = \frac{5.2\% \ (5.1\%)}{92.7\% \ (96.2\%)}$$

$$\frac{Sales}{Assets}$$

$$\frac{Motor \ van}{Sales} = \frac{£1,000}{£37,000} = 2.70p \ (1.00p)$$

$$\frac{Plant}{Sales} = \frac{£3,000}{£37,000} = 8.10p \ (6.20p)$$

$$\frac{Land}{Sales} = \frac{£10,000}{£37,000} = \frac{27.02p \ (25.00p)}{37.82p \ (32.20p)}$$

$$\frac{Stocks}{Sales} = \frac{£3,000}{£37,000} = 8.10p \ (8.00p)$$

$$\frac{Debtors}{Sales} = \frac{£4,000}{£37,000} = 10.81p \ (9.75p)$$

$$\frac{Cash}{Sales} = \frac{£1,000}{£37,000} = \frac{2.70p \ (2.50p)}{21.61 \ (20.25p)}$$

Fig. 16.—Example of profitability analysis.

should immediately examine the production area to establish the reason for the unfavourable variance of 2·3 per cent. This may reveal the following:

		1972	1973
$\dfrac{\text{Production costs}}{\text{Sales revenue}}$	× 100	74%	76·6%
$\dfrac{\text{Labour costs}}{\text{Sales revenue}}$	× 100	36·6%	37·7%
$\dfrac{\text{Material costs}}{\text{Sales revenue}}$	× 100	37·4%	38·9%

The explanation may lie in higher wage rates or overtime working and higher prices of materials, which, if controllable, demand immediate remedial action in the area of work schedules to avoid costly overtime payments and in the buying department to obtain cheaper supplies.

Similarly, the higher administration costs should be investigated. Fortunately small economies in establishment costs and general costs have been made, which partly offset the diseconomies within production and administration.

Furthermore, the right-hand side of Fig. 16 reveals a more efficient use of both fixed and current assets in 1973. Asset turnover is higher so that in total 52·25p of assets are needed to produce £1 of sales revenue compared with 59·43p in 1972. Dealing firstly with fixed assets, we see that although a lower value of motor vans is required to support the sales revenue (1·00p compared with 2·7p in 1972) relatively less capital per £1 of sales revenue is tied up in plant and land, i.e. 6·20p and 25·00p respectively compared with 8·10p and 27·02p in 1972. Furthermore, less money is tied up in all current assets, so that only 20·25p is required in 1973 (21·61p in 1972).

CONTROLLING CURRENT ASSETS: STOCK-IN-TRADE

4. Introduction. Ceteris paribus, any improvement in the asset turnover ratio produces a corresponding improvement in the profitability percentage. Thus in this section, we concentrate our attention on the analysis and control of stocks consisting of raw materials, W.I.P. and finished goods, to investigate possible ways of improving the asset turnover by maintaining a given sales revenue from a smaller value of stocks.

5. Factors influencing stock levels. There are basically two factors influencing the optimum level of stocks to be held by an organisation:

(a) *Demand.* There must be sufficient stocks to satisfy:

(i) normal production demands determined by the production cycle,

(ii) anticipated growth in sales and production,

(iii) abnormal demands, *i.e.* buffer stocks to allow for the unexpected.

These variables may be illustrated by reference to Fig. 17, which indicates a hypothetical re-order level bearing in mind

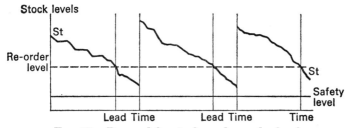

FIG. 17.—Demand for stocks and re-order levels.

the assumed lead time, *i.e.* the time taken to order, receive and inspect stocks ready for use.

The line St–St represents irregularity and abnormality in sales and hence production demands over time; the required safety stock level or buffer stocks and the lead time determine the stock level when re-ordering must take place.

(b) Economic quantities. Orders should be made bearing in mind the following:

(i) There are costs involved in ordering and carrying stocks. Naturally, any savings in this respect is of benefit to the organisation and directly improves the stock turnover ratio, but any decision to place small orders must be made by reference to (a) above, and

(ii) economies of bulk purchases.

6. The re-order level. This is calculated as follows:

Re-order level (R.O.L.) = Average consumption rate × Lead time

However, if materials already ordered are awaiting delivery when further re-orders are being considered, then the R.O.L. will have to be adjusted accordingly.

R.O.L. = Average consumption rate − Goods in transit × Lead time

7. The costs of carrying stocks. There are three elements in the costs of carrying stocks. They are:

(a) Costs of holding stocks,[1] *e.g.*

    (*i*) Cost of tied-up capital.
    (*ii*) Storage costs.
    (*iii*) Insurance.
    (*iv*) Spoilage costs, etc.

(b) Out of stock costs, *e.g.*:

    (*i*) Lost revenue from being out of stock.
    (*ii*) Lost future sales because of damaged goodwill.
    (*iii*) Spoilage, damage caused by hold-ups in production.

(c) Administrative and financial costs:

    (*i*) Costs of placing, processing orders.
    (*ii*) Handling costs.
    (*iii*) Costs of forgoing bulk purchase discounts.
    (*iv*) Cost of failing to anticipate price increases.

8. The optimum order quantity. An alternative way of classifying these costs is to express them according to how they behave in relation to order size and stock levels. Clearly, certain costs rise (perhaps directly) with the amount of stocks, *e.g.* cost of capital tied up, storage, spoilage, etc.; on the other hand, some costs will vary inversely, *e.g.* costs of being out of stock, the costs of ordering and processing through the operation of economies of large-scale buying. If we now graph these relationships then we have Fig. 18 that contains the hypothetical curve ATC–ATC which is the sum of the two curves (Cc and Oc) representing these increasing and decreasing costs. The slopes of the two curves Cc–Cc and Oc–Oc are

[1] Managers should resist the temptation of issuing an instruction to cut all stocks by, say, 10 per cent as an economy measure. Instead they should first analyse stocks by value to find that some 80 per cent of the total stock value is tied up in about 20 per cent of certain stocks; consequently, tighter control on these particular items alone is likely to produce substantial savings without the interruptions to production caused by being out of stock of less valuable but essential items.

identical at OA, where the marginal increasing costs and the marginal decreasing costs are equal. At this unique point, average total costs are at a minimum value. At stock levels below OA, marginal decreasing costs exceed marginal increasing costs so that average total costs (A.T.C.) are falling. Above OA, marginal increasing costs are greater, so that A.T.C. rises. Thus total costs are neither increasing nor decreasing and at their lowest value at OA, which represents the optimum

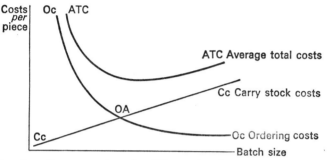

FIG. 18.—Costs *per* piece for different batch sizes and optimum order sizes.

or Economic Ordering Quantity (E.O.Q.) or Economic Batch Quantity (E.B.Q.) if the goods are produced within the organisation's production department.

A formula for the E.O.Q. for a single independent inventory is as follows:

$$\text{E.O.Q.} = \sqrt{\frac{2SD}{CI}}$$

Where D = consumption rate *per annum*
S = ordering/handling costs *per* order
C = cost *per* unit
I = percentage stock carrying charge

9. Examples.

PROBLEM 1

(*i*) If an organisation uses 300 units of the material at a cost of £1 *per* unit when carrying costs are 20 per cent of the stock value and ordering and preparation costs are £10, then:

$$\text{E.O.Q.} = \sqrt{\frac{2SD}{CI}}$$

$$= \sqrt{\frac{(2 \times 300 \times 10)}{0 \cdot 2 \times 10}}$$

$$= \sqrt{\frac{6000}{2}}$$

$$= \quad 54 \text{ units}$$

(*ii*) If we now assume that sales are doubled, and all other assumptions are unchanged, then:

$$\text{E.O.Q.} = \sqrt{\frac{(2 \times 600 \times 10)}{0 \cdot 2 \times 10}}$$

$$= \sqrt{\frac{12,000}{2}}$$

$$= 77 \text{ units (note E.O.Q. has not doubled)}$$

(*iii*) If we assume that sales treble, then:

$$\text{E.O.Q.} = \sqrt{\frac{(2 \times 900 \times 10)}{0 \cdot 2 \times 10}}$$

$$= \sqrt{\frac{18,000}{2}}$$

$$= 95 \text{ units (note E.O.Q. has not trebled)}$$

PROBLEM 2

If the assumptions are unchanged except that the cost of ordering/handling the order is doubled to £20, then the re-worked examples for sales of (*i*) 300, (*ii*) 600 and (*iii*) 900 units are as follows:

$$(i) \qquad \text{E.O.Q.} = \sqrt{\frac{(2 \times 300 \times 20)}{0 \cdot 2 \times 10}}$$

$$= 77 \text{ units}$$

$$(ii) \qquad \text{E.O.Q.} = \sqrt{\frac{(2 \times 600 \times 20)}{0 \cdot 2 \times 10}}$$

$$= 110 \text{ units}$$

(*iii*) $$\text{E.O.Q.} = \sqrt{\frac{(2 \times 900 \times 20)}{0\cdot2 \times 10}}$$

$$= 134 \text{ units}$$

PROBLEM 3

Finally, if the stock-holding charge is doubled to 40% of the stock value, with the same assumptions, then:

(*i*) $$\text{E.O.Q.} = \sqrt{\frac{(2 \times 300 \times 10)}{0\cdot4 \times 10}}$$

$$= 39 \text{ units}$$

(*ii*) $$\text{E.O.Q.} = \sqrt{\frac{(2 \times 600 \times 10)}{0\cdot4 \times 10}}$$

$$= 55 \text{ units}$$

(*iii*) $$\text{E.O.Q.} = \sqrt{\frac{(2 \times 900 \times 10)}{0\cdot4 \times 10}}$$

$$= 67 \text{ units}$$

SUMMARY OF PROBLEMS 1, 2 AND 3

		1	2	3
		S = £10	S = £20	S = £10
		I = 20%	I = 20%	I = 40%
		E.O.Q.s	E.O.Q.s	E.O.Q.s
Sales	300	54	77	39
	600	77	110	55
	900	95	134	67

This confirms one's intuitive judgment that E.O.Q.s are lower when stock-carrying costs are higher (Problem 3) and that E.O.Q.s are higher when ordering/preparation costs are lower. Furthermore, these are clearly economies of scale, in that stock levels do not rise in proportion to sales whatever the assumptions for S or I.

10. Value of the E.O.Q. In practice, it is certainly more difficult to calculate the E.O.Q. and re-order level than is demonstrated in these examples. Nevertheless, these illustrations show the nature of the variables in stock control, the different costs which need quantifying and give an introduction to the principles that the stock controller must master if he is to implement an efficient inventory policy. A more ambitious treatment of stock control systems is outside the scope of this study and lies within the province of operations research.

11. Work-in-progress. The principles underlying E.O.Q. and E.B.Q. that we have discussed in relation to stocks apply equally to work-in-progress and finished goods. However, one aspect of efficient stock control that has not been mentioned is ratio analysis, *i.e.* comparison of the production cycle with the balance sheet stock-in-trade values. For instance, if stock-in-trade is as follows:

Raw materials	£6,000
Work-in-progress	£5,000
Finished goods	£9,000

and we assume that the manufacturing cycle is five days and that fifteen days stocks are held, then clearly the business is overstocked (assuming readily available supplies of materials). Furthermore, assuming that W.I.P is valued halfway between raw materials and finished goods values then on a fifteen-day cycle it is £7,500; but on a five-day cycle it should be one-third, *i.e.* £2,300, under half of the actual W.I.P. figure.

Ideally, for optimum stock-in-trade levels and for positive contributions towards profitability, a manufacturing company should employ ratio analysis to establish trends within the company and to compare their performance with similar companies in their industry. To this end, the following ratios are commonly employed:

Sales to material stocks
Sales to W.I.P.
Sales to finished goods stock

CONTROLLING CURRENT ASSETS: DEBTORS

12. The value of debtors. The Annual Abstract of Statistics shows clearly the annual increase in trade credit and the trend in the ratio of debtors/capital employed over the years 1964–1971 (*see* Table XXIII(B)).

13. Reasons for granting credit. The reasons for granting credit to customers are varied.

(*a*) *It is customary in the trade*. However, this may be argued to be a negative attitude. More positive reasons are:

(*b*) *To increase the company's market*. In fact, it may be the only way to increase turnover if marginal customers are only attracted and secured by the prospect of buying on credit. Indeed, if fixed costs are already fully covered, then these marginal sales may be contemplated if they are expected to make only a small contribution to overall profit.

(*c*) *To increase profit*.

(*d*) *To realise funds earmarked for specific uses, e.g.* investment in new plant.

14. The costs of granting credit. There are basically three elements in the cost of granting credit:

(*a*) *The financial cost*.

   (*i*) To a borrower of funds, this is the interest charge on the loan or overdraft.

   (*ii*) Otherwise, it is the opportunity cost of the funds, *i.e.* the revenue the company could have earned by using it in some alternative investment.

(*b*) *The administration cost, i.e.* the cost of employing a credit control and collection department (covering staff salaries, accommodation expenses and other related costs).

(*c*) The insurance cost, which includes the expenses of factoring or invoice discounting or simply charging provisions for bad debts against profits.

15. Debtors and the growing firm. It is not uncommon for profitable fast-growing companies to experience cash flow problems: the amounts required for investment in raw materials, work-in-progress, finished goods, and debtors as well as for extra fixed assets may very well exceed available cash. An efficient debtor control policy can alleviate the problem. Figure 19 illustrates a typical cash flow problem for a fast-growing company. Assuming that the firm pays for supplies within the month, that debtors are given two months' credit (Column (*i*) in Fig. 19) and sales invoiced to debtors expand initially by some 5 per cent per month but that total payments increase faster because of the additional purchases of goods and services needed in order to gear up production to the higher anticipated levels, then the company must find considerable external funds to finance its day-to-day trade. Alternatively (Column (*ii*) in Fig. 19), by cutting down on

Month	Sales £	Total payments £	(i) Credit term two months			(ii) Credit term one month		
			Cash receipts £	Cash flow Net £	Cash flow To date £	Cash Receipts £	Cash flow Net £	Cash flow To date £
Jan.	20,000	18,000	—	(18,000)	(18,000)	—	(18,000)	(18,000)
Feb.	21,000	19,500	—	(19,500)	(37,500)	20,000	500	(17,500)
Mar.	22,000	21,000	20,000	(1,000)	(38,500)	21,000	—	(17,500)
Apr.	23,000	22,000	21,000	(1,000)	(39,500)	22,000	—	(17,500)
May	24,000	22,500	22,000	(500)	(40,000)	23,000	500	(17,000)
June	25,000	23,000	23,000	—	(40,000)	24,000	1,000	(16,000)
July	26,000	23,500	24,000	500	(39,500)	25,000	1,500	(14,500)
Aug.	29,000	24,000	25,000	1,000	(38,500)	26,000	2,000	(12,500)
Sept.	31,000	24,500	26,000	1,500	(37,000)	29,000	4,500	(8,000)
Oct.	34,000	25,000	29,000	4,000	(33,000)	31,000	6,000	(2,000)

Fig. 19.—Anon Co.: Cash flow and credit terms.

the period of credit allowed to debtors, *i.e.* one month, it can reduce its borrowings dramatically and has excellent prospects of a positive cash flow for November. In summary, a shorter credit period improves company liquidity.

16. How credit control improves profit and profitability. An efficient credit control system reduces the costs of extending credit to customers outlined in (**14**) and improves the R.O.C.E. percentages. For example, we can construct a hypothetical balance sheet of Anon. Co. as at 31st October (*see* Fig. 20) to

	Situation 1		Situation 2	
Fixed Assets		£10,000		£10,000
Current assets				
Debtors	£65,000		£34,000	
Other current assets	25,000		25,000	
Total current assets		90,000		59,000
Total assets		£100,000		£69,000
Financed by:				
Equity		£67,000		£67,000
Bank borrowing at 15%		33,000		2,000
		£100,000		£69,000
Sales turnover Jan.–Oct.		£255,000		£255,000

Fig. 20.—Anon Co.: Balance Sheet as at 31st October.

illustrate these cost savings and the attendant improvement in profit and profitability by making certain assumptions:

(*i*) Profitability is defined as (*a*) the ratio of profits to total assets employed in the business and (*b*) as profits as a percentage of the equity.

(*ii*) Cash-in-hand and stock-in-trade is constant and total £25,000.

(*iii*) Net fixed assets are £10,000

(*iv*) Profits are 15 per cent of sales

(*v*) Debt collection costs are initially £500, and bad debts are 2 per cent of debtors.

Thus as a result of a more efficient credit control system whereby the credit period is reduced (situation 2 in Fig. 21), and where credit controllers carefully scrutinise debtors and

	Situation 1			Situation 2	
Profit 15% on turnover		£38,250			£38,250
Less Bad debts 2% of debtors	£1,300		(say, 1%) £340		
Bank interest	4,950			300	
Collection costs	500	6,750		250	890
Assumed profit attributable to the equity		£31,500			£37,360

$$\text{Profitability (a) R.O.C.E.} = \frac{£31,500}{£100,000} \times 100 \quad \frac{£37,360}{£69,000} \times 100$$
$$= 31\cdot5\% \qquad\qquad = 54\cdot1\%$$

$$\text{(b) Return on equity} = \frac{£31,500}{£67,000} \times 100 \quad \frac{£37,360}{£67,000} \times 100$$
$$= 47\cdot0\% \qquad\qquad = 55\cdot7\%$$

Fig. 21.—Anon Co.: Adjustments to Profit and Loss Account.

thereby minimise bad debts (say 1 per cent of debtors) the following benefits accrue:

(a) The improved cash flow reduces bank interest payable on the overdraft.

(b) If the company is self-financing, i.e. other activities are contributing the funds locked up in debtors, then they are more quickly released for profitable reinvestment.

(c) Careful selection of credit customers avoids bad debts.

(d) There are savings in management and staff time in pursuing and collecting debts.

Clearly profits are improved (in situation 2 in Fig. 21) as too is profitability. In summary, a more efficient credit control system increases profits and profitability, which is further improved by earlier settlement of debt. Indeed, this confirms our original conclusions on profitability that a smaller investment in debtors for a given value of sales improves the asset turnover and thereby the R.O.C.E. value.

| | 31st January | | 28th February | |
	£k	%	£k	%
Age of debtor balances				
0–30 days	81	80	87	79
31–45 days ⎫ overdue between	12	12	18	16
46–60 days ⎭ 1 and 2 months	5	5	2	2
61–90 days ⎫ at least 2	2	2	2	2
91– days ⎭ months overdue	1	1	1	1
	101	100	110	100

FIG. 22 Ageing Analysis of Debtors. (Normal term: thirty days.)
The percentage columns reveal the trends shown in Fig. 23.

17. Analysis of credit. A comprehensive credit control system includes the following techniques:

(a) *Ratio analysis.*

(*i*) Debtors ÷ capital employed, *i.e.* the proportion of company capital tied up in debtors.

(*ii*) Debtors ÷ sales, *i.e.* the asset turnover.

(*iii*) Average debtor collection period, *i.e.* how quickly debtors pay.

Certainly trend analysis and preferably comparative analysis should be carried out, so that the credit department's performance can be compared over time and with other companies in similar industries.

(b) *Ageing analysis of debtors.* This involves the credit controller or responsible accountant preparing a schedule of debtor balances analysed by age groups. Fig. 22 contains a typical example of age analysis that conveys to the credit controller trends in age-debts that reflects in part the effectiveness of the credit control system in customer selection and in collecting debts. It is axiomatic that excess amounts of old debts deprive the organisation of its most scarce resource, *i.e.* finance, and must be minimised.

(*i*) Marginally overdue accounts 31–45 days have increased from 12–16 per cent.

(*ii*) Debts aged 46–60 days have slightly improved, *i.e.* 2 per cent compared with 5 per cent in January.

The next step is to prepare a schedule that identifies the

overdue accounts and summarises remedial action on the part of the credit controller (*see* Fig. 23).

Thus in the case of Brown and Smith & Co., letters have been sent reminding them of the outstanding amounts and the terms of credit: Lord has had a second: Hogg and Slough Eng. have had their deliveries stopped following a letter threatening legal action and Horsebrass has all orders refused.

Days overdue: 46–60			Days overdue: 61–91			Date: 1st Feb. Days overdue: 90+		
Debtors	£k	Action	Debtors	£k	Action	Debtors	£k	Action
J. Brown	2·5	1 reminder	I. Hogg Eng.	1·7	Deliveries stopped	Horse brass Co.	1·0	No new orders
B. Smith & Co.	0·5	1 reminder	Slough Eng.	0·3	Deliveries stopped			
I. Lord Ltd.	2·0	2 reminders						
	5·0			2·0			1·0	

Fig. 23.—Ageing analysis of debtors.

Obviously, the next course of action, *i.e.* whether further reminders are sent or legal proceedings commenced, depends on the standing of the customer and the amounts involved in relation to the cost involved in recovering the debts (*see also* Fig. 24).

CONTROLLING CURRENT ASSETS: CASH

18. Motives for holding cash and bank balances. The reasons or motives why individuals hold funds in liquid form proposed by John Maynard Keynes, the eminent economist, apply equally to corporations. Keynes' reasons for "liquidity preference", *i.e.* a certain proportion of savings kept in liquid form, were

(*a*) In order to meet current commitments, *i.e.* the transactionary motive. For example:

(*i*) To buy materials.
(*ii*) To pay staff and indirect expenses.

(*b*) To guard against future contingencies, *i.e.* the precautionary motive. For example:

(*i*) To finance promotional schemes in order to match competitors' actions.

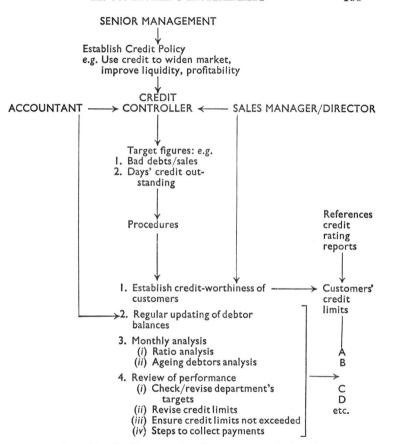

FIG. 24.—Credit control policy/system relationships.

(ii) To settle legal actions.

(iii) To minimise risk in uncertain financial and trading periods, e.g. Slater Walker 1974.

(c) To exploit profitable opportunities that may arise, i.e. the speculative motive. For example:

(i) To accomplish a take-over.

(ii) To exploit an innovation.

In addition to these general motives, we may add specific reasons why corporations, as profit-dependent organisations, hold cash.

(a) To take advantage of cash discounts which may represent significant savings. (see VI, 3).

(b) To maintain credit-worthiness and goodwill.

It is of paramount importance to maintain adequate liquid assets and thereby satisfactory liquidity ratios, since these are increasingly regarded by suppliers as the yardstick of credit-worthiness. Furthermore, criticism regarding liquidity on the part of analysts or city editors would certainly damage the organisation's financial standing and goodwill in the eyes of the investing public, which would cause a fall in the share price (viz. secondary banks, property and insurance companies in July–August 1974) and difficulties if acquiring additional external funds is contemplated.

Accepting the need for adequate liquid funds, we now turn our attention to the employment of such assets.

Clearly the disposition of funds will vary between companies and certainly between industries because of their special characteristics, e.g. the very nature of financial institutions as custodians of depositors' funds demands that they maintain a far larger proportion of assets in a highly liquid form in order to meet withdrawal demands than, say, manufacturing companies, whose short-term liabilities are slight by comparison. Moreover, liquidity preference will vary over time and is certainly influenced by rates of interest and the company's expectations regarding future sales, e.g. transferring more cash into short-term investments when rates of interest are high. However, we can conclude that the profit-dependent organisation should try to achieve a compromise between the conflicting needs to hold non-earning cash for the reasons advanced above and the need to invest cash in profitable opportunities (see VII). Indeed, from a viewpoint of pure profitability the less cash held the better, because of the higher cash asset turnover ratio, *i.e.* a higher sales cash balance ratio multiplied by the company's profit margin magnifies the R.O.C.E. percentage.

19. Measuring liquidity. The conventional yardsticks of liquidity are as follows:

(a) Current ratio $= \dfrac{\text{Current assets}}{\text{Current liabilities}}$

(b) Quick ratio $= \dfrac{\text{Current assets} - \text{stock-in-trade}}{\text{Current liabilities}}$

Both are discussed in detail in X.

20. Liquidity in British industry. It is interesting to examine the liquidity performance measured by the current and quick ratios of British industry, represented by some 2,000 quoted companies from data supplied in the Annual Abstract of Statistics. Their performance over the period is contained in Table XXIV.

TABLE XXIV. TRENDS IN LIQUIDITY RATIOS IN
BRITISH INDUSTRY

Year	Current ratio	Quick ratio
1961	2·01	1·02
1962	1·98	1·01
1963	1·93	1·00
1964	1·90	0·99
1965	1·83	0·94
1966	1·79	0·93
1967	1·84	1·00
1968	1·72	1·00
1969	1·60	0·92
1970	1·53	0·88
1971		

Source: Annual Abstract of Statistics. H.M.S.O.

Clearly the restrictive Government economic policies of 1964 and "dear" money after 1969 had a real impact on company liquidity.

21. What determines company liquidity? Basically the factors determining company liquidity are:

(a) *Management's success in controlling stocks and debtors.* Failure to control these inevitably means more funds tied up.

(b) *The level of trade.* Sales require financing by way of additional raw materials, work-in-progress and finished stock and debtors if customers take credit. Although extra sales may be profitable, they do not necessarily generate cash and thereby contribute to liquidity. An understanding of the distinction between cash flow and profitability is fundamental —ask any one of the many businessmen who owned quite profitable firms that went into liquidation in the severe economic freeze following devaluation because they were unable to pay their way and meet immediate debts!

EXAMPLE:
Assume that a company is established with a capital of £10,000. During the first year's operations sales total £20,000, purchases £15,000 and administrative and selling costs £2,000. Fixed assets are purchased for £6,000, which are to be depreciated at 20 per cent *p.a.* Over the year £19,000 is received from customers, while payments to creditors total £12,000. Stocks are valued at £1,000 at the year-end. Cash flow from the enterprise is:

Total receipts from debtors		£19,000
Less Payments:		
Fixed assets	£6,000	
Purchases	12,000	
Expenses	2,000	
		£20,000
Cash Flow		(1,000)

The profit from the enterprise is:

Total sales		£20,000
Less Cost of sales		
Purchases	£15,000	
Less stock at end	1,000	14,000
Gross Profit		£6,000
Less Expenses	£2,000	
depreciation	1,200	3,200
Net Profit		£2,800

In year 2, sales total £20,000, purchases £16,000 and expenses £2,000. Total receipts from debtors are £20,000 while payments to creditors total £14,000. Year-end stocks are £2,000. Cash flow for the second year is:

Total receipts from debtors		£20,000
Less Total payments		
Purchases	£14,000	
Expenses	2,000	16,000
Cash Flow		£4,000

Profits for the second year are:

Sales		£20,000
Less Cost of sales		
Stock at beginning	£1,000	
Purchases	16,000	
	£17,000	
Less Stock at end	2,000	£15,000
Gross Profit		£5,000
Less Expenses	£2,000	
depreciation	960	2,960
Net Profit		£2,040

This clearly shows that there is a fundamental distinction between cash and profits in the short term (since they vary inversely over these two years) although over the long term profit is eventually made equal to a net inflow of cash when debtors pay up and creditors are satisfied.

(c) *The relationship between movements in fixed and current assets* with long- and short-term sources of funds. If additional funds invested in fixed assets are in excess of new long-term funds received, then the short-fall must necessarily be drawn out of current assets. New investment in fixed assets on a large scale can spell illiquidity for the company. On the other hand, a surplus of long-term funds over new fixed-asset investment spills over into current assets, which improves the liquidity ratios.

A source and use of funds statement provides a control document to ensure that a correct relationship is maintained between working capital and fixed assets and in particular identifies changes in the cash or liquidity areas of the organisation and isolates the various reasons for them. In general terms, it shows historically where funds have come from, both

		£
Sales		9,822,450
Profit before tax is arrived at after charging:		1,859,088 (v)
Depreciation	147,287 (vi)	
Lease rentals	13,412	
Directors' remuneration	35,527	
Auditors' remuneration	8,910	
Interest payable		
Bank overdraft and short-term loans	59,875	
Long-term loans	46,411	
Less Taxation		711,150 (xvi)
Profit after taxation		1,147,938
Less Dividends		351,038 (vii)
		£796,900

(a) Profit and Loss for the 52 weeks ended 31st December 1973.

	Notes		31.12.73		31.12.72
Fixed Assets	(1)		£2,571,422		£1,962,241
Development expenditure	(2)		846,457 (xii)		523,964 (xii)
Current assets	(3)	£4,074,767		£3,664,698	
Less Current liabilities	(4)	3,348,171		3,232,328	
Net current assets			726,596		432,370
			4,144,475		2,918,575
Less					
Taxation		957,000 (xvii)		610,500 (xvii)	
Secured loans	(5)	537,900 (ix)		495,000	
			1,494,900		1,105,500
			2,649,575		1,813,075
Representing:					
Issued share capital	(6)		948,750		948,750
Undistributed profits	(7)		1,700,825		864,325
			£2,649,575		£1,813,075

(b) Balance Sheet as at 31st December 1973.

FIG. 25.—Triumph Electro-Mechanical Ltd.: company accounts.

Notes to the Accounts.

(1) Fixed assets	Freehold land and buildings	Leasehold and land buildings	Plant and Machinery	Motor vehicles	Furniture and fittings	Total
Cost						
At 1st Jan. 1973	£1,578,312	£81,733	£454,941	£156,791	£193,962	£2,465,739
Additions	447,666	81	204,651	260,137	11,814	924,349 (xi)
Less Disposals	—	—	41,464	170,740	442	212,646 (a)
At 31st Dec. 1973	2,025,978	81,814	618,128	246,188	205,334	3,177,442
Depreciation						
At 1st Jan. 1973	76,996	5,420	255,479	35,966	129,637	503,498
Less Disposals	—	—	23,347	21,245	173	44,765 (b)
Charge for period	29,280	5,456	54,214	41,854	16,483	147,287
At 31st Dec. 1973	106,276	10,876	286,346	56,575	145,947	606,020
Net book value						
At 31st Dec. 1973	1,919,702	70,938	331,782	189,613	59,387	2,571,422
At 1st Jan. 1973	1,501,316	76,313	199,462	120,825	64,325	1,962,241

$(xi) = (a) - (b)$.

(2) Developmental expenditure. This relates to expenditure on a new model of electro-mechanical machine and to major variations on existing model.

(3) Current Assets	1973	1972
Stocks (a)	£2,570,431	£2,357,347
Debtors	1,263,690	1,068,768
Cash at Bank and in hand	2,954 (xiv)	1,773 (i)
Loan to XYZ Ltd.	237,692 (xiii)	236,810 (ii)
	£4,074.767	£3,664,698

(a) Stock is valued at lower of cost or net realisable value

(4) Current liabilities	1973	1972
Creditors	£2,777,691	£2,266,296
Dividends payable	351,037	260,906
Current taxation	18,178	9,181
Bank overdraft (secured)	201,265 (xv)	200,945 (iii)
Secured loans	—	495,000 (iv)
	£3,348,171	£3,232,328

(5 Secured loans £537,900
£495,000 payable 1986 interest at 8·5% p.a
£42,900 payable 1990 interest at 10·5% p.a.

(6) Share capital		1973	1972
Authorised 2,000,000 shares @ £1·00 each		£2,000,000	£2,000,000
Issued	948,000 shares @ £1·00 each	948,750	948,750

(7) Undistributed profit	1973	1972
Balance at 1st Jan. 1973	£864,325	£486,195
Undistributed profit for period	796,900	336,880
Tax provision no longer required	39,600 (xviii)	41,250
	£1,700,825	£864,325

	1973	1972
Capital commitments		
Contracted	£12,164	£7,641
Authorised but not contracted	9,412	706
Directors' remuneration		
(ignoring pension contributions)	1973	1972
Chairman	16,400	16,400
Other directors		
Under £2,501	4	2
£7,501–£10,000	2	2

FIG. 25.—contd.

Opening liquid position:	Cash		£ 1,773 (*i*)
	Short-term loan receivable		236,810 (*ii*)
	Bank overdraft		(200,945) (*iii*)
	Short-term loan repayable		(495,000) (*iv*)
			(457,362)

SOURCES

		£	
Net profit for the year		1,859,088 (*v*)	
Depreciation		147,287 (*vi*)	
		2,006,375	

	£		
Less Dividends	351,038 (*vii*)		
Taxation†	325,050 (*viii*)	676,088	
		1,330,287	
Sale of Plant		167,881 (*ix*)	
Additional secured long-term loan		42,900 (*x*)	
Decrease in working capital			
(excluding liquid item)		202,517*	
			1,743,585
			1,286,223

USES

Purchase of plant		924,349 (*xi*)	
Development expenditure		322,493 (*xii*)	1,246,842
			£39,381

Closing liquid position
made up as follows:

Loan receivable (XYZ)		237,692 (*xiii*)	
Cash		2,954 (*xiv*)	
Overdraft		(201,265) (*xv*)	

Change in working capital
(excluding liquid items)

	Source	Use
Stocks (cf working capital items in balance sheets)	—	£213,084
Dividend payable	£90,131	—
Taxation	8,997	—
Creditors	511,395	—
Debtors		194,922
	£610,523	£408,006
Decrease in working capital	£202,517*	

(*c*) Source and Use of Funds Statement for the year ended 31st December 1973.

* The foregoing example clearly illustrates the movements in sources and uses of funds for this company. By comparing the opening and closing liquid position we notice that the company has improved its position significantly from (£457,362) to £39,381 over the year, due largely to the reduction in working capital (non-liquid items). A statement of the change in working capital is included to identify the relative movements in the non-liquid items that contribute to this net decrease of £202,517.

† Tax charge in the P & L			£711,150 (*xvi*)
less change in B/S provision			
	(*xvii*)	£346,500	
tax provision not required			
	(*xviii*)	39,600	386,100
			£325,500

long- and short-term, and how they have been employed between fixed and current assets.

22. Source and use of funds statement. Each year an increasing number of public companies are including in their published accounts a source and use of funds statement. Indeed it is one of the most useful methods to give shareholders an idea of where company funds have come from and how they are being employed. If sufficiently detailed, it will highlight company progress and problems.

Alternatively, it explains why working capital changes between two dates or if based on a future date provides a cash forecast and is useful in financial planning, showing how much surplus cash is likely to be available to meet capital expenditure requirements.

Basically, one is comparing the balance sheets of a company at two different dates and noting the changes that have occurred over the period. For example, if an examination reveals that the value of an asset has fallen, then less money is now tied up so it must represent a source of funds. Similarly, if a liability has increased then money or money's worth has been received by the company and again it is a source of funds. Conversely, an increase in an asset or decrease in a liability represents a use of funds. This is summarised below:

Source of funds:

   (a) Decrease in an asset.
   (b) Increase in a liability.

Use of funds:

   (a) Increase in an asset.
   (b) Decrease in a liability.

23. Format of the source and use of funds statement. These statements take a variety of forms. One common approach is to start with the opening cash balance. Next, all sources and uses are considered, the relative change being absorbed into the closing cash balance. Thus if total use exceeds the sources, then more funds have been applied than those generated internally or externally, so that the short-fall is met out of cash. Consequently, the closing cash balance is lower than that at the start of the period (*see* Fig. 25).

24. The cash forecast. The cash forecast is an integral part of efficient corporate financial planning. Management needs to forecast the cash position at a future date, say, in one year's time divided into monthly or even weekly intervals to find out how the money is coming in. More specifically, the purpose is to:

(a) Ensure that the company's working capital and cash are *sufficient to carry out day-to-day transactions*. If growth is envisaged, then sufficient funds must be made available to finance it. Extra stocks are needed to service increasing production and the higher sales turnover.

(b) Confirm that adequate cash is *available to the corporate financial plan*, e.g. projected capital investments for expansion or replacement.

(c) Indicate whether *surplus cash exists*.

(d) Indicate *deficiencies in cash balances* which might necessitate a reappraisal of the financial plan. Calling in debts, using bank facilities and running down stocks may alleviate the cash flow problem, although if it persists a serious reconsideration of the planned expenditure is called for or more permanent funds must be raised to meet the short-fall.

Methods of cash forecasting.

(a) *Receipts/payments forecast.* Fig. 26(b) illustrates a typical cash forecast layout, in which are inserted cumulative monthly cash receipts and payments.

(b) *The balance sheet cash forecast.* The balance sheet (Fig. 26(c)) is forecast as at the end of the period under consideration and serves as a check on the cumulative receipts/payments forecast. Naturally, it does not indicate the cash balance situation in the interim.

The balance sheet items are prepared from the various operating and financial budgets and the cash balance inserted as the balancing figure.

(c) *Profit-cash forecast.* This third method of forecasting the cash balance at a predetermined date also serves as a check on the accuracy of the first methods cumulative total. (Fig. 26(d)). First, the profit figure for the period under consideration is forecast. Next, adjustments are made; depreciation is added back since it is a non-cash charge against profits; similarly the reduction in debtors and increase in creditors are added back, increases in stocks are deducted as are appropriations of profit and capital expenditures. The net effect of these adjustments is to convert the profit figure into cash receipts, which when added to the opening cash balance gives the balance at the end of the period.

Electron Minor Co. Ltd.
Balance Sheet as at 1.1.73

	1.1.73	Forecast 28.2.73				1.1.73	Forecast 28.2.73
Share capital				Fixed assets			
90,000 £1 ordinary shares	£90,000	£90,000		Land and buildings		£35,000	£35,000
Reserves	30,000	30,000		Plant and			
				machinery	£50,000		
Profit and loss balance	10,000	84,000		*Less* Deprec.	10,000		
	£130,000	£204,000				£40,000	£44,200
Deferred taxation	20,000	10,000		Vehicles	20,000		
Current liabilities				*Less* Deprec.	5,000		
Trade creditors	70,000	75,000				15,000	14,800
Current tax	10,000	20,000		Current assets			
Dividends	20,000	—		Stocks		60,000	70,000
				Debtors		80,000	75,000
				Cash		20,000	70,000
	£250,000	£309,000				£250,000	£309,000

NOTES: (*i*) Depreciation for the two-month period is as follows:

Plant and machinery £800
Vehicles £200

(*ii*) Tax payable is paid on 1st Jan. 1973
(*iii*) Dividends payable are paid in Feb. 1973
(*iv*) Stocks at Feb. 28th are expected to be £70,000
(*v*) Tax reserve against profits for the period is £10,000.

	1.1.73	28.2.73
Information from budgets:		
Receipts:		
Cash sales	£25,000	£40,000
Debtor receipts	70,000	90,000
Payments:		
Materials	25,000	50.000
Wages	25,000	30,000
Salaries	5,000	5,000
Plant and machinery	—	5,000
Debtor balances	70,000	75,000
Creditor balances	65,000	75,000

(*a*) Balance Sheet as at 1.1.73.

Figure 26 illustrates the principles underlying the cash forecast using these three methods. The balance sheet of the Electron Minor Co. Ltd. as at 1st January 1973 (Fig. 26 (*a*)) is supplied with information from operating and financial budgets. Clearly, the accuracy of the cash forecast depends on the accuracy of these budgets and in particular the sales forecast. In view of the importance of sales, methods of demand estimation are dealt within the following sections (25–27).

Cash forecast for two months ending 28.2.73

	Jan. 31st	Feb. 28th	Total
Cash receipts			
Cash sales	£25,000	£40,000	£65,000
Credit sales	70,000	90,000	160,000
Total receipts	£95,000	£130,000	£225,000
Cash payments			
Materials	£25,000	£50,000	£75,000
Wages	25,000	30,000	55,000
Salaries	5,000	5,000	10,000
Plant and machinery	5,000	—	5,000
Dividends	—	20,000	20,000
Taxation	10,000	—	10,000
Total payments	£70,000	£105,000	£175,000
Surplus/(Deficit)	£25,000	£25,000	
Cash balance at beginning of month	20,000	45,000	
Cash balance at end of month	45,000	70,000	

(b) Receipts/payment method.

FIG. 26.—Electron Minor Co. Ltd.: Balance Sheet and cash forecasts.

Profits anticipated for two-month period end 28th Feb. 1973

Sales invoiced in Jan. and Feb.			£225,000
Less reduction in debtors 1.1.73		£80,000	
	28.2.73	75,000	5,000
			£220,000
Add increase in stock	28.2.73	70,000	
	1.1.73	60,000	10,000
			£230,000
Less costs associated with sales			140,000
			£90,000
Less increase in creditors			5,000
			£85,000
Less depreciation			
Plant and machinery		£800	
Vehicles		200	£1,000
Profit			£84,000
Appropriation of profit			
Tax reserve			10,000
			£74,000
Profit balance brought forward			10,000
Profit and loss balance at 28.2.73			£84,000

The above calculation provides the profit and loss balance at Feb. 28th for the forecast balance sheet of Electron Minor Co. Ltd. In addition the schedule of budget data and notes to the opening balance sheet gives the expected values of deferred tax, creditors, stocks and debtors. Plant and machinery at cost at 28th Feb. is £55,000 *less* depreciation of £10,800 (an additional £800 charged for the two-month period) so that written-down value is £44,200. Vehicles W.D.V. is £14,800 (£20,000 cost *less* £5,200 depreciation). As all other assets and liabilities are assumed unchanged, the balancing figure of £70,000 is cash which confirms the cumulative receipt-payment figure of Fig. 26(*b*).

FIG. 26—*contd:* (*c*) Balance Sheet method.

Profit (*see* Fig. 26 (c) £84,000		
+ depreciation	£1,000	
reduction in debtors	5,000	
increase in creditors	5,000	11,000
		£95,000
— capital investment	5,000	
increase in stock	10,000	
dividends paid	20,000	
taxation paid	10,000	£45,000
Profit/cash		£50,000
+ cash balance at 1.1.73		20,000
Cash balance at 29.2.73		£70,000

FIG. 26.—*contd:* (*d*) Profit-cash forecast.

IMPROVING PROFIT MARGINS

25. Introduction. In this section, we now turn our attention to techniques to improve the profit margin which may be effected by reducing costs and/or raising price as a means of raising profitability. However, we confine our examination to pricing and assume that the company under consideration has discretion as to the selling price for its product; either it is a price-fixer or if in a market dominated by a price leader it has some degree of control over its volume of sales by altering price.

26. Optimum price/sales combination. Below is a hypothetical demand schedule for a product.

Price (p)	Quantity demanded
125	2,000
100	2,800
75	3,300
50	4,000
25	4,500

Moreover, fixed costs identifiable with this product are assumed to be £1,000 and variable costs *per* unit 25p. We can now graph the cost information showing the relationship between volume and total costs (*see* Fig. 28). Furthermore, by graphing total revenues assuming the selling price to be 25, 50, 75, 100 and 125p, we have the familiar break-even graph which shows that break-even occurs at:

1,000 units at a selling price of 125p
1,300 units at a selling price of 100p
2,000 units at a selling price of 75p
4,000 units at a selling price of 50p

Obviously at no point can sales break even at a selling price of 25p or less, since this exactly covers average variable costs and therefore makes no provision for fixed costs.

Finally, we plot the anticipated demand at the various prices to arrive at the curve DD. Comparison of the total revenue and total cost curve at a particular price–output combination indicates the profit or loss; in particular, the vertical distance between a location on the total cost curve and the corresponding point on the demand curve DD represents profit. Thus, if selling price is 75p total revenue is £2,475, total costs £1,825 and profit £650.

Selling price	125p	100p	75p, etc.
Marginal cost (variable)	25p	25p	25p
Contribution	100	75	50
Anticipated sales	2,000	2,800	3,300
Total contribution	£2,000	£2,100	£1,650
Less Fixed costs	£1,000	£1,000	£1,000
Profit	£1,000	£1,100	£650

27. Establishing demand. The foregoing presupposes an accurate demand schedule. However, although precision is impossible in practice it is possible to achieve significantly accurate results.

(*a*) Market research has a proven success record adopting quantitative and scientific methods, *e.g.* probability analysis.

(*b*) Surveys may be adjusted to take account of the marketing staff's experience of the industry and their intuitive judgment.

(*c*) To reduce error, the "demand curve" or contribution curve may be drawn as a band to allow for the more optimistic, most pessimistic and most likely estimates of demand. Thus for any one price there may be several output, revenues and profits or contributions (*see* Fig. 27).

	Pessimistic estimate		Most likely estimate			Optimistic estimate	
Price (p)	125	100	125	100	75	125	100
Marginal cost (p)	25	25	25	25	25	25	25
Contribution (p)	100	75	100	75	50	100	75
Quantity	1,800	2,500	2,000	2,800	3,300	2,100	3,000
Total contribution (£)	1,800	1,875	2,000	2,100	1,650	2,100	2,250

FIG. 27.—Hypothetical market research results.

If the company currently sells 3,300 units at a price of 75p and contemplates a price increase of 100p, marketing staff and accountants should feel confident on the basis of the market suitably amended to take account of experts' intuitive

BFM—H

judgment (*see* Fig. 27). There is the highest probability that total contribution will increase to £2,100 and even to £2,250 if the market is underestimated. Even the most pessimistic

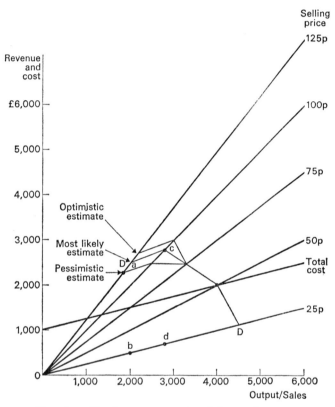

FIG. 28.—Total revenue, cost and demand curves.

estimate of a contribution of £1,875 is a significant improvement on the current level of contribution of £1,650.

Moreover, assuming that the objective is to maximise profit the marketing strategy will be to sell 2,700 units at a price of 100p where the corresponding point on the curve DD in Fig. 28 is furthest away from the total cost line.

This method has clear advantages over the conventional approach of the economist to cost-demand analysis.

(a) It represents virtually the whole relationship between price, costs, profit and volume in total terms which is immediately more meaningful to the business man who is probably unfamiliar with marginal analysis.

(b) It facilitates understanding of the marketing or product manager's difficulties of efficient pricing. Certainly cost-plus pricing is unlikely to arrive at the unique profit maximising price–output combination except by accident.

(c) It is an approach readily appreciated by marketing men and accountants and should provide the basis for discussion of the financial implications of marketing.

(d) It may be adapted to express the contributions made by the product towards fixed costs. Indeed, there is a very powerful argument that managers should be forward-looking, concerning themselves with future marginal costs and revenues rather than total costs that include fixed cost which are sunk and unavoidable in the short run.

Thus the 25p revenue line becomes the variable cost line (since average variable cost is also 25p) and contributions towards fixed costs of £1,000 can be read off for given selling prices, *i.e.* a contribution of a–b at a price of 125p, c–d at a price of 100p, etc. These values may be confirmed by calculation.

PROGRESS TEST 11

1. Explain the nature of the factors that directly affect company profitability. (1–2)

2. Describe the structure of the pyramid of ratios. (3)

3. Explain the following:

   (i) R.O.L.
   (ii) E.O.Q. (5–10)

4. Why is credit important to firms and what are its costs? (12–14)

5. Using hypothetical data, show how an efficient credit control policy improves profitability. (15–17)

6. Define "liquidity preference" and its relevance to the business organisation. (18)

7. Explain the essential difference between profit and cash flow. (21)

8. "A source and use of funds statement if sufficiently detailed can highlight company progress and problems." Discuss. (22–23)

9. Examine three methods of forecasting the cash position. (24)

10. "The profit margin may be improved either by raising price or by lowering costs. Admittedly the former is the least reliable method but may be used in conjunction with demand analysis." Discuss. (25–27)

11. Prepare a Source and Use of Funds statement for the year ended 31st March 1974 for the Auto Co. Ltd. from the Profit and Loss and Balance Sheets contained in Fig. 15. Include a statement of the changes in working capital.

12. Similarly, prepare a Source and Use of Funds statement for P. P. Refrigeration Ltd. from the data supplied in Progress Test 10 Question 7.

CHAPTER XII

CONTROLLING FIXED ASSETS

FINANCIAL PLANNING

1. Financial planning. Financial planning—generally regarded as the means whereby the company ensures immediate and future solvency and liquidity and adequate finance generated internally or externally at the best possible terms for revenue and capital commitments—forms an essential part of the overall company plan. In other words, predetermined and quantified company objectives are the prerequisites for an effective corporate plan or strategy in which the quality of the integral financial plan plays a vital role. Obviously a strategy formulated without consideration for the sources and availability of finance is nonsense; funds must be matched against expenditure, both in amount and timing if strategy and objectives are to be met.

Furthermore, the relationship between strategy and the financial plan implies a dialogue: a two-way relationship. For instance, in addition to the "requests" that financial planners provide adequate funds at appropriate times, feedback responses, as for example when funds are unavailable or available only at unacceptably high cost, may necessitate compensatory adjustments to corporate strategy.

2. Finance a scarce resource. Finance is an economic resource both in the macro-economic sense (hence its price, or rate of interest it commands in the financial markets) and at the micro or company level because of its limited supply in relation to the competing uses the company may put it to. In general terms, this scarcity of finance is influenced by a number of factors:

(*a*) *Company performance.* Clearly the supply of funds generated internally depends on how successful the company is at present and in the future in employing its capital.

(*b*) *The company's financial plan.* This may act as a constraint on the company's potential supply of finance.

(*i*) Company controllers may adopt a high pay-out policy.

(*ii*) Planners may be reluctant to increase capital gearing beyond a certain level because of the extra risk.

3. Adjustments to the financial plan. In the event of a short-fall between planned expenditure and actual funds, financial managers may resort to predetermined contingency plans designed to secure the corporate objectives by other means. Alternatively it may mean:

(*a*) Capital rationing, where projects are selected by comparison of:

  (*i*) Risk, or
  (*ii*) Return on investment, or
  (*iii*) Pay-back.

(*b*) Postponement of investment.

(*c*) Review of strategy to see whether alternative courses of action are consistent with the selected objectives, *e.g.* securing use of equipment by means of H.P. instead of buying, or buying parts from sub-contractors as a short-term solution.

4. Generation of investment projects. The process of selecting investment projects can be analysed into the following stages:

(*a*) The project is conceived, *i.e.*

  (*i*) Internally generated in response to company strategy or from opportunities created by company activities.
  (*ii*) Externally generated by environmental forces.

(*b*) The proposal for specific expenditure.

(*c*) Appraisal of the proposal on the basis of the following:

  (*i*) Specifications of project.
  (*ii*) Estimate of costs. In particular, accurate investment appraisal depends on the reliability of these estimates, and correct forecasts of capital.

    i. Capital expenditure required.
    ii. The life of the project.
    iii. Working capital required.
    iv. Residual value of the equipment.
    v. Tax rates and allowances.

  (*iii*) Estimates of revenues generated by the investment.

    i. The selling price of the article.
    ii. The volume of sales.
    iii. The operating costs.

(*iv*) Consistency with corporate and appropriate departmental strategy.

(*v*) Availability of funds.

(*d*) Testing using investment appraisal techniques.

(*i*) Pay-back.

(*ii*) Rate of return.

(*iii*) Discounted cash flow (D.C.F.).

(*e*) Selected projects introduced into capital budget.

(*f*) Authorisation.

(*g*) Implementation.

(*h*) Feedback to check actual performance against anticipated performance.

5. Nature of investment. Investment in this context may be defined generally as "the commitment of company resources in the expectation that this will realise a profit or gain." Clearly investment decisions must never be made lightly, but only after rigorous appraisal of the alternative project, because investment once made is often irreversible and thus commits management to a fixed policy in the future. Furthermore, it introduces risk since the anticipated profit or gain cannot be guaranteed at the outset. In summary the nature of company investment is such that:

(*a*) A decision is often irreversible since abandonment would probably involve considerable financial loss if the asset is resold.

(*b*) It introduces inflexibility into future company policy.

(*c*) It means that the expenditure is at risk because future incomes cannot be forecast exactly.

With the need for cost-consciousness on the part of management and increasing capital intensiveness in industry, it is vital that managers should understand the principles underlying the various techniques of capital appraisal to secure the optimum use of company and departmental resources. The principal investment appraisal techniques available to managers are now considered in detail.

METHODS OF MEASURING THE PROFITABILITY OF CAPITAL PROJECTS

6. Accounting rate of return method. This measures the return on an investment as a percentage of the capital expenditure.

$$\% \text{ rate of return} = \frac{\text{Total revenue} - \text{Total operating costs}}{\text{Capital expenditure}} \times 100$$

or
$$\frac{\text{Net earnings}}{\text{Investment}} \times 100$$

The principles underlying the accounting rate of return method may be illustrated by an example. Assume that a company buys an automatic press for £12,000 which is expected to have an operational life of six years, at which time it will have no scrap value. Gross earnings arise by way of savings in wages and present operating costs and are expected to amount to about £2,500 *per* year. The calculations involved in this example are as follows:

Year	(i) Gross earnings £	(ii) Depreciation (straight line) £	((i)–(ii)) Net earnings £
1	2,500	2,000	500
2	2,500	2,000	500
3	2,500	2,000	500
4	2,500	2,000	500
5	2,500	2,000	500
6	2,500	2,000	500
	£15,000	£12,000	£3,000

Here net earnings (ignoring taxation) are increased by £500 *per* year by the reduction in labour and operational costs after charging depreciation on a straight-line method over its operational life, *i.e.* £2,000 *per* year. Thus we are attempting to remove the replacement part of the cash flow and calculate the true profit element of cash flow in relation to the cost of the project.

$$\text{Thus } \frac{\text{Net earnings}}{\text{Investment}} \times 100 = \frac{£3,000}{£12,000} \times 100$$
$$= 25\% \quad \text{(or 25p } per \text{ £1 of investment)}$$

The return measured on a yearly basis is:
$$= \frac{£500}{£12,000} \times 100$$
$$= 4 \cdot 16\% \text{ } per \text{ } annum$$

If the company had a choice of several automatic presses all equally acceptable in terms of performance, then we could calculate the profitability of each and seriously consider the one showing the highest percentage rate of return. However, because of the disadvantages of this method (*see* **7**) it is dangerous to use this method alone for making investment decisions, but rather as a guide to performance of alternative investments.

7. Disadvantages of the method. The disadvantages of the rate of return method are that:

(*a*) It disregards the incidence of cash flow, *i.e.* it fails to take time into account, weighing each £ equally. However, £1 received in Year 1 is obviously worth more than £1 in Years 2, 3, 4, 5 and 6, since it can be invested immediately to earn interest. Similarly, money received in Years 3, 4, 5 and 6 is worth less than money received in Years 1 and 2.

(*b*) Bearing in mind this important limitation experienced, it is misleading to compare two projects which have different earning profiles, *i.e.* where income accrues at different times over the operational life of each project.

EXAMPLE:

	Project A *Alpha Automatic Press* *Net earnings*	*Project B* *Beta Automatic Press* *Net earnings*
	£	£
Year 1	1,000	2,000
Year 2	1,000	2,000
Year 3	1,500	1,000
Year 4	2,000	500
	£5,500	£5,500

Obviously, since the total net earnings are identical the accounting rate of return method will give identical answers for both machines if their capital costs are identical; but project B is preferred on the grounds that the bulk of the net earnings are received in the very early years and can be reinvested for additional earlier profits.

Throughout this example, we have ignored taxation and thus the return is gross. However, taxation may be taken into account and the net return calculated by deducting tax from the net earnings and adding savings through capital allowances to the next taxed earnings.

8. Advantages of the yield method.

(a) It is simple to understand and calculate.

(b) It gives an indication of overall profitability, since it measures savings over the entire life of the project and relates it to the investment.

9. Pay-back method. This second method measures the length of time it takes to recoup the capital outlay out of the expected earnings, usually defined as pre-tax profit plus depreciation (note that in 1964–5 96 per cent of companies used pay-back gross of tax (A. J. Merret and A. Sykes)). It is a simple concept to operate and can be illustrated by way of example.

Assume that a company is about to launch a new product which is thought by the marketing manager to have a reasonably long product life cycle. He illustrates this by means of Fig. 29.

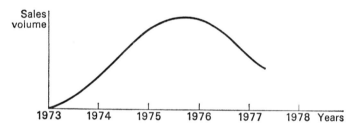

FIG. 29.—Product life cycle of Swallow brand cassette tape recorder.

The marketing manager explains this typical product life cycle curve as follows:

1973—*Period of product innovation when sales increase slowly.* Development and launching costs are being incurred so that profits are low.

1974—*Period of maximum growth in sales.* The public quickly appreciate the novelty of the product and a high sales volume generates high profits.

1975—*Period of maturity of the product.* In a competitive market rivals are launching similar goods which slows down the growth in sales. Higher marketing costs to counteract rival products tend to reduce profits.

1976—*Period of decline.* Profits fall rapidly as customers prefer competitors' products instead as they are newer and probably incorporate technological improvements.

10. Pay-back: example. In the light of the Swallow Brand's product life cycle let us imagine that the initial capital outlay (column (ii) of Table XXV) on manufacturing equipment is £200,000 and net profits from sales are as shown in column (i) of Table XXV.

TABLE XXV. PAY-BACK CALCULATIONS

Year	(i) Net annual earnings (inflow) £	(ii) Investment (outflow) £	(iii) Cumulative net inflow £
1973	10,000	200,000	− 190,000
1974	100,000	—	− 90,000
1975	70,000	—	− 20,000
1976	50,000	—	+ 30,000
1977	40,000	—	+ 70,000

Here the project pays for itself during 1976, assuming that the projected net annual earnings are achieved. In other words, the project breaks even in the third year, when the net revenue balances with the capital outlay. This is shown graphically in Figs. 30 and 31.

11. Advantages of the pay-back method. The main advantages of this method are:

(*a*) It is simple to calculate.

(*b*) It recognises the timing of cash flow.

(*c*) It is particularly appropriate and informative for a company short of liquid assets, in which case projects with short pay-back periods are preferred.

(*d*) It is valuable as a method for investment decisions for companies operating in high-risk markets. Companies whose products tend to be overtaken by changing technology or fashion and therefore have short product life cycles, will prefer short pay-back periods to lessen risk.

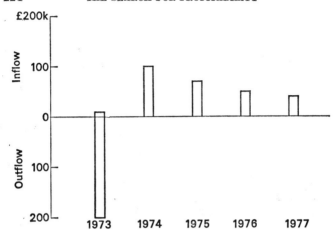

FIG. 30.—Cash flows for Swallow cassette tape recorder.

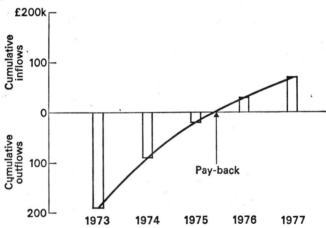

FIG. 31.—Culmulative net cash flows and pay-back period for Swallow cassette tape recorder.

12. Disadvantages of the pay-back method. The chief disadvantages are:

(a) It ignores the value of receipts after the point of recovery of original capital outlay (pay-back).

(b) It fails to consider the timing of receipts beyond this break-even point.

(c) It ignores the profitability of the project, since it is preoccupied with speed of repayment.

(d) If the company is concerned with liquidity, then pay-back measured gross of tax understates the true cash flow and is therefore inaccurate.

13. Compound interest. The investment appraisal methods that we next consider have one thing in common. They are all based on the concept of "present value", *i.e.* they overcome the objections raised against pay-back and accounting rate of return by considering the "time value of money," which means that more weight is given to immediate cash flows than to future cash flows. To appreciate the real significance of this concept, let us look first at compound interest.

If an investor deposits £100 in a deposit account of a bank that pays 10 per cent interest then the total investment will grow as follows:

	Initial deposit	*Interest* 10%	*Total deposit*
	£	£	£
at start of year 1	100	—	100·00
at end of year 1	—	10·00	110·00
at end of year 2	—	11·00	121·00
at end of year 3	—	12·10	133·10
at end of year 4	—	13·31	146·41

A visual presentation, as in Fig. 32, may help the reader to appreciate the nature of compound interest.

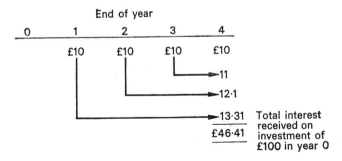

FIG. 32.—Compound interest calculations.

Of course in practice it is unnecessary to go through this tedious process; instead we use a formula. The formula for calculating compound interest per unit of principal is

$$(1 + i)^n$$

where i is the rate of interest and n is the number of years that the principal sum is invested.

Thus to calculate the interest that £1 will earn at 10 per cent over four years so as to check the above table, we substitute the values of i and n in the formula.

$$
\begin{aligned}
\text{Compound interest} &= (1+i)^4 \\
&= (1+\cdot10) \\
&= 1\cdot1 \times 1\cdot1 \times 1\cdot1 \times 1\cdot1 \\
&= 1\cdot461
\end{aligned}
$$

If we extend the formula to include the initial sum invested (Principal) then the total sum invested at the end of a period is calculated by the formula:

$$P(1+i)^n$$

$$
\begin{aligned}
&= £100(1+i)^n \\
&= £146\cdot41 \quad \text{This is the sum invested at the end of fourth year}
\end{aligned}
$$

In conclusion of this brief analysis of compounding, it is worth stating two principles, which, if appreciated at the outset of the examination of discounting that follows, will avoid difficulties that might arise.

(a) £1 now is worth more than £1 in the future because the present £1 can be invested and will in time be equal to £1 plus interest.

(b) We are interested only in the monetary value of £s and not the real or economic value. Consequently, the analysis is not intended to compensate for the depreciation in the value of future money caused by inflation. However, this does not mean that inflation is not taken into account: under conditions of inflation interest rates tend to rise and the stream of expected receipts and payments expected to arise from a project are adjusted upwards for the anticipated rate of inflation.

14. Discounting. Discounting is essentially compound interest in reverse, and tells us the present value of a future sum of money. For example, if an investor wants exactly £100 at the end of year 1 when the rate of interest is 10 per cent then he must invest £90·91 now. The reader is probably wondering where this figure of £90·91 came from. The answer is simple. We know that £100 with interest of 10 per cent will grow to £110 at the end of one year, and £121 at the end of year two. Then if we divide

£100 by £110, then we obtain 0·9091 for Year 1.
and   £100 by £121, then we obtain 0·8264 for Year 2.

These figures are called discount factors, and inform us that:

£1·00 at the end of Year 1 is worth £0·9091 now at 10 per cent
and   £1·00 at the end of Year 2 is worth £0·8264 now at 10 per cent.

Using these factors we can reduce any future sum of money back to present-day value: at 10 per cent interest £127 at the

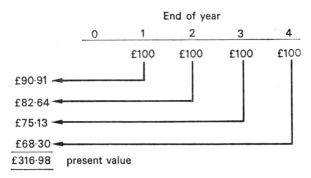

End of year

FIG. 33.—Present-value calculations.

end of Year 1 has a present value of £115·45 (£127 × 0·9091); £146,000 at the end of Year 2 has a present value of £121,894 (£147,500 × 0·8264).

Returning to a visual presentation, if £100 is received at the end of each year for four years then in present-value terms the total cash flow discounted at 10 per cent is worth £316·98 (*see* Fig. 33).

A formula for calculating the discount factor is

$$\frac{1}{(1+i)^n}$$

so that if we substitute the information for Year 1 in this example as a check on the above calculation we have:

$$\left(\frac{1}{1+0\cdot10}\right)^1 = \frac{1}{1\cdot1} = 0\cdot9091,$$

i.e. £1 at the end of Year 1 is worth £0·9091 now: the investor is indifferent between receiving £0·9091 immediately or £1·00 at the end of one year.

15. What the discount rate means. Let us assume that Ivor Hogg borrows £200 from a building society at 11 per cent and repays the loan over two years. The transactions are as follows:

		(i)		(ii)
Start of Year 1	Capital outstanding	£200		
	Interest on this capital (11%)	22		
		£222	11% discount factors	
End of Year 1	Repayments	117 × 0·9009	= £105·4	
Start of Year 2	Capital outstanding	105		
	Interest on this capital (11%)	12		
		117		
		(i)		(ii)
End of Year 2	Repayments	117 × 0·8116	=	94·9
	Capital Outstanding			200·3 (£200)

Ivor has repaid a total of £117 + £117 = £234 which represents a repayment of the loan of £200 plus interest payments of 11 per cent on the capital balance outstanding at the start of each year. Column (ii) confirms that the repayments repay the £200 capital when brought back to present values. This relationship between compounding and discounting can be clarified and the full implications of the D.C.F. percentage used in capital appraisals appreciated if the above example is explained in a different way, *i.e.* a businessman borrowing £200 for investment can just afford to pay compound interest on this sum of 11 per cent if it generates an equal return of 11 per cent because the actual cost of the investment equals the present value of the investment, measuring the time value of money as 11 per cent. However, an 11 per cent return does not make any allowance for risk; the businessman might expect a return of 13–14 per cent to compensate for slight risk and correspondingly higher returns over 11 per cent for more risky investments.

16. Present value tables. If one is to have a sound grasp of the concept of discounting, it is crucial to understand the meaning of discount rates and how the discount factors are determined. Indeed this has been the purpose behind these numerous examples. Fortunately, however, the chore of calculating individual discount factors is unnecessary in

Year	Net annual earnings £	Discount factor (10%)	Discounted net annual earnings £	Cumulative net inflow (discounted) £
1973	10,000	0.9091	9,090	−190,910
1974	100,000	0.8264	82,640	−108,270
1975	70,000	0.7513	52,590	−55,680
1976	50,000	0.6830	34,150	−21,530
1977	40,000	0.6209	24,830	+ 3,300
			£203,300	

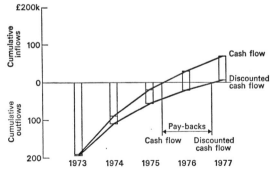

FIG. 34.—Effect of discounting cash flow on pay-back.

practice because they are already calculated and available in present value tables which can be found in most books on management accounting and capital budgeting (*see* Appendix II).

17. Present value of future earnings. So far, we have applied discounting to investment income resulting from a deposit of money at compound interest, but in fact it has a far wider application. If we now reconsider the financial data set out in Table XXV we can apply this discounting technique to future earnings arising from a company's investment, that are unlike bank deposit interest in that they are positively skewed as reflected by the product life cycle diagram. By assuming that the time value of money is 10 per cent we discount future earnings at 10 per cent and thereby give greater weighting to earnings achieved in the immediate periods. The result is a new break-even point: pay-back is put back one year and now occurs during 1977 (*see* Fig. 34).

18. Definition of discounted cash flow method. The next method of capital appraisal to consider is the Discounted Cash Flow (D.C.F.) rate of return on an investment, which is defined as the annual return on the outstanding capital balance at the end of each year. The D.C.F. rate of interest is unique because it is that rate that makes the present-day value of future cash flow equal in aggregate to the present-day capital cost of the project.

We can illustrate its operation by using the estimated annual sales, costs and capital outlay of the Swallow brand Cassette Recorder set out in Table XXV. In (**17**) we discounted the net earnings at 10 per cent to arrive at total net earnings measured at present-day values of £203,300 which exceeded the present-day value of the cost of the project (£200,000) by £3,300 (called net present-day value). Therefore a 10 per cent discount factor is too low; the return must be greater than 10 per cent. A little thought will show that this must be so since the cash flow pays for the original investment and earns a 10 per cent return on this outlay with an additional surplus of £3,300 over and above this return. The next step, therefore, is to discount the earnings at a higher rate of interest.

Let us now discount the earnings at 11 per cent

Year	Net annual earnings	Discount factor 11%	Discounted net earnings
	£		£
1973	10,000	0·9009	9,000
1974	100,000	0·8116	81,160
1975	70,000	0·7312	51,180
1976	50,000	0·6587	32,930
1977	40,000	0·5935	23,740
			£198,010

In comparison with the previous calculation, this calculation produces a negative balance (or net present value) of £1,090 and shows that a 11 per cent discount rate is too high, so that the true rate lies between 10 per cent and 11 per cent where the discounted cash flow exactly equals the cost of the investment. In summary:

(a) The D.C.F. is too high if present value of future earnings is less than the cost of the original investment.

(b) The D.C.F. rate is too low if the present value of future earnings is more than the cost of the original investment.

(c) The true D.C.F. rate is that when present value of future earnings equals the cost of the original investment.

19. D.C.F. rate by interpolation. This method, shown in (**17 and 18**), is appropriately known as the "trial and error" method, since at least two calculations must be made that straddle the true rate. This rate is then found by interpolation, *i.e.*:

Net present value of earnings at 10%	= + £3,300
Net present value of earnings at 11%	= − £1,090
Overall difference	£4,390

Therefore the true discount is found by interpolation; it lies at a point $\frac{3,300}{4,390}$ of the difference between 10 per cent and 11 per cent, *i.e.* 10 per cent + 0·75 per cent or 10·75 per cent.

Thus the profits from the project are sufficient to repay the cost of the investment and earn a rate of interest on the capital of 10·75 *per annum*. However, one note of caution regarding interpolation to establish the D.C.F. rate of return. This method assumes a linear trend (in fact it is non-linear) in net present values between 10 and 11 per cent and therefore tends to overestimate the true D.C.F. return. The error is too small to worry about in the above example, but would produce less accurate results if we were to interpolate between extreme values of, say, 10–15 per cent or more. This is apparent from the example in Fig. 35.

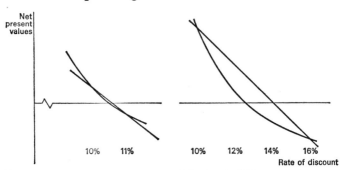

FIG. 35.—Interpolation to establish the D.C.F. rate of return.

In the first situation, the error is insignificant, but not in the second case; the answer is to avoid large extremes in D.C.F. rates of returns straddling the true return when interpolating with the trial and error method.

20. Net present value method. This method also makes use of discount factors, but is less onerous than the previous trial and error method where several calculations are needed. Here, one simply discounts the cash flows at a stipulated rate of discount to give their present-day values, selecting the project showing the largest surplus of earnings at present-day values. An example serves to illustrate this technique.

Assume that a company can borrow sufficient funds at 10 per cent to finance one or two projects it has under consideration: the minimum acceptable return on capital for the company is 12 per cent. This difference of 2 per cent represents the return to compensate for the risk inherent in the project, discussed in (**17**). The capital expenditure required for projects A or B is £25,000 and net cash flow is as follows:

	Project A	Project B
	£	£
Net cash flow		
Year 1973	7,000	12,000
1974	12,000	10,000
1975	15,000	8,000
Total net cash flow	£34,000	£30,000

Calculations of net present values at discount rate of 10 per cent *p.a.*:

	Project A			Project B		
Year	Net cash flow	Discount factor	Discounted net present value	Net cash flow	Discount factor	Discounted net present value
	£		£	£		£
1973	7,000	0·9091	6,363	12,000	0·9091	10,909
1974	12,000	0·8264	9,916	10,000	0·8264	8,264
1975	15,000	0·7513	11,269	8,000	0·7513	6,010
	£34,000		£27,548	£30,000		£25,183
	Less Capital cost		25,000	*Less* Capital cost		25,000
		N.P.V. =	2,548		N.P.V. =	183

Calculations of net present values at discount rate of 12 per cent:

Year	£		£	£		£
1973	7,000	0·8929	6,250	12,000	0·8929	10,714
1974	12,000	0·7972	9,566	10,000	0·7972	7,972
1975	15,000	0·7118	10,677	8,000	0·7118	5,694
	£34,000		£26,493	£30,000		£24,380
	Less Capital cost		25,000	*Less* Capital cost		25,000
		N.P.V. =	1,493		N.P.V. =	(620)

The calculation shows that both projects achieve a return in excess of the 10 per cent, the cost of capital, but only Project A passes the threshold return of 12 per cent and is therefore preferable to B. In other words, the size of the net present value indicates that the project earns a true return in excess of the discount percentage selected for the exercise; the larger the N.P.V., the larger the rate of return.

21. The choice of discount rate.

(a) The stipulated rate of interest may be the organisation's R.O.C.E. percentage. Possible projects that fail to meet this test should be disregarded, projects whose profitability exceeds this figure will tend to improve the organisation's overall profitability.

(b) It may be the company's cost of capital. It goes without saying that a profit-dependent organisation should never invest funds if the expected return is lower than the cost of the capital. Indeed, judging by the lack of corporate investment it is apparent that many decision-makers appreciate this, and the corollary is that consideration should be given to the opportunity cost of investment, for in the summer of 1974 substantial sums were transferred into the more profitable money markets at the expense of industrial expansion.

Let us assume that a hypothetical company has the following capital structure (column (i))

(i)		(ii) Per- centage	(iii) Post-tax cost	(iv) Weighted cost
Ordinary shares £100,000		40	20%	80
Undistributed profits	25,000	10	20%	20
8% Debenture	75,000	30	4%	12
6% Loan Stock	50,000	20	3%	6
	£250,000	100		118

Average cost of capital $= 11.8\%$ $(118 \div 100)$ %

Column (iii) indicates the post-tax cost of the various categories of capital employed by the company. The loan capital needs no further mention except that the interest is tax-deductible where tax is assumed to be 50 per cent. The cost of the equity capital, however, does require comment; here, the opportunity cost of investment is used on the basis that the shareholders expect a return consistent with the yield on similar equity shares and given the opportunity would transfer their investments if company returns failed to match these alternative returns. Thus assuming that ordinary shareholders traditionally expect, say, 7 per cent, and with a rate of inflation of 13 per cent, a total cost of 20 per cent is required.

Thus the weighted cost of capital is 11·8 per cent, which should be the minimum acceptable rate of return figure for projects. Preferably returns should exceed this figure if the organisation is to grow, but should never be lower on the grounds that the debt capital is very low cost capital (*see* (*d*)).

(*c*) It may be based on the cost of capital plus a percentage for uncertainty or the degree of risk.

(*d*) Certain projects or capital expenditure produce a nil return, as for example expenditure on safety installations. Naturally they cannot be rejected merely on profitability grounds.

A company possessing limited resources and faced with several projects each competing for funds may select projects by ranking them in order of:

(*a*) Pay-back.

(*b*) Accounting rate of return.

(*c*) Net present value.

(*d*) Profitability index, which is the net present value of net earnings divided by the present value of the capital outlay. Thus at 10 per cent discount rate the profitability indices for projects A and B described in (**20**) are:

$$\overset{A}{\frac{\text{Net present earnings}}{\text{Capital outlay}} \frac{£27,548}{£25,000}} = 1·101 \quad : \quad \overset{B}{\frac{£25,183}{£25,000}} = 1·007$$

This confirms our conclusions reached in (**20**) that at a 10 per cent discount rate both projects succeed, but if they are mutually exclusive then A is preferred to B on the basis of its higher profitability index number.

22. Ranking projects and D.C.F. Perhaps the reader will have noticed that the D.C.F. method does not appear above as a means of ranking investment projects. This is because,

		A			B	
Year	Net earnings	Discount 10%	Discounted net earnings	Net earnings	Discount 10%	Discounted net earnings
	£		£	£		£
1	40,000	0·9090	36,360	58,000	0·9090	52,722
2	40,000	0·8265	33,060	58,000	0·8265	47,937
3	40,000	0·7513	30,052	58,000	0·7513	43,575
4	40,000	0·6830	27,320	58,000	0·6830	39,614
5	40,000	0·6209	24,836	58,000	0·6209	36,012
			151,628			219,860
	Less Capital outlay		120,000	*Less* Capital outlay		180,000
		N.P.V.	£31,628		N.P.V.	£39,860
	By trial and error D.C.F. = 19·8%				D.C.F. = 18·5%	

unlike the other methods, it fails to take into account the cost of the capital expenditure. However, this is not a serious obstacle and in view of D.C.F.'s significant overall advantages (*see* 23) should not appear to be deficient in this respect. Consequently, a ranking procedure for D.C.F. follows.

Assume that management has two alternative projects under consideration. A requires a capital outlay of £120,000 but B needs £180,000. Both are estimated to provide a cash flow for five years; A £40,000 *per* year and B £58,000 *per* year. The cost of capital is 10 per cent.

Calculation would show that A is preferable, in that it earns a higher D.C.F. rate, but it must be remembered that the two projects require different capital investments. Thus we are not comparing like with like.

However, we may usefully employ the economist's concept of the margin, and by comparing the two projects calculate the marginal or incremental capital outlay and marginal net earnings.

	Capital outlay	*Annual net earnings*
A	£120,000	£40,000
B	180,000	58,000

Marginal investment $= £60,000$

Marginal earnings $= £18,000$
D.C.F. $= 15\cdot7\%$

Thus the marginal capital of £60,000 invested in project B generates marginal earnings of £18,000 *p.a.* which earns a D.C.F. rate of 15·7 per cent.

To conclude, the second project performs as well as project A, but the incremental investment of £60,000 generates additional earnings that yield 15·7 per cent, which is to be preferred bearing in mind that the cost of the capital is only 10 per cent.

23. Advantages of D.C.F. rate. The D.C.F. rate has certain advantages over other capital appraisal techniques:

(*a*) It is expressed as a percentage.

(*b*) As a percentage it is easily understood by managers who conventionally measure profitability and yields in this way.

(*c*) It can be readily compared with the cost of capital, which is also expressed as a percentage.

24. Determination of annual rentals. Goggle Box Services Limited wish to rent out a black-and-white TV set to a new customer. Their policy is to charge an annual rental that within four years pays for the set (£60) and in addition generates a 15 per cent return. The rental is determined as follows (ignore tax and capital allowances).

Year	Discount factor 15%
0	1·0000
1	0·8695
2	0·7561
3	0·6575

3·2831 total factors

$$\frac{\text{Capital investment}}{\text{Total factors}} = \text{Rental/year}$$

$$\frac{£60}{3·2831} = £18·28 \, p.a.$$

25. Lease or buy. The owner-manager of the Wayside Garage is interested in installing a diagnostic-tuning system and establishes that such a machine can be bought for £4,000 or rented for £600 *p.a.* In both cases operating costs and maintenance are borne by the garage. The anticipated life of the equipment is ten years. Obviously the running costs and sales revenue are identical, whether the equipment is bought or leased, so the decision rests on the relative capital costs of acquiring the system. The garage at present earns 16 per cent return on capital. (Tax and capital allowances are ignored.)

Cost of purchase	*Cost of rental*	
Cost = £4,000	Rental cost	£600 *p.a.*
Present value = 4,000	Present value of £1 for 10 years at 16% =	4·883
	Present value of £600 =	4·833 × £600
		= £2,899

Therefore, on these comparative costs the rental agreement is preferable as it produces the lower present value.

NOTE:
In this example the rental agreement requires the garage to pay a regular fixed sum of £600 *p.a.* for ten years (which is like an annuity). We could employ the same method as in

(24,) but this would be tedious considering the life of the project. Fortunately there is a short cut. We look therefore in a compound interest table called "Present Value of an Annuity of £1"—for the appropriate term (ten years) and at the appropriate rate of interest, in this case 16 per cent—(4·833).

TAXATION

26. Taxation considerations. Throughout this chapter we have ignored taxation in the capital appraisal calculations in order to clarify understanding of the essential principles underlying the different methods. However, we are now in a position to introduce taxation and capital allowances and consider the effect on a typical investment decision. The basic rules for dealing with taxation are as follows:

(a) The net earnings before depreciation arising from the capital outlay should be adjusted for corporation tax liability.

(b) Any capital allowances must be set off against tax liability.

The reader is advised to study thoroughly the following example, which is self-explanatory as long as he remembers that the 100 per cent capital allowance reduces tax liability in the year of purchase (1973) and that a capital charge is made against the receipts from the sale of the plant.

27. Example.

P. P. Refrigeration is considering the purchase of a machine to make pressings for its domestic refrigerators. It is estimated that the machine, which costs £40,000, will have a life of five years, at the end of which it will have a scrap value of £6,000. In addition, the project involves an investment in working capital of £2,000 at the commencement of operations and an additional £4,000 one year later, all of which is released at the end of the projects life. Overheads and commissioning expenses are expected to be £2,000, payable at the end of the first year. This is summarised in the Profit and Tax Calculation Sheet shown in Fig. 36.

Corporation tax is 50 per cent; 100 per cent capital allowance for 1973 which is applied to the operating profit of that year to calculate the tax *which is payable the following January*. The company carries on other manufacturing activities from which it derives taxable profits.

						Project:	Machine Press
Year ending	1973	1974	1975	1976	1977	1978	1979
Sales revenue	—	£20,000	£40,000	£50,000	£60,000	£60,000	—
Costs							
Variable costs	—	£15,000	£30,000	£35,000	£40,000	£40,000	—
Fixed costs	—	500	500	500	500	500	—
Other overheads	—	2,000	—	—	—	—	—
Costs of project	—	£17,500	£30,500	£35,500	£40,500	£40,500	—
Profit before depreciation	—	£2,500	£9,500	£14,500	£19,500	£19,500	—
Capital allowances	£40,000	—	—	—	—	—	(£6,000)
Taxable profits	—	2,500	9,500	14,500	19,500	19,500	—
Taxation at 50%	(£20,000)	1,250	4,750	7,250	9,750	9,750	(3,000)
		Note: Outflow ( )					

(a) Profit and tax calculations.

					Project:	Machine Press
Year	Fixed assets	Working capital	Operating profit	Corporation tax	Net total	Cumulative total
1973	£40,000	(£2,000)	—	—	(£42,000)	(£42,000)
1974	—	(£4,000)	£2,500	£20,000	18,500	(23,500)
1975	—	—	9,500	(1,250)	8,250	(15,250)
1976	—	—	14,500	(4,750)	9,750	(5,500)
1977	—	—	19,500	(7,250)	12,250	6,750
1978	—	—	19,500	(9,750)	9,750	16,500
1979	6,000	6,000	—	(9,750)	2,250	18,750
1980	—	—	—	(3,000)	(3,000)	15,750

(b) Cash flow summary.

Project: Machine Press

Net cash flow out

	0%		10%		20%	
Year	Actual cash	Factor	Present value	Factor	Present value	
1973	£42,000	1·0	£42,000	1·0	£42,000	
1974	—		—		—	
1975	—		—		—	
Total	£42,000		£42,000		£42,000	

Net cash flow in

	£		£		£	
1973	—	1·000	—	1·000	—	
1974	18,500	0·909	16,816	0·833	15,410	
1975	8,250	0·826	6,814	0·694	5,725	
1976	9,750	0·751	7·322	0·579	5,645	
1977	12,250	0·683	8·367	0·482	5,904	
1978	9,750	0·621	6·055	0·402	3,919	
1979	2,750	0·564	1,269	0·335	754	
1980	(3,000)	0·513	(1,539)	0·279	(837)	

Totals			£45,104	£37,035
Profitability index			1·07	·88
Net present value			+ £3,104	− £4,965

Yield by interpolation:

$$+ 10\% + \frac{3104}{3104 + 4965} \times 10\%$$

$$= 13 \cdot 8\%$$

(c) Discounted cash flows.

FIG. 36.—Profit and tax calculations for a machine press project.

CAPITAL APPRAISAL AND RISK

28. Introduction. So far in this chapter we have examined the principles of investment appraisal techniques and the relative pros and cons of each method. Perhaps the precision with which estimated costs and revenues, and therefore cash flow, were stated caused readers to wonder at the remarkable confidence of the forecasts! However, let us now introduce a degree of realism into the calculations by considering the risks and uncertainties that underlie investment appraisal.

29. Risk and uncertainty. It is axiomatic that in a dynamic situation no forecast, however accurate, can precisely predict future events; nor can a company completely avoid the risks and uncertainties present in an unpredictable world.

    (*a*) Risk in this context is defined as the situation where events can to some extent be quantified so that the probability that a specific investment will yield a certain return can be calculated.

    (*b*) Uncertainty on the other hand is the situation where no probability estimates are possible.

30. Analysis of risk. Let us imagine that a company has sufficient surplus management, staff and productive capacity to produce one additional product and must decide which one of two new restyled products (A and B) to select. As a first step in evaluating the products it conducts extensive research to obtain objective judgments supported by expert opinion on the expected sales revenue in the first year if sales are made at a predetermined price. Admittedly, this assumes certain subjective judgments, as must any situation involving the sale of a product, because the data needed to calculate probabilities cannot be obtained with the same precision as when a sample of electric-light bulbs are life-tested, and the results used to calculate the probability of one bulb selected at random failing at x hours. Nevertheless, we can assume that the product has a very short life cycle of one year, that the experts are well experienced in selling similar products and that there are no changes in Government economic policy or in competitors' reactions within this time span.

Once the estimated sales are known they can be recorded and presented in the form of normal curves and the standard deviations and coefficients of variation for A and B compared.

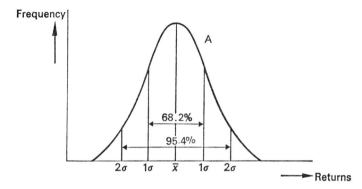

(a) Area under the normal curve.

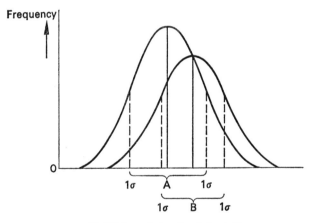

(b) Risk and standard deviation.

FIG. 37.—Risk and standard deviation.

Fig. 37(a) represents a typical normal curve and the relationship between σ, the standard deviation, and the area beneath the curve. Thus 68·2 per cent of the total area lies inside the 1 standard deviation limit so that two out of three events lie within 1 standard deviation of the mean. If this figure relates to product A showing the anticipated sales revenues on the horizontal axis against recorded frequencies (*i.e.* how often each sales revenue figure was selected) on the vertical axis then we can directly compare their standard deviation, as in Fig. 37(*b*). It appears that on the grounds of risk, product A is superior (*i.e.* less risky) in that the majority of the sales values are more concentrated around the average observation, compared with B's which are more variable (although this must be confirmed by comparing their coefficients of variation) (*see* **31**) and therefore more risky. On the other hand, product B is judged to perform better on the average in terms of returns and whether management proceeds with A or B depends on their relative attitudes to risk.

31. Formula for comparing risk.

(*a*) The standard deviation provides a comparison of risks between projects, *i.e.* a lower standard deviation indicates lower risk when return is expressed in percentage terms. Its formula is:

$$\text{Standard deviation} = \frac{\Sigma f(x - \bar{x})^2}{\Sigma f}$$

(*b*) Where returns are expressed in revenue terms the coefficient of variation is needed

$$\text{Coefficient of variation} = \frac{\text{Standard deviation}}{\text{Mean}} \times 100$$

32. Uncertainty.
There may be situations where highly subjective or arbitrary weighting must be used. For example, two mutually exclusive projects are considered (X and Y); both are evaluated scientifically on accurate costing and sales figures assuming certain rates of economic growth resulting from possible Government economic policies. Their net present values are:

			Project X	Project Y
(*i*)	Pessimistic forecast	(nil growth)	£15,000	£18,000
(*ii*)	"Neutral" forecast	(2% growth)	27,000	25,000
(*iii*)	Optimistic forecast	(4% growth)	40,000	38,000

If the weight or probability of any one forecast of proving correct is assumed equal (i.e. $\frac{1}{3}$), then the weighted average for Project X is £27,070 and £26,680 for Project Y.

X				Y		
0·33	×	£15,000 =	£4,960	0·33	×	£18,000 =	£5,940
0·33	×	27,000 =	8,910	0·33	×	25,000 =	8,250
0·33	×	40,000 =	13,200	0·33	×	38,000 =	12,540

X total: **£27,070**   Y total: **£26,730**

Thus project X shows a marginally better return.

However, if the economic situation deteriorates and remedial government economic controls are expected then additional weighting can be applied to the pessimistic forecast. Assuming the following subjective weightings for situations (*i*), (*ii*) and (*iii*) to be. 0·5, 0·3 and 0·2 respectively, then we have

Project X			*Project Y*		
(*i*) 0·5 × £15,000 =	£7,500		0·5 × £18,000 =	£9,000
(*ii*) 0·3 × 27,000 =	8,100		0·3 × 25,000 =	7,500
(*iii*) 0·2 × 40,000 =	8,000		0·2 × 38,000 =	7,600

X total: **£23,600**   Y total: **£24,100**

Consequently the position is reversed, and project Y is selected.

For a different approach to uncertainty let us reconsider the earlier example of the cassette tape recorder. Thus if the

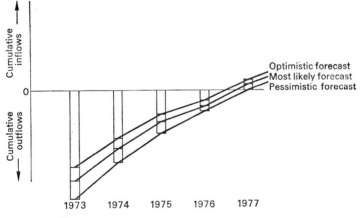

FIG. 38.—Forecasts and discounted cash flows.

forecasts of profits from their sales are thought to be realistic, in that they are based on the most accurate costing and sales figures and on the probable growth in the economy, then we can regard the figures as the most likely to occur. However, we may estimate that there is a likely range within which actual profits may fall. The most optimistic level of profits may lie 5 per cent above the expected level; the most pessimistic level may lie say, 10 per cent below the most likely level.

The profits or cash flows can then be calculated for these two extreme levels and D.C.F. or net present values calculated to see in particular whether the most pessimistic level meets the investment criterion. If the minimum acceptable return for the organisation is 10 per cent and the return at the least favourable level is, say, 8 per cent, then the capital may be invested elsewhere for higher returns at less risk. If, however, it suggests a minimum return of 12 per cent then the project is viable, since it satisfies the minimum requirement and stands a very high chance of exceeding this most pessimistic figure. Figure 38 illustrates the three assumptions of expected cash flows.

33. Decision trees. Decision tree analysis is particularly appropriate to capital budgeting problems where the pattern of complex quantifiable relationships between decisions, *e.g.* investments, and chance events, *e.g.* change in demand, and their conditional consequences, *e.g.* sales revenues, can be illustrated visually and thereby simplified.

The decision tree is so called because of its resemblance to a tree, the branches representing a decision or outcome each with symbols indicating whether the branch is due to a possible alternative outcome or an alternative decision becoming available. Conventionally, decision points are represented by O and chance outcomes by □.

In order to illustrate the construction and nature of a decision tree and its utility in capital budgeting the data contained in 32 is reproduced in Fig. 39 in the form of a decision tree.

34. Dealing with risk. There are a number of ways of dealing with one risk inherent in a particular investment decision.

(a) *Rule of thumb.* After the evaluations regarding costs, revenues, life of project, etc. have been undertaken, and the calculations made to establish the return on the investment, there still remains the decision whether to proceed in preference to alternative investments. In contrast to the scientific methods of appraising capital projects, this is often done by rule of thumb whereby mutually exclusive projects are listed in order of priority on the basis of an unquantified trade-off between profitability or pay-back and the degree of risk associated with each one. Some projects are considered "too risky" and given low priority regardless of the anticipated return, others carrying an "acceptable risk" will eventually be ranked according to

FIG. 39.—Application of simple decision tree to investment analysis.

relative performance, while "low-risk" projects may be afforded highest priority, assuming the return exceeds the cost of capital. Clearly, this basis is highly subjective and therefore makes any analysis of the way risk is dealt with very difficult.

(b) *Necessity/postponability.* A company starved of capital may be forced to employ all funds becoming available to service existing investments coming up for replacement or repair.

(c) *Discounting for risk.* The decision-maker may well add a premium on to the accepted rate of discount for low-risk projects in order to compensate for the degree of extra risk associated with a particular investment. For example, if the cost of capital is, say, 12 per cent, this same figure may be used for risk-free investments, but 3 per cent may be added for marginally risky ventures, 8 per cent for moderately risky ones and, say, 18 per cent for high-risk ones. Naturally the choice of these risk premium values depends on the subjective attitude of the individual risk-averter towards risk and his evaluation of the degree of risk inherent in each project.

(d) *Sensitivity analysis.* This is a complex computer-based exercise. Briefly, it involves the following:

(i) Identification of the variables.

(ii) Evaluation of probabilities for these variables.

(iii) Selection and combination of variables to calculate net present value or rate of return of the project.

(iv) Substituting different values for each variable in turn while holding all others constant to discover the effect on the rate of return.

(v) Comparison of original rate of return with this adjusted rate to indicate the degree of sensitivity of the rate to changes in the variable.

(vi) Subjective evaluation of the risk involved in the project, *e.g.* chance of unfortunate change of a key factor causing deterioration on highly sensitive rate of return.

PROGRESS TEST 12

1. Carefully explain the nature of financial planning, its purpose and advantages. (**1–3**)

2. How do capital investment proposals arise? (**4**)

3. Discuss the pros and cons of the accounting rate of return method of investment appraisal. (**6–8**)

4. How do you account for the widespread use of "pay-back" in investment decision-making. (**9–12**)

5. Compare and contrast compounding and discounting, using examples. (**13–17**)

6. Explain the following terms:

D.C.F.	(**18**)
Interpolation.	(**19**)
N.P.V.	(**20**)
Trial and error method.	(**19**)
Profitability index.	(**21**)
Decision trees.	(**33**)

7. Distinguish between risk and uncertainty and explain how the decision-taker achieves a trade-off between risk and return. (29–34)

8. The P. P. Refrigeration Co. are considering the purchase of a new moulding machine which will cost £40,000. It is estimated that the machine will have a life of seven years, at the end of which it will have a scrap value of £1,000. This will involve an investment in working capital of £10,000. The net pre-tax cash inflows which this will produce are:

Year	£
1	8,000
2	10,000
3	14,000
4	13,000
5	11,000
6	12,000
7	10,000

This company has a target return on capital (after tax) of 12 per cent and on this basis you are required to prepare a statement evaluating the above project.

Taxation: Assume the following:

1. Corporation tax 40 per cent.
2. Full allowance of 100 per cent in first year.

The company carries on other trading activities from which it derives taxable profits.

CHAPTER XIII

MERGERS AND TAKE-OVERS

MOTIVATION AND TERMS OF MERGERS

1. Company environment. Companies operate in a dynamic environment created and influenced by a variety of forces. Let us illustrate the nature and impact of some of these influences on the fortunes of a company by taking a company statement at random from the financial press.

TUBE INVESTMENTS LTD. INTERIM STATEMENT
21ST AUGUST 1974

Comments and Prospects

Demand for the Group's products continued strong, from home and overseas markets, with the exception of home demand for consumer durables which weakened noticeably towards the end of the period. This weakness was reflected in the results of the Domestic Appliance Division which was also the chief sufferer from restricted working during the power crisis. Demand on the Cycle Division, which sells more than two-thirds of its output of bicycles and components overseas, remained firm.

The Steel Tube Division's results benefited from high utilisation of the increased capacity installed over recent years.

In many parts of the Group, shortage of labour is a limitation on performance.

The Overseas Division maintained the higher contribution to Group profits established in the latter half of last year.

Sales in the first half of 1974 increased by 24 per cent compared with the corresponding period of 1973 and profits before tax increased by 21 per cent. However, owing to the raising of United Kingdom Corporation Tax to 52 per cent the earnings for the period increased by only 7 per cent. Since it is the earnings that provide the basis for financing the total cash requirements of a business—to provide for dividends for investment for expansion generally, and to cover the effects of inflation—the heavy tax burden imposed on industry is a severe handicap. With inflation at present running in the United Kingdom at an annual rate of well over

15 per cent the real burden of taxation is much heavier than the nominal rate applied to historical accounting profits.

Profits for the second half of the year are expected to be comparable with the first half, although the outlook is overshadowed to an unprecedented degree by political and economic uncertainties.

In summary, these influences on industrial and company environment referred to above and others that are generally identifiable are:

(a) *Political, e.g.* uncertainty over timing of general election, tax policy.

(b) *Economic, e.g.* shortage of labour, power crisis, inflation, actions and reactions of competitors.

(c) *Social, e.g.* changes in income, demand.

(d) *Technological, e.g.* innovation, new energy-saving processes.

2. Company strengths and weaknesses. These changes in a dynamic environment, while creating uncertainty and risk, also create opportunities for management to exploit the situation for profit objectives or whatever their criterion of success, *e.g.* Wilkinson Sword's innovation of the revolutionary stainless steel razor blade. However, success cannot be guaranteed and there are many instances in recent history where companies have recognised opportunity but failed to exploit it, sometimes at considerable expense, by reacting too slowly to change so that they are overtaken by new and different market forces or by failing to interpret correctly the nature of their environment, *e.g.* the Ford Edsel.

In view of the risk inherent in a dynamic market, it is vital that management correctly appraises the industry, its prospects and the relative strengths and weaknesses of the organisation in relation to its competitors. Ideally, management should first ensure that there is a current and future demand for the product, that production is generally viable in terms of supplies of materials, labour and capacity and that it is potentially profitable. Thereafter, assured by the above, management should draw up a list of company strengths and weaknesses to establish its competitive position by asking such questions as:

(a) What is the company's general standing in the eyes of customers?

(b) Are there competitors who dominate?

(c) How efficient is production?

(d) Has the company sufficient financial resources to finance sales?

(e) Is management up to the task?

3. Company strategy. Finally, management devises a plan of campaign, a strategy to exploit the opportunity (*see* Fig. 40).

(a) Products are selected, *e.g.* innovative products such as new efficient fuel injection system for internal combustion engines.

(b) Production methods are decided, e.g. make rather than buy because of the need for secrecy and in view of the shortage of sub-contracting capacity.

(c) Timetable of operations agreed.

    (i) Acquire the know-how, and productive capacity, by merging with the company developing the system.

    (ii) Decide on and implement the terms of the merger.

    (iii) Set up the organisation and detail production and marketing plans to achieve the anticipated benefits.

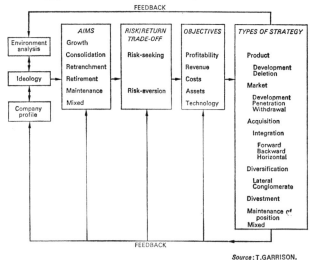

Source: T. GARRISON.

FIG. 40.—Strategy determination.

4. A model of strategy determination. It is appropriate at this stage to extend our thoughts on company strategy beyond the take-over situation to consider a model of how companies generally determine their strategy. Figure 40 provides a valuable insight into this process and facilitates understanding of this complex subject.

(a) The company's board of management has an ideology either implicit or explicit. If implicit, the ideology is expressed in the form of appropriate objectives. On the other hand, if the ideology is explicit, perhaps formulated in the manner described by the Cyert and March behavioural theory of the firm, and influenced by its analysis of the company's environment and company strengths and weaknesses, then the board has definite aims.

(b) These aims in summary cover the areas of corporate growth, consolidation, retrenchment, retirement from operations, maintenance of position or a mixture of these.

(c) Next is the Risk/Return trade-off. The board adopts an attitude towards the risk/return conflict. At one extreme is the risk-seeking board which for the prospect of high returns is prepared to accept high risks; at the other extreme, is the ultra-cautious risk-averting board.

(d) In the light of the board's compromise between risk and return, the aims are qualified and quantified and expressed as an objective or mix of objectives. Specific targets or standards are set in the areas of:

 (i) Profitability.
 (ii) Revenue.
 (iii) Costs.
 (iv) Assets.
 (v) Technology.

(e) Next a strategy is formulated to achieve these objectives. In particular, plans are drawn up in the areas of products, markets, acquisitions, diversification, divestment, for the maintenance of the company's position or for a mixture of these.

(f) Finally, strategic actions cause reactions. The environment and company strengths and weaknesses are affected and perhaps ideology changes. Clearly the board should then review its aims; its attitude towards risk/return; its objectives and type of strategy. However, the feedback may call only for a reconsideration of objectives (if ideology, aims and attitude towards risk are unchanged) when for instance company profit targets are not met or if the latest technology proves to be too expensive.

A hypothetical example will illustrate the steps in the model.

STEP 1

The management of Economy Propulsion Ltd. believe that shareholders will leave management to pursue a policy that satisfies their monetary, authority and reputation aspirations if their demands for above-average payments of dividends and capital growth are met. Moreover, they believe that workers will accept the organisations' objectives for the price that satisfies their monetary demands, *i.e.* above-average pay.

Moreover, the energy crisis creates a demand for a low fuel consumption propulsion unit which Economy Propulsion might exploit. Management's view is that the organisation has substantial financial resources, capable management, efficient though limited production facilities and a good reputation among customers. However, it lacks the know-how to develop a suitable unit within the near future.

STEP 2

Management decides to consolidate its position as a leader in the field of economy motors and to expand its share of the total market.

STEP 3

Management collectively have an aversion to risk and prefer a course of action whose worst possible outcome provides the highest pay-off. Thus, faced with two alternatives A and B,

	Returns to Economy Propulsion	
Alternatives	(*i*) *Maximum*	(*ii*) *Minimum*
A. Buy out competitor who possesses the technology and modify for own use	£2,000,000	£2,000,000
B. Develop technology independently	£5,000,000	£500,000

management will prefer project A.

STEP 4

Management formulates objectives to:

(*i*) Acquire the technology.

(*ii*) Achieve a target return on capital employed based on sales revenue of £x and costs of £y which satisfy the explicit ideology, aims and attitude to risk.

STEP 5

Strategy is determined.

(*i*) Acquisition of the company possessing the know-how, *i.e.* horizontal integration.

(*ii*) Penetration of the market.

(*iii*) Development of the fuel-saving motor, *i.e.* product development.

FEEDBACK

(*i*) A successful strategy may cause management to revise their profitability objective upwards.

(*ii*) Management's success may cause them to be slightly less cautious and accept a slightly higher risk for greater returns. Consequently, profitability objectives are again revised.

(*iii*) On the other hand, an adverse feedback, when for instance competitors react by introducing similar or superior products, or when unforeseen teething troubles cause costs to rise, may cause management to amend its ideology. Perhaps retirement becomes the general aim, conservation of assets the objective and divestment of the product and productive facilities the new strategy.

5. Definitions.

(*a*) *Take-over.* This is where a party gains control over a company by acquiring a controlling interest in its voting share capital.

(*b*) *Merger.* This is an arrangement where the assets of two companies are placed under the control of a single company which is owned jointly by the shareholders of the original companies.

The distinction between these is not clear-cut, as in the past offerors would bid for control without reference to the board of directors and perhaps successfully take over the company against their wishes.

6. Possible methods. Take-overs and mergers may be brought about by the following means:

(*a*) An agreement between the parties, especially when the shares are held by a small number of persons.

(*b*) Buying up shares on the Stock Exchange.

(*c*) A take-over bid, *i.e.* a general offer to the body of shareholders which may be against the wishes of the offeree's directors. It takes the following forms:

(*i*) An offer to buy shares for cash.

(*ii*) An offer to exchange shares for shares.

(*iii*) A combination of these.

7. Advantages and disadvantages of purchase considerations.
The consideration given by the acquiring company to the shareholders of the acquired company may take the form of ordinary shares, preference shares, loan stock or cash or any combination. The pros and cons of each method are as follows:

Advantages	*Disadvantages*
Cash	
(a) Simple.	(a) Offerees may be liable to capital gains tax.
	(b) Offeror may lack sufficient liquid funds (although rights issue is possible).
Fixed interest securities	
(a) No capital gains liability for offerees.	(a) Offeree may hold equities as a hedge against inflation and prefer equities in exchange.
(b) Interest is tax-deductible.	(b) If he sells these securities to realise equities then liable to capital gains tax.
(c) A lower coupon possible with convertible loan stock.	(c) Issue of fixed-interest securities limits offeror's borrowing capacity.
(d) Does not dilute equity.	(d) Expensive if interest rates are high.
	(e) May affect the company's gearing ratio adversely.
Equities	
(a) May take advantage of high share price to finance transaction.	(a) New issue may exceed authorised capital.
(b) Increased share capital is a check against take-overs.	(b) Company must increase earnings to maintain dividends on enlarged share capital.
(c) No refunding problem.	
(d) No capital gains liability for offeree.	
(e) Does not limit offeror's borrowing capacity.	
(f) Acceptable by inflation-conscious offerees.	

8. Valuation of the business. To effect a purchase or amalgamation the parties must first establish the value of the
undertaking's shares, quoted, unquoted or controlling.

9. Valuation of quoted shares. The Stock Exchange price of
the shares is a useful guide to their valuation. This will be de-

termined by investors' attitudes towards security, yield and the marketability of the securities.

Naturally the offeror will bear in mind these same considerations, but will also pay regard to any voting rights, increasing his offer price accordingly to secure the benefits which control affords.

10. Valuation of unquoted shares.

(a) The offeror wishing to value unquoted shares which are in a minority (i.e. control is exercised by others) uses as a criterion the company's true earning record compared with the opportunity cost of his capital. He will expect a yield comparable to other investments in similar fields, adjusted accordingly for reduced marketability of shares and the degree of risk associated with this investment.

For example, X Co. has an issued share capital of 50,000 £1 ordinary shares. Profits for distribution average £20,000 *per annum*. An offeror who has considered the above factors estimates a satisfactory rate of return on capital employed to be 25 per cent.

$$\text{Value of 50,000 ordinary shares} = \frac{£20,000}{1} \times \frac{100}{25}$$
$$= £80,000$$

$$\text{Value of one share} = \frac{£80,000}{50,000}$$
$$= £1\cdot60$$

(b) The assets valuation method is generally used (as for assessment of estate duty) to value shares that control the company. Creditors, debentures and preference capital are deducted from total assets (realistically valued on a current replacement basis) to give the capital balance for ordinary shareholders. For example:

Total assets	£80,000	
Goodwill	8,000	£88,000
Less Debentures	1,000	
Preference shares	5,000	
Creditors	2,000	8,000
		£80,000
Value of each ordinary share		
(50,000 £1 shares issued)		= £80,000
		50,000
		= £1·60

Naturally, the offeror places a higher valuation on these shares, and the offeree too expects a higher consideration. In addition to a compensatory payment, he may insist that:

(i) he continues in an executive capacity (if he is a director);

(ii) existing staff are retained.

(c) A third and more accurate though problematic method of valuing unquoted shares is to compare the unquoted company with an otherwise identical quoted company. The first step is to analyse thoroughly the financial performance of quoted companies engaged in the same activities, ideally companies which are similar in terms of balance sheet values, earnings and dividend policy so as to develop a feel for the current climate of investment opinion regarding the industry.

Calculations are required to establish the dividend yield and cover, earnings yield and P/E ratio, to provide a standard against which the unquoted company's performance may be compared.

The next stage is to select from the list one company which most closely resembles the unquoted company under consideration and value its shares on an asset basis (see (b)). Thus if its 25p shares are quoted at 250p and asset value per share is, say, 110p, then the company is commanding a premium in the market, i.e. benefiting from goodwill of 140p per share.

Finally, assuming that the unquoted company's performance is comparable and that there are no exceptional circumstances causing distortion to the twin quoted company's share price, we may assume 250p to be a fair and reasonable price for the unquoted shares. On the other hand, this can be marked up or down if current and future earnings are, or are expected to be, significantly higher or lower.

However, in one important respect, the companies are different. The shares under consideration are not freely marketable and are therefore less valuable, so that a discount must be applied to the share price of 250p. This is clearly a matter of judgment; a 15 per cent discount may be thought reasonable in a stable trade and perhaps 30–40 per cent to compensate for additional risk where trade is volatile.

11. Determination of the consideration price. The selling price, which must be acceptable to both the offeror and offeree, is based on their evaluation of the company's earning power, adjusted according to their attitudes to other factors, as follows:

(a) Offerees will naturally not accept a bid price which differs greatly from the market price of the shares, although they may demand a premium in the following circumstances:

(*i*) If other bids are expected.

(*ii*) If higher returns are anticipated from future investment projects.

(*iii*) If the offeree is a controlling shareholder, in which case he may expect compensation for giving up the benefits which control affords (*e.g.* determining the company's distribution or trading policy).

(*b*) Offerors will naturally wish to pay the lowest price to acquire the company, but may be prepared to exceed the financial evaluation in the following circumstances:

(*i*) The offeree's company has products which will complement the offeror's product range.

(*ii*) The offeree possesses new processes.

(*iii*) The offeree possesses competent management.

(*iv*) The offeree has assets which are inefficiently used.

(*v*) He has efficient R. & D., marketing, advertising and promotion departments.

(*vi*) Self-development by the offeror of these could incur considerable efforts, costs and time. It might be easier to buy them instead.

On the other hand, the offeror may offer a lower price for a highly specialised organisation or one whose shares are less readily marketable.

12. Factors determining the basis of a share for shares amalgamation.

(*a*) The pre-offer market values of the offerors' and offerees' shares when they are unaffected by amalgamation hopes or fears.

(*b*) The cover and dividend records of the two companies. If the offeror's record is unattractive to offeree shareholders, they may be induced to exchange their shares by:

(*i*) preference shares and their guaranteed dividends;

(*ii*) debentures and their guaranteed interests;

(*iii*) convertible debentures. These may be included as part of the consideration of the exchange transaction.

(*c*) The value of the assets of the companies. Offerees will expect a consideration which at least equals the break-up value of assets owned by their company.

(*d*) The growth potential of the two companies.

(*e*) The capital gearing factors of the two companies. A

shareholder in the offeree company might refuse shares in a lower-geared company on the grounds that earnings are diluted.

(f) The vote-gearing factors of the two companies. Share-holders in the offeree company will not readily accept a situation where they exercise reduced voting powers in an enlarged company, although some compensation may persuade them to accept.

13. Example of merger terms. The following example of the Boots offer to Glaxo shareholders in January 1972 (following a bid by Beecham Group Ltd.) illustrates reasons for mergers and the nature of the terms of a typical offer and the calculation of the premium offeree shareholders are offered, and goes some way to value the benefits expected to accrue from the amalgamation (synergy) or that the offerors expect to realise by acquisition.

NOTE:
In fact the Monopolies Commission stopped this proposed merger.

(i) *Reasons for the merger.*

"The merger is a logical combination of two of the strongest British pharmaceutical companies. Their product ranges, research activities and manufacturing capacities complement each other to such an extent that overlap is minimal. Boots, in addition to its massive retail business, has considerable manufacturing capacity in the United Kingdom. Despite the progress that Boots has made over the past few years in its sales overseas, there is still much potential abroad. Glaxo has operating subsidiaries in over thirty countries and is particularly strong in the Common Market where it already has powerful organisations. This structure will enable the products of Boots' research and development and manufacture —which will complement those of Glaxo—to reach a wider market.

Boots has assets and financial resources of a similar size to those of Glaxo, and together they will have ample means to achieve the further growth and development which the combined group will now seek.

The fact that the Board of the merged Company will be formed by uniting the present Boards of both Glaxo and Boots will ensure the creation of a joint enterprise which will be to the advantage of stockholders and staff alike. It is intended to change the name of Boots to reflect the merger of the two companies, and the new group will continue to uphold the traditions of both partners."

Source: Glaxo Chairman's letter contained in Boots offer document recommending Glaxo stockholders to agree to the merger.

(*ii*) *The offers.*
. . . to acquire all the 68,840,720 issued Ordinary stock units of 50p each and all the 335,070 issued 6 per cent Cumulative Preference stock units of 50p each of Glaxo.

(*iii*) *Terms of the offers*

| For EACH Ordinary stock unit of 50p of Glaxo | 2 Ordinary shares of 25p each
AND
£1 nominal of 5 per cent Convertible Unsecured Loan Stock 1985 ("Convertible stock") of Boots (both credited as fully paid) | (the "Ordinary Offer") |

and so in proportion for any greater number of Ordinary stock units of Glaxo.

| For EACH 6 per cent Cumulative Preference stock unit of 50p of Glaxo | 40p in cash | (the "Preference Offer") |

The Ordinary and Preference stock units of Glaxo will be acquired free of all liens, charges and encumbrances, and with the benefit of all rights attached thereto, including the right to all dividends hereafter declared or paid.

(*iv*) *Effects of acceptance*
The market values shown in the following tables are based on the middle market quotations in the *Daily Official List* of The Stock Exchange London, except as regards the Convertible stock which, based on the valuation of Cazenove & Co., has been taken to be worth £103 per cent.

Boots—on the forecast of the total dividend of 22 per cent in respect of the financial year ending 31st March 1972.

Glaxo—on the total dividend of 16 per cent paid in respect of the financial year ended 30th June 1971.

(*v*) *Ordinary offer*
A holder of 200 Ordinary stock units of Glaxo who accepts the Ordinary Offer will receive, upon that Offer becoming

unconditional, 400 Ordinary shares in and £200 nominal of Convertible stock of Boots, and his position would be as follows:

	Total	*Per Glaxo Ordinary stock unit*
Market value		
The market value of the Ordinary stock units of Glaxo on 1st December 1971 (the day before the announcement that Beecham Group Ltd. intended to make an offer) was	£735	367½p
On 28th January 1972 (the latest practicable date before printing this letter) the securities of Boots offered in exchange would have been worth:		
Ordinary shares . . .	£932	466p
Convertible stock . . .	206	103p
Total	£1,138	569p
Being an INCREASE of . .		54·8 per cent
Annual Income		
Ordinary dividend of Glaxo .	£16·00	8p (*i.e.* 16% dividend 1971)
Ordinary dividend of Boots .	£22·00	11p
Interest on Convertible stock of Boots . . .	£10·00	5p
Total	£32·00	16p
Being an INCREASE of . .		100 per cent

Preference Offer
The market value of a holding of 200 Preference stock units of Glaxo on 1st December 1971 (the day

before the announcement
that Beecham Group Ltd.
intended to make an offer)
was £56

Upon the Preference Offer
becoming unconditional an
acceptor will receive in cash .   £80

Being an INCREASE of .   .   42·8 per cent

(vi) Stock Exchange quotations
The middle market quotations, based on the *Daily Official List* of the Stock Exchange, London, for the Ordinary Shares in Boots for the Ordinary and Preference stock units of Glaxo on the first dealing day in each month from July 1971 to January 1972 inclusive and on certain other relevant dealing dates were as follows:

	Boots	Glaxo	
	Ordinary shares of 25p	*Ordinary stock units of 50p*	*Preference stock units of 50p*
1971 1st July	192p xd	369½p	28p
2nd August . . .	205p	382½p	28p
1st September . . .	205p	402½p	28p xd
1st October . . .	207½p	402½p	28p xd
1st November . . .	207½p	372½p xd	28p
1st December* . .	235p xd	367½ xd	28p
1972 3rd January . . .	245p xd	430p	35p
11th January† . .	237p	460p	35p
21st January‡ . .	232p	507½p	35p
26th January§ . .	225p	522½p	35p
28th January‖ . .	233p	527½p	35p

* 1st December—Day before the announcement by Beecham of its intention to make an offer
† 11th January—Day before the announcement by Boots of its intention to make an offer
‡ 21st January —Day before the announcement by Beecham of its intention to increase the terms of its offer
§ 26th January—Day before the announcement by Boots of its intention to increase the terms of its offer
‖ 28th January—latest practicable date before printing this document

(vii) Profits and dividends
The Board of Boots expect that, in the absence of unfore-

seen circumstances, the results for the financial year ending 31st March 1972 will be:

Years to 31st March

	1972 £ million	1971 £ million
Profit before taxation	33·50	24·95
Less: Taxation	14·25	10·65
Profit after taxation	19·25	14·30
Less: Minority interests	0·10	0·08
Profit attributable to Ordinary shareholders	19·15	14·22

On this basis, they intend to recommend a final dividend of 14 per cent which, with the interim dividend of 8 per cent (1971, 7 per cent) already paid will make a total dividend for the year of 22 per cent (1971, 19 per cent).

The assumptions on which this profit forecast is based are that:

(*i*) There will be no adverse change in the present rates of exchange between sterling and the foreign currencies of the countries in which the Company has major subsidiaries.

(*ii*) Consumer expenditure in the United Kingdom will not be adversely affected henceforth by significant changes to the present economic conditions, by industrial disputes and consequential disruptions, or by abnormal weather.

(*iii*) There will be no material changes in the bases and rates of direct and indirect taxation in the United Kingdom.

Upon the Ordinary Offer becoming unconditional, Ordinary shares in Boots to be issued to accepting Ordinary stockholders of Glaxo will rank for the final Ordinary dividend of Boots.

14. Arithmetic of a take-over. Let us now consider the situation where a purchaser acquires assets at a discount because assets are under-utilised and management is poor (*see* Fig. 41). His intention is to sell surplus assets and install new management to raise profits significantly.

Clearly the purchaser is keen to buy in the region of 540p per share although he is prepared to go higher on the basis of the anticipated higher earnings and the profit on the sale of surplus assets, but obviously no higher than the total cash flow he believes his investment can generate.

Victim Co. Balance Sheet

Fixed Assets			
Land and buildings			£100,000
Plant and machinery			200,000
			£300,000

Current Assets			
Stocks		£150,000	
Debtors		100,000	
Cash		50,000	
		£300,000	

Less current liabilities			
Creditors	£130,000		
Current taxation	30,000		
Current dividend	20,000	180,000	

Net current assets			£120,000

Net assets			420,000
Represented by:			
Ordinary £1 shares			200,000
Preference shares £1 @ 6%			200,000
Deferred liabilities			20,000
			£420,000

NOTE: (*i*) Market value of land is £300,000.
        (*ii*) Earnings currently £60,000 can be raised to £200,000 by Year 4.
        (*iii*) Shares are selling at 10 times earnings, *i.e.* 300p.

(a) Net assets attributable to equity

Net assets		£420,000
less deferred liabilities	£20,000	
preference shares	200,000	220,000
		£200,000
Plus: increase in value of land	300,000	
less potential tax liability 40%	120,000	
Net increase in value		180,000
Net assets		£380,000

(b) Market valuation of shares at a P/E of 10

Earnings forecast		£200,000
less tax, say, 40%		80,000
		£120,000
less preference dividend		12,000
		£108,000*

E.P.S.	54p
Share value	540p

Fig. 41.—Victim Co.: Balance Sheet.

Victim Co. Balance Sheet—*continued:*

(c) Range of bid prices:
   (i) On earnings forecast   540p

   (ii) On basis of higher earnings   540
        and higher land valuation
        i.e. 9p per share × 10 P/E   90
                                       ────
                                       630p

Another way of calculating the maximum purchase price for an income maximiser, assuming that the accurate forecasts of profits are available for the next four years, is to use D.C.F. analysis. Thus, assuming that the surplus assets are sold at the end of Year 1, and the profit distributed, that forecast profits distributed to the purchaser are as shown *below,* that the cost of capital to the company is 15 per cent, then by discounting this cash flow to present values, we have the cash payment needed to secure a post-tax return of 15 per cent on the purchaser's investment which he regards are the minimum acceptable return to justify the acquisition.

	Sale of assets	Distributed profits	Total receipts	Discount factors 15%	Present values
Year					
0					
1	£180,000	£40,000	£220,000	0·8696	£191,312
2		60,000	60,000	0·7561	45,366
3		80,000	80,000	0·6575	52,600
4	{108,000*	1,008,000		0·5717	576,273
	{900,000				
					£865,551

* Reorganisation completed and anticipated gross profits of £200,000 are secured. Thereafter profits available for distribution are expected to grow by 3 per cent p.a.: at this time, year 4, these future profits are valued at £108,000 discounted at 15 per cent less the anticipated growth rate of 3 per cent i.e. £108,000÷0·12=£900,000.

Thus in year zero, the income maximiser interested in a minimum return of 15 per cent would fix the maximum price at £865,551, or 433p *per* share (*i.e.* present value of all receipts).

REASONS FOR MERGERS AND TAKE-OVERS

15. Defensive motives. There are three varieties of amalgamations undertaken for defensive reasons. They are as follows:

(a) Horizontal integration.
(b) Lateral integration.
(c) Vertical integration.

16. Horizontal integration. Firms may integrate horizontally by means of take-overs and mergers for a number of defensive reasons, as follows:

(a) Trading difficulties. The rationalisation schemes of the 1920s and 1930s, where firms merged to remove excess capacity and to maintain prices, helped solve the problems facing the shipbuilding and cotton industries.

(b) Economies of scale.

(c) The desire to eliminate competitors. A firm may react to competition or potential competitors by eliminating them by means of take-overs.

17. Lateral integration. Possible defensive motives are:

(a) To counter competition by extending the product range.
(b) To secure economies of scale.
(c) To solve a financial problem, *e.g.* Bats' acquisition of

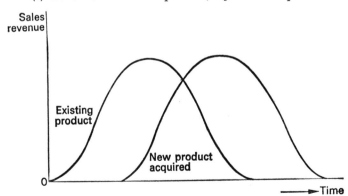

Fig. 42.—Acquisition of new product to compensate for declining sales revenue.

Pricerite and International Stores to augment earnings to offset advance corporation tax.

(d) To acquire new potentially profitable products when present products are at the maturity stage in their life cycle (*see* Fig. 42).

18. The reverse take-over. This is a rare type of bid which may be used by a firm to get a Stock Exchange quotation. For example, an unquoted company, X, wishing to acquire Y, a quoted company, may arrange with Y's directors that they offer a share-for-share exchange of equity so that X becomes Y's subsidiary. The motive is defensive, to avoid the costs of formal quotation and the exacting disclosures demanded by the Stock Exchange Council and the possibility of an unfavourable reaction in the capital market. But success is by no means guaranteed, for the Council may now suspend quotation where a take-over materially alters the style of the company, until information regarding its new form is forthcoming, *e.g.* the Clubman's Club and City Tote, 1969.

19. Vertical integration. Firms may attempt to integrate vertically through mergers and take-overs of firms at different stages of the production process to secure the following:

(a) *Sources of supplies.* These may be endangered if competitors are integrating backwards or if a monopoly situation already exists.

(b) *Marketing outlets.* These may be especially desirable if competition is severe. The firm may feel that it needs to protect its retailing outlets, increase its selling points or deal directly and perhaps more effectively with consumers.

(c) *Trading advantages.* These may be secured when the manufacturer/retailer has control over his products' prices. He may prefer stable prices to price competition, something which has increased following the *Resale Prices Act*, 1964, and which aggravates the difficulties of production planning.

20. Offensive motives. There are three main groups of causes for take-overs and mergers for offensive motives:

(a) The acquisition of assets at a discount (*see* **21**).
(b) Trading advantages (*see* **23**).
(c) Personal reasons (*see* **24**).

21. Acquisition of assets at a discount (reduced value). A frequently cited reason for take-overs is that the offeror finds available cash or other liquid assets in the offeree to finance the transaction. Alternatively, speculators sell fixed assets, usually land, to realise the cash and then arrange for the company to lease them back. In the past, balance sheets and share prices have often understated the true value of the business in order to produce the classical take-over situation. Experience has now made companies more careful to revalue assets periodically, although the Department (then Board) of Trade estimated the value of gross (pre-depreciation) assets of the quoted company sector in 1963 to be £31,199m at current prices and the gross book value as £20,398m, an impressive discount of 53 per cent. But one factor diminishing this apparent attractiveness for take-overs is the considerable premium over the pre-bid share price which has exceeded 33 per cent on occasions.

22. Reasons for this discount. Assets may be available at a discount for various reasons, as follows:

(a) *Dividend restraint.* The offeree retains a larger than normal proportion of profits, which tends to depress the share price. This may be due to the following factors:

(i) Government tax policy. Up to 1957 and with corporation tax since 1965, high taxation on distributed profits makes for conservative distribution policies.

(ii) Company controllers may determine the company's distribution policy to suit their own tax position, *e.g.* high-rate tax payers will prefer profit retention.

(iii) Company controllers may aim at complete ownership and control. A low dividend policy will affect the share price to their advantage as buyers.

(b) *Inefficient management.* The offeror may feel that his management can realise the asset's full potential, *e.g.* public houses have been acquired and redeveloped profitably by breweries.

(c) *Inefficient capital structure.* When the return on assets is high, it is to the advantage of shareholders to finance long-term capital requirements by means of lower fixed-interest securities, *i.e.* debentures or preference shares. (Although, since corporation tax, debentures are preferred since the interest is allowable against taxation.) Consequently a company which is low-geared and has issued preference shares would be attractive to a bidder who can profitably reorganise the company's capital structure.

(d) *Unrealistic valuation of assets.* The balance sheet may understate the true value of assets because:

(i) fixed assets may be valued at original cost less an over-generous adjustment for depreciation; or

(ii) the company may fail to appreciate the true worth of its land and the effect of inflation since the war.

This places the company in the classic take-over situation.

(e) *"Tax-loss" companies.* Companies may set off accumulated losses against taxation due on future profits, so that a company having insufficient capital or ability to restore profitability may find itself taken over by another company in the same trade. The offeror may take over control cheaply, run the company profitably without "discontinuing" the business and offset the past losses against profits, thereby increasing the effective return on capital.

23. Capital reconstructions. The offeror may carry out, with the members' agreement and the Court's sanction, an internal capital reconstruction which alters the rights of members as set out in the articles of association. They may do so for the following reasons:

(a) Additional share capital is required and it can only be attracted by offering securities on advantageous terms to prospective investors.

(b) Circumstances may demand a change in capital gearing.

(c) The existing structure may be unnecessarily complex and can be simplified, *e.g.* by reducing the number of share classes.

(d) Circumstances may demand a "reduction in capital." For example, a company might be in a weak financial position, dividends may be passed over or assets may have fallen below book values. One solution might be to reduce the nominal value of ordinary shares and the dividend on preference shares. This will reduce the prior charges on profits and give the company a better chance of paying dividends out of current earnings and improve its standing in the eyes of investors. However, it is the ordinary and not the preference shareholders who are expected to bear the main burden of the capital reduction. Any loss of income on the latter's part should be made good by giving them ordinary shares or allowing them to participate in profits. The exact form which the scheme takes will depend on the respective rights of share classes (*e.g.* participating preference shares bear a greater burden than fixed dividend preference shares).

24. Trading advantages. Firms may amalgamate to improve their competitive position to secure the following advantages:

(*a*) *Economies of scale.* The synergy principle explains why companies make offers for others operating in the same industry. The enlarged company may be worth more than the sum of the two companies (in effect $1 + 1 = 3$) and these economies, reflected in lower unit costs, should improve its competitiveness (*e.g.* I.C.I.'s bid for Courtaulds in 1962 on the grounds that they needed a strong, efficient unit to face international competition).

(*b*) *Diversification.* It is argued that multi-product firms are able to stabilise their overall trade and spread the risk of demand variations, so that a decline in one sector may be compensated for by increases in others. Obviously profit opportunities are relevant too. For example, Unilever is a company which has diversified its interests to a remarkable extent, producing a variety of branded goods varying from soap powders and perfumes to frozen foods.

Diversification may be an answer for industries whose traditional trade has been overtaken by modern technology. Textiles and tobaccos are good examples: Courtaulds has moved into nylon and paint, Imperial Tobaccos into confectionery and cosmetics.

(*c*) *Purchasing management.* An expanding company may acquire "new blood" for its top management with the new company.

25. Personal motives. There are men who strive to build and extend financial or industrial empires for personal reasons of power, interest, achievement and satisfaction.

ADVANTAGES AND DISADVANTAGES OF TAKE-OVERS AND MERGERS

26. Introduction. It is no exaggeration to say that the majority of mergers and take-overs proceed smoothly with agreement on both sides. Not infrequently it is the offeree who takes the initiative. Its management may be ambitious yet growth may be restricted by insufficient capital or technical know-how and it realises that an amalgamation, preferably with a company whose operations are complementary, provides a solution. The offeror may fulfil these requirements and both may benefit from greater economies of scale. There are companies today which specialise in advising firms in the choice of partners, timing and negotiation and who will provide funds to realise the full potential of the amalgamation. An example is Industrial Mergers Limited, a subsidiary of I.C.F.C.

27. Advantages to shareholders.

(*a*) A take-over bid may cause the board to end a policy of "dividend restraint" with the result that higher dividends are paid and share prices climb. Even if the bid succeeds, the shareholder will probably receive a premium over the pre-bid price. Either way, he gains.

(*b*) A bid reminds directors that the voting shareholders are important and it should make them pay greater attention to their interests.

(*c*) A merger by means of an exchange of shares may bring future financial rewards in the enlarged company.

(*d*) All are given an equal opportunity to sell.

28. Disadvantages to shareholders.

(*a*) A minority shareholder may find himself compelled to sell his shares if the bidder gains 90 per cent of the shares (*see s*. 209, *Companies Act* 1948).

(*b*) The offer may be a "partial bid," in which case some shareholders will be unable to sell all their shares. The take-over code regards partial bids as generally undesirable.

(*c*) It is just conceivable that the offeror might prevent opposition to its policy through a reconstruction or by the issue of non-voting securities.

29. Advantages to directors.

(*a*) If the offeror requires their services then there may be greater scope in the larger company for:

(*i*) promotion,
(*ii*) remuneration, and
(*iii*) achievement in the field of management.

(*b*) They may relinquish control on favourable terms.

30. Disadvantages to directors.

(*a*) The possibility of dismissal and the loss of future remuneration

(*b*) The loss of power, status and other benefits which the position offered.

31. Advantages to bidders. Where the bid is successful the bidder increases his scale of operations and secures trading or other benefits.

32. Disadvantages to bidders.

(*a*) When the bid fails, the bidder suffers heavy irrecoverable capital losses.

(*b*) The acquiror may himself be vulnerable to bids from other sources.

(*c*) The amalgamation may be refused by the Department of Trade and the Monopolies Commission on the grounds that it is against the public interest. This acts as a control over irresponsible bids.

33. Advantages to the national economy.

(*a*) Bidders who promote take-overs and mergers have frequently shown great ability in putting the group assets to the most profitable use.

(*b*) As a consequence new firms entering the industry must set a standard at least as high as that of the group in order to compete successfully.

(*c*) Larger-scale production, marketing, purchasing, financing and distribution may produce lower average costs and prices.

(*d*) Large firms tend to invest more heavily than small ones, which could set higher productivity standards for the industry.

(*e*) Large firms may be more willing to export and finance import substitution projects in the national interest or for prestige purposes, even when the profit margins are low.

Thus amalgamations can be regarded as being in the national interest if they result in more efficient production, and if this leads to a more efficient redeployment of the nation's resources, lower consumer prices or a better balance of payments.

34. Disadvantages to the national economy.

(*a*) Increasing returns to scale are not assured in every take-over or merger. Technical economies may be exhausted, so that instead of lower prices, consumers may be faced with rising prices, especially if administration becomes less efficient in the larger organisations.

(*b*) Amalgamations may result in monopolies which exercise their potential power over suppliers, who are forced to enter into contracts favouring the monopolist, or over consumers who find that choice is restricted through reductions in quality, selection or the life of the product.

(*c*) Amalgamations may stifle competition and so check the stimulus for increased efficiency.

(d) Any deterioration in the performance of the enlarged company has a proportionally more significant effect on the economy.

METHODS OF AVOIDING A TAKE-OVER POSITION

35. Defences against take-overs. Ideally, companies should organise and conduct themselves so as to avoid situations which attract bids. The following measures make for a complete defence against take-over bids:

(a) *The issue of non-voting or "A" shares.* This arrangement allows companies to raise capital from the general public without affecting corporate control.

(b) *The issue of shares to a friendly partner.* It is possible to do this by:

(i) exchanging shares with another company, so making it difficult for an outsider to acquire a controlling interest; or

(ii) issuing a block of shares to a company which is uninterested in control, *e.g.* E.D.I.T.H.

(c) *The defensive merger.* An amalgamation may make companies more secure from outside interference because a controlling interest of the enlarged share capital may be beyond the financial resources of many bidders.

36. Countering take-over bids. There are a number of measures management can take when faced with a take-over bid, although at this stage it is frequently a case of too little being done too late.

(a) The board may remove the object of the bid by:

(i) revaluing fixed assets to current values; or

(ii) capitalising reserves to bring share capital into line with current values.

(b) The board might announce a higher dividend to improve the attractiveness of shares to their owners. It might also raise the share price, thereby making the bid more expensive.

(c) It may recommend rejection of the bid with reasons and promise projects expected to improve future earnings. Consequently, shareholders may consider the shares and the board more favourably.

(d) A capital reconstruction may frustrate a bid, based on an inefficient capital structure. Higher gearing might benefit ordinary shareholders, whilst a substitution of debentures for preference shares would improve post-tax profits.

(e) The board may improve earnings by disposing of unprofitable assets and reinvesting the proceeds for a higher return.

(f) The board may plead to the present directors for loyalty or for patriotism in the case of an overseas bid.

More drastic action may be possible:

(g) The board may resort to the sale and leaseback of assets. Although Savoy Hotel Ltd. (1953) was not a legal precedent, it showed how courts might judge similar issues (*i.e.* unfavourably).

(h) The board may introduce restrictive clauses into the company's articles to modify voting rights or to limit the transferability of shares, all of which may or may not be valid. However, company law, *ultra vires*, and directors' responsibilities towards shareholders, all severely limit the scope for such desperate actions in the face of a bid.

37. Arguments against "A" shares.

(a) They are undemocratic in that some ordinary shareholders are not given voting rights in return for risk-bearing.

(b) They are against the national interest if they check take-overs which create more efficient industrial structures.

38. Arguments for "A" shares.

(a) Company controllers secure from outside interference can concentrate on developing and running the business (*e.g.* J. Lyons and Co. Ltd.).

(b) Investors, even when aware of their non-voting features, may be prepared to buy them as they are generally cheaper than shares with full voting rights.

(c) Some individuals, on balance, tolerate "A" shares on the following grounds:

(i) Prohibitive legislation is unjustified as only a handful of shareholders are affected.

(ii) Legislation is undesirable because it would unnecessarily restrict and complicate company law.

(iii) Shareholders are not forced to buy these shares.

(iv) Shareholders tend to be apathetic whether they have votes or not.

(v) "A" shares are now less common, for many companies, respecting either public opinion or the financial power of institutions, have granted voting rights to these shares or exchanged them for shares with rights.

PROGRESS TEST 13

1. Describe how you think companies arrive at a company strategy. (1–4)

2. Why do some companies develop strategy to acquire other companies? (4)

3. Discuss the advantages and disadvantages of the various purchase considerations used in company amalgamations. (5–8)

4. Compare the take-over and merger as a means of amalgamation and the possible methods by which each may be accomplished. (5–8)

5. How is the consideration price determined in amalgamation negotiations? (5–14)

6. You are asked to advise an investor on the valuation of three classes of shares in which he is interested. They are the following:

    (a) Ordinary shares in a quoted company.

    (b) Ordinary shares in an unquoted company.

    (c) Ordinary shares (in a minority) in an unquoted company.

Outline the nature of your recommendations. (9–10)

7. "Firms expand horizontally, laterally or vertically for defensive motives." Discuss this claim. (15–19)

8. Indicate the main reasons why firms expand by acquisitions and mergers for offensive motives. (20–24)

9. A frequently cited reason for take-overs is "acquisition of assets at a discount." Explain this term, giving reasons for this discount. (21–22)

10. What is the economic justification for a "take-over bid"? Illustrate your answer by reference to any recent case. (26–38)

11. Discuss the pros and cons of take-overs from the viewpoint of:

    (a) shareholders;

    (b) directors; and

    (c) bidders. (26–32)

12. Consider the advantages and disadvantages of take-overs from the viewpoint of the national economy. (33–34)

13. What measures can a company adopt to avoid a take-over situation? (35–38)

CHAPTER XIV

FINANCIAL DECISION-MAKING TECHNIQUES

NATURE OF BREAK-EVEN ANALYSIS

1. Introduction. Throughout this Chapter, we examine the various financial aids that can be used in decision-making: in particular break-even and marginal analysis, the two most widely-used techniques, will be the focus of our attention. In fact, we have already referred to break-even in VII in connection with the economist's approach to revenue, costs and profit and the firm's typical revenue–cost–volume relationship: however, we now regard it from the accountant's or manager's viewpoint to consider its value as a practical tool.

2. Definition of break-even. Break-even is defined as the level of activity where no profits are made or losses incurred. In other words, that level of operations where total costs equal total revenue.

3. Break-even: the accountant's viewpoint. In contrast with the economist, who analyses the behaviour of continuous total costs and revenue over the company's entire output/sales range, the accountant is directly concerned with supplying management with past and future information of costs and revenue for a limited range of activities. Furthermore, since he is primarily interested in the operational range, he considers the nature of costs and revenue at very low and high levels of activities to be irrelevant to immediate management decisions.

Consequently, the accountant uses break-even analysis suitably modified in the following ways:

(*a*) Total costs are represented by a straight line which tends to approximate to the actual values over the narrow sales/production range.

(*b*) Total revenue is represented by a straight line on the assumption that moderate percentage increases in sales may be achieved without price cutting.

(*c*) These curves may be extended outside the narrow operational range and may illustrate the approximate cost/revenue/volume relationship as long as the limitations are remembered, *i.e.* revenue and costs are, in fact, non-linear over the entire range of activities.

Figure 43 illustrates a typical break-even diagram.

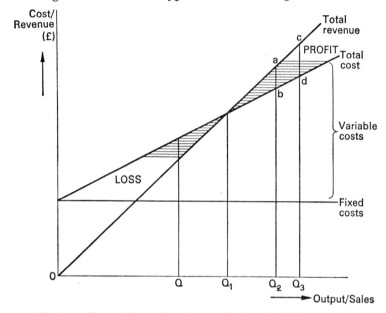

(*i*) Assumed normal operational range of output is Q–Q_2.
(*ii*) Profit at an output of OQ_2 is £a, b.
(*iii*) The graph shows that if output could be increased to OQ_3, then profit could be increased to £c, d.
(*iv*) Any level of output beyond OQ_1 (the break-even) is profitable.
(*v*) It shows the revenue cost relationship at different levels of output and not that the company initially makes losses and profits later in the year. Time is ignored and does not appear on the horizontal axis.

FIG. 43.—Straight line break-even graph.

4. Calculation of break-even. The break-even level of activity can be calculated by formulae as a check on the accuracy of the graph. The formulae are as follows:

(a) Break-even sales revenue $= \dfrac{\text{Fixed cost}}{1 - \dfrac{\text{Variable cost}}{\text{Selling price}}}$

(b) Break-even sales volume $= \dfrac{\text{Fixed cost}}{\text{Selling price} - \text{Variable cost}}$

5. Limitations of straight line break-even. Before we examine the application of break-even graphs to decision-making, it is important to remember that the graphs are a simplification of a complex relationship and are subject to several limitations which, if appreciated, are less likely to result in faulty diagnosis and poor decisions. These limitations can be summarised as follows:

(a) In practice, the cost/volume relationship is not necessarily linear.

(b) In practice, the revenue/volume relationship is not necessarily linear. In other words, it is dangerous to extrapolate the curves outside the normal range of activity. To resist this temptation, one should be aware of the economist's analysis on the behaviour of cost, revenue and volume and the relationship between each.

(c) Profits are not necessarily maximised at maximum output (OQ_3) since in practice:

(i) The revenue curve may be lower than shown because of discounts and price cuts to achieve this high level of sales.

(ii) The cost curve may be higher than shown, because of disproportionate increases in variable costs, *e.g.* overtime, shift work payments, to achieve this high output.

(d) It is a static illustration of a dynamic situation and therefore must be updated regularly.

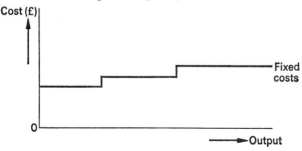

FIG. 44.—"Stepped" fixed cost curve.

(e) It assumes that sales and output are in balance, *i.e.* all that is produced is sold within the same time period.

(f) Fixed costs may in fact change. For example, to obtain high levels of output additional machines or staff may be taken on. Thus the fixed cost curve is not perfectly horizontal but is "stepped" (*see* Fig. 44); the total cost curve is similarly stepped.

APPLICATIONS OF BREAK-EVEN

6. Contribution break-even graph. Contribution is simply the difference between selling price and variable costs, consisting of direct wages, materials and other direct expenses. Thus if selling price is £6·00 and variable costs amount to £3·00,

$$\text{Contribution} = \text{Selling price} - \text{Variable costs}$$
$$\text{£3·00} = \text{£6·00} - \text{£3·00}$$

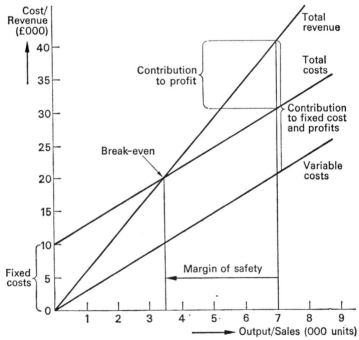

FIG. 45.—Contribution break-even for Product A.

This £3·00 along with other contributions go into a fund which is used to meet the fixed costs and to provide a profit. For example, if fixed costs amount to £10,000 and 7,000 units are sold, then

$$\text{Total contribution} - \text{Fixed cost} = \text{Profit}$$
$$£3\cdot00 \times 7,000 \quad - £10,000 \quad = £11,000$$

The contribution break-even is graphed (*see* Fig. 45) in the following steps:

(*a*) Draw in the variable cost curve.
(*b*) Add fixed costs to the variable cost curve. This line represents total costs (TC = FC + VC).
(*c*) Draw in the sales revenue line.

7. Analysis of contribution break-even graph.

(*a*) Examination of the graph shows that break-even is 3,333 units and sales value of £20,000. The accuracy of the graph is checked by calculation (*see* 4).

$$
\begin{aligned}
(i)\ \text{Break-even} &= \frac{\text{Fixed cost}}{1 - \dfrac{\text{Variable cost}}{\text{Selling price}}} \\
\text{(sales revenue)} \\
&= \frac{£10,000}{1 - \dfrac{3}{6}} \\
&= £20,000
\end{aligned}
$$

$$
\begin{aligned}
(ii)\ \text{Break-even} &= \frac{\text{Fixed cost}}{\text{Selling price} - \text{Variable cost}} \\
\text{(sales volume)} \\
&= \frac{£10,000}{6 - £3} \\
&= 3,333\ \text{units}
\end{aligned}
$$

(*b*) Furthermore, the contribution towards fixed costs can be read off for a given level of activity. Thus the contribution measured by the vertical distance between the variable cost line and the revenue line is:

£6,000 at output and sales of 2,000 units, and
£15,000 at output and sales of 5,000 units, etc.

Clearly a separate contribution break-even graph can be drawn for each product to facilitate comparisons (*see* Fig. 46).

8. Need for caution. These graphs present the cost/revenue/volume relationship simply, providing data that, if

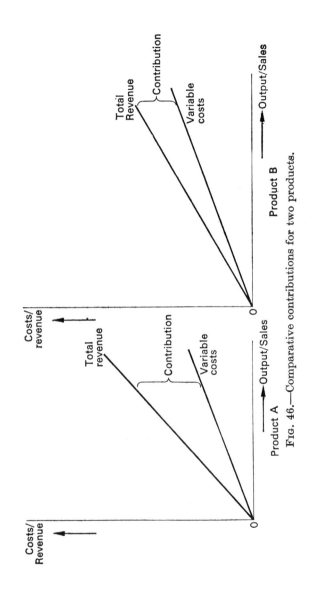

Fig. 46.—Comparative contributions for two products.

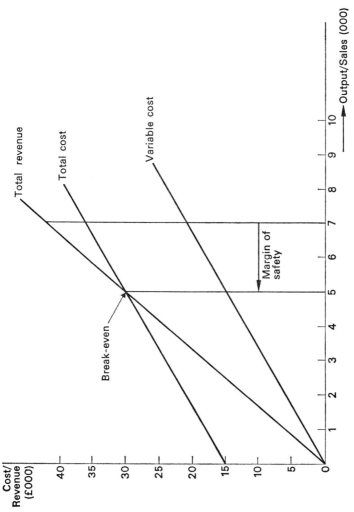

FIG. 47.—Contribution break-even for Product B.

used wisely, allows a more flexible approach to decision-making, particularly in the pricing area. However, they should not be used independently as an absolute measure. For example, consider Figs. 45 and 47 and the respective contributions of products A and B.

Both product A and B make a contribution of £21,000 at a level of sales of 7,000. However, further investigation of both charts reveals that product A possesses significant advantages over product B.

(a) Product A's profit is £11,000; B's is only £6,000 because the contribution must cover higher fixed cost (£15,000 as opposed to £10,000 for A).

(b) Product A's superior profits are confirmed by the fact that it has a broader profit wedge than B.

(c) Product A has a lower break-even level than B. This means that if the level of activity is 7,000 units for both products then sales of A can fall significantly before losses are incurred. This is termed the "margin of safety."

(i) The margin of safety of product A is 3,667 units, £22,002 sales value or 53 per cent.

(ii) The margin of safety of product B is 2,000 units, £12,000 sales value or 28 per cent.

9. Cash break-even. Today, inflation and anti-inflationary policies, with attendant high interest rates, has increased the cost of cash and made it more important than ever before to control cash effectively. Success in this respect demands a full appreciation of the probable values of cash inflows and outflows in relation to the level of business activity: a relationship that is clarified by means of a cash break-even graph. The only difference between this graph and the normal break-even graph is in the treatment of fixed costs. They are distinguished as follows:

(a) Costs requiring immediate cash payments are included, *i.e.* administration, salaries, rent and rates.

(b) Other costs are ignored for this purpose. These consist of book or non-cash costs, *i.e.*:

(i) Depreciation.

(ii) Writing-off charges on capitalised research and development expenditure.

(iii) Nominal depreciation charges on fully depreciated assets.

Figure 48 illustrates a typical cash break-even graph.

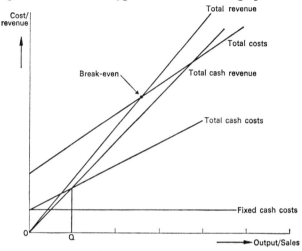

(*i*) Only immediate cash payments are included.

(*ii*) Variable costs are assumed to be for cash. Where credit is taken such purchases should be eliminated.

(*iii*) Sales revenue is assumed to be for cash. Credit sales should be eliminated.

The figure shows that at a level of output/sales of OQ, sufficient cash revenue is generated to pay immediate cash expenses.

FIG. 48.—Cash break-even point and comparison with ordinary break-even point.

MARGINAL ANALYSIS: DEFINITIONS

10. Marginal costs. Marginal cost or incremental cost is the additional cost of producing one extra unit. Thus if 100 units are produced for a total cost of £250 and 101 units for £252, then the marginal cost is £2. In fact, marginal cost is the same as variable cost, which can be seen from the following:

$$\text{Fixed costs} + \text{Variable costs} = \text{Total costs}$$
$$£50 \quad + \quad £200 \quad = \quad £250 \text{ (for 100 units)}$$
$$50 \quad + \quad 202 \quad = \quad 252 \text{ (for 101 units)}$$

Clearly the additional cost is £2(£252−£250) and results directly from the extra wages and material costs involved in producing the extra unit (since fixed costs are constant).

Marginal revenue. This is the additional revenue gained from the sale of one extra unit, *i.e.* the selling price of the good.

11. Contribution. Contribution is the difference between selling price and marginal (variable) cost.

Contribution = Selling price − Marginal cost or variable cost *per* unit

But contribution to what? To answer this, we must consider the special treatment of fixed costs in marginal costing. They are not apportioned to units of output as in full-cost pricing, but are set aside and eventually covered by a fund of contributions realised by the sale of individual units of output. Clearly, if total contributions exceed fixed costs, then profits are made.

Product A

Sales revenue − Variable costs
(price × sales volume)
              = Contribution
£5·00 × 4,000 − £6,000 =   £14,000

Product B

Sales revenue   − Variable costs
              = Contribution
£3·00 × 3,000 − £7,000 =   £2,000

Product C, etc.

Sales revenue   − Variable costs
              = Contribution
£2·00 × 3,000 − £5,000 =   £1,000

Total contributions £17,000   fixed cost £12,000

Therefore profit = Total contribution − Fixed cost
              = £17,000   − £12,000
              = £5,000

12. Importance of marginal costing. Marginal costing and contribution analysis are extremely useful tools for management in decision-making and cost control, providing the decision-maker with a very high degree of flexibility and scope for application in the areas of pricing, costing and resource allocation generally.

APPLICATION OF MARGINAL ANALYSIS

13. Range of application. Examples of areas where this may be applied are:

    (a) Pricing.
    (b) Allocation of scarce resources between competing uses.
    (c) Make or buy analysis.
    (d) Close-down decisions.
    (e) Comparisons of production methods.

14. Pricing decisions. Marginal costing allows management greater flexibility in setting selling price than full-cost pricing permits. In fact, price may be set below total cost.

For instance, let us consider a hypothetical example. Marginal (variable) costs are £20 *per* unit and fixed costs are £40,000 and anticipated sales are 3,900 units at £30 each: the total cost *per* unit is the sum of the average fixed and variable costs.

$$\begin{aligned} \text{Total cost } per \text{ unit} &= \text{AFC} & + \text{AVC} \\ &= £40{,}000 \div 3{,}900 + £20 \\ &= £30{\cdot}25 \end{aligned}$$

Assuming that the company is working below capacity and is in the course of tendering for a contract for the supply of 300 units, it might base its tender price on a full-cost basis of £29·52, *i.e.*

$$\begin{aligned} \text{Total cost } per \text{ unit} &= £40{,}000 \div (3{,}900 + 300) + 20 \\ &= £9{\cdot}52 \quad + £20 \\ &= £29{\cdot}52 \end{aligned}$$

As one would intuitively expect, the total cost *per* unit has fallen because the fixed costs of £40,000 are now being spread over a larger output.

However, using marginal pricing, a lower price is possible: a price of £27 might be low enough to secure the contract and yet provide an overall profit of £1,100.

    EXAMPLE:

      (i) Anticipated sales: contribution

               Contributions

Selling price		Variable cost		= *Unit*		*Total*
£30	−	£20	=	£10/unit	£10 × 3,900 units	= £39,000

(*ii*) Tender sales: contribution

£27	—	£20	= £7/unit	£7 × 300
				units = 2,100
				41,100
		less Fixed costs =	40,000
			Profit	£1,100

A good example of the application of marginal pricing is found in the travel industry. Package tour operators who book hotels for the whole year earn sufficient revenue in the peak periods to cover fixed costs and to provide profit so that they can then offer off-season rates at marginal cost (the cost of travel, accommodation, food, etc.). Obviously this is preferable to closing down the hotels.

(*a*) Off season rates of, say, £5 *per* week cover marginal costs and may make additional, if small, contributions to total profit.

(*b*) Overall profits are increased as long as peak bookings are maintained. However, this example illustrates the danger inherent in marginal pricing, for if holidaymakers substitute the cheaper off-peak holidays for peak period holidays, fixed cost will not be covered, so that losses are incurred.

(*c*) Hotel services are maintained and hotel staff retained.

Similarly, air carriers offer cheaper charter rates based on marginal cost of transport which makes a contribution to the airlines' overheads.

15. Allocation of scarce resources. The second example where marginal analysis may be applied to good effect is in the allocation of company resources. All these resources, whether management's time, materials, plant capacity, machine time or money, are limited in supply and some may be very scarce, so that decisions affecting their allocation are vitally important. Bad decisions resulting in sub-optimal allocation between the competing uses directly contribute to poor performance and reduced profitability. Therefore, if management is faced with a scarcity of a factor of production (termed a limiting or key factor), it must ensure that these resources are used in such a way so that profits *per* unit of key factor are maximised. This is where contribution analysis comes in, for if fixed costs remain constant, maximum contributions *per* unit of this limiting factor automatically secure maximum profits.

16. Example.

Veneered Table Tops Limited manufacturers coffee- and telephone- table tops for the furniture industry. Costing details are as follows:

Coffee-table tops				*Telephone-table tops*			
Variable costs							
Wood	2 cu. ft @ £3·00 =	6·00		2·25 cu. ft	@ £3·00	£6·75	
Labour	2 hours @ 75p =	1·50		1½ hours	@ 75p	1·12	
Expenses	2 hours @ 50p =	1·00		1½ hours	@ 50p	75	

Total variable costs per unit	8·50	8·62
Contribution: Selling price	10·00	10·00
less Variable cost	8·50	8·62
	£1·50	£1·38

NOTE:

Management must organise output to take into account the following circumstances:

(*i*) Staff holidays in August, when labour hours will be the key or limiting factor, acting as a constraint on production.

(*ii*) A shortage of wood in September brought about by fire at the local wood stockist.

These problems can be solved by analysis of the contributions *per* unit of limiting factor.

(*a*) Contribution *per* unit of labour $= \dfrac{\text{Contribution}}{\text{labour hours}}$

    (*i*) Contribution *per* unit of labour (coffee table) $= \dfrac{£1·50}{2}$

    $= 75\text{p}$

    (*ii*) Contribution *per* unit of labour (telephone table) $= \dfrac{£1·38}{1·5}$

    $= 92\text{p}$

(*b*) Contribution *per* unit of wood $= \dfrac{\text{Contribution}}{\text{Cubic ft of wood}}$

    (*i*) Contribution *per* unit of wood (coffee table) $= \dfrac{£1·50}{2}$

    $= 75\text{p}$

    (*ii*) Contribution *per* unit of wood (telephone table) $= \dfrac{£1·38}{2·25}$

    $= 61\text{p}$

Thus, faced with this allocation problem, management should concentrate on telephone tables in August and coffee tables in September, which thereby maximises contributions and profits of these two limiting factors.

17. Make or buy analysis. The third application of marginal analysis is in the make or buy area, where managers may occasionally be faced with the problem of whether to continue to make a product or to buy from an outside supplier. The decision obviously depends on the relative profitability of either course of action, which is measured by comparison of the purchase price and marginal cost of production. The justification of using only marginal costs in this calculation is that fixed costs exist in the short term, whether the goods are produced or not, and are therefore irrelevant to the analysis. Let us assume that the company producing two products, X and Y, has limited machine capacity and that the comparative cost data is as follows:

	Product X	Product Y
Marginal (variable) costs	£5	£7
Purchase price	£7	£10
Difference	£2	£3
Machine times	45 min	25 min
Difference *per* machine hour	£2·66	£7·20

This shows that to purchase products X and Y costs £1·50 and £1·25 *per* machine hour respectively, in excess of the cost of making them in the factory. Consequently, greater cost savings and perhaps higher profits would be secured if product Y were purchased and the machine capacity so realised used for the production of X.

18. Close-down decisions. A fourth example of marginal analysis is where management faces the problem of temporarily closing down a department or factory which is making losses. On cost grounds, there is a strong case for maintaining operations while sales revenue exceeds variable costs, since a contribution is made towards fixed costs because to close down would not avoid the fixed costs and so any contribution to fixed costs, however small, which reduces the amount of the trading osls, is preferred.

Figure 49 illustrates this point. Break-even occurs at a selling price of OP and output and sales of OQ, *i.e.* total revenue (price, OP × quantity, OQ = the area bounded by the points OPTQ) is equal to total cost (cost *per* unit, OP × quantity, OQ = OPTQ). Whenever selling price is below OP,

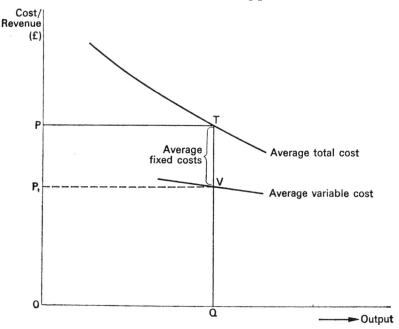

FIG. 49.—Break-even graph.

then total revenue is less than total cost, so that losses are incurred.

If price is OP_1 then total revenue is OP_1TQ, total cost is OPTQ and the loss is P_1PTV which is equal to the fixed cost, *i.e.*:

$$
\begin{aligned}
\text{Total cost} &= \text{Total variable cost} + \text{Fixed cost} \\
\text{OPTQ} &= \text{OP}_1\text{VQ} \qquad\qquad + \text{Fixed cost} \\
\text{Fixed cost} &= \text{Total cost} - \text{Total variable cost} \\
\text{Fixed cost} &= \text{OPTQ} \qquad - \text{OP}_1\text{VQ} \\
&= \text{P}_1\text{PTV}
\end{aligned}
$$

It follows that:

(a) If selling price is below OP_1, fixed cost and part of variable costs are not covered. The firm on cost grounds should close down and minimise the size of the loss to the value of fixed costs.

(b) If price is above OP_1 but below OP, variable costs are covered and a contribution is made to fixed costs. Here, losses are less than the value of fixed costs and are therefore minimised if the company continues to operate.

Non-cost considerations. However, non-cost factors must be considered in arriving at a closure decision.

(a) Suspension of activities may adversely affect customer goodwill and loss of business in the future.

(b) The firm may get a reputation as a bad employer, which will cause difficulties in the future when staff are recruited.

19. Comparisons of production methods. Management may have a choice between methods of production. For instance:

	Method 1		Method 2
Sales 1,000 units @ £20	£20,000		£20,000
Variable costs 1,000 units @ £10	10,000	@ £14	14,000
Contribution	£10,000		£6,000
Fixed costs *per* method	7,000		2,000
Contribution to factory overheads	£3,000		£4,000

Here, Method 1 makes the larger contribution to fixed costs associated with the production method, but Method 2 secures a larger overall contribution to factory overheads and is therefore preferable to Method 1.

20. Profit/volume (P/V) ratio. The value of the contribution concept has already been discussed in the previous section on break-even, where graphical comparisons were made between two products. However, this method compared absolute contributions only and made comparisons of relative contributions or profitability very difficult. Fortunately, this can be remedied by examining the Profit/volume (P/V) ratio. This ratio, more accurately described as the Contribution/sales ratio, measures contribution as a percentage of sales value.

$$P/V = \frac{\text{Contribution}}{\text{Selling price}} \times 100$$

$$= \frac{\text{Selling price} - \text{Variable cost}}{\text{Selling price}} \times 100$$

TABLE XXVI. APPLICATIONS OF P/V RATIO

Product	Selling price (£)	Variable cost (£)	Contribution (£)	P/V (%)	Sales value (£)	Total contribution (£)
A	10	5	5	50	80,000	40,000
B	8	3	5	62	70,000	43,400
C	7	2	5	71	60,000	42,600

Table XXVI shows applications of the P/V ratio. Applying the formula, the P/V ratio for product A is 50 per cent $\left(\dfrac{(£10 - £5 \times 100)}{£10}\right)$ and 62 per cent and 71 per cent for B and C respectively. The comparative profitabilities of these products are immediately revealed. For a given £1 of sales, A makes a contribution of 50p to fixed costs and profits, B 62p and C 71p. Furthermore, since contribution and sales are in direct proportion, total contributions can be calculated (P/V × Sales value) for a given amount of sales value. Clearly, product C is preferred to A and B on the grounds that it makes the highest unit contribution to overheads and profits and therefore management should try either to improve the ratios for A and B or transfer resources from A and B to the production of C. In other words, the P/V ratio enables management to rank products in terms of contributions: hence the preference for product C:

Product	P/V ratio	Ranking
A	50%	3
B	62%	2
C	71%	1

The P/V method of analysis may be usefully employed in any type of activity involving sales, and is a valuable complement to the contribution *per* unit of limiting factor methods of appraisal and ranking that we have discussed. Thus, P/V analysis is particularly appropriate in the following areas:

(a) Product lines, as *above*.

(b) Divisions or factories, where the contributions to division sales or factory sales are calculated.

(c) Salesmen or sales areas.

21. Dangers of marginal costing. As shown by the foregoing example, marginal costing provides technique for decision-making in a wide range of business situations. However, it must be applied with caution, for example in pricing decisions:

(a) One must not lose sight of the fact that in the longer term prices must be sufficient to cover total costs.

(b) Its usefulness is limited where a manufacturer makes a standard product that sells in a single market. Clearly there is no possibility of price discrimination in this situation: to base price on variable cost would mean disaster.

(c) Customers might react unfavourably to a price policy based on marginal costs that continually changes because of movements in labour and material costs.

(d) Additional sales secured through marginal costing must be justified, and not become an end in themselves. Thus, if sales have to be diverted from profitable markets in order to meet contracts priced on a marginal basis, overall contributions and profits are reduced.

PROGRESS TEST 14

1. Compare and contrast the accountant's and economist's approach to break-even curves. (1–3)

2. "Break-even analysis may be usefully employed in the areas of contribution and cash forecasting." Discuss. (6–9)

3. Define marginal pricing and compare with the cost-plus method. (10–12)

4. "Marginal analysis provides a flexible approach to the problem of securing optimum resource allocation but not without dangers." Comment. (13–21)

5. What is the meaning of Profit/volume ratio? (20–21)

EXAMINATION TECHNIQUE

Examination questions may be classified as follows:

(a) Text-book questions which test your memory of your text-books and your ability to marshal and organise information. For example, "Explain the following terms in relation to investment: (i) P/E ratio; (ii) Earnings yield, etc."

(b) Applied questions which test your knowledge and your ability to apply it to the facts in the question or which test your appreciation of current financial problems and policies. For example, "Compare and contrast factoring and invoice discounting and their relevance to a firm with a turnover of say £75,000 p.a. with average sales values of £500."

Procedure at the examination.

(a) Read all the questions to get the "feel" of the examination paper and to establish precisely what is required.

(b) Select the questions which you feel you can answer best, bearing in mind your knowledge and ability. Your choice may be limited, as when questions have to be selected from sections within the paper, e.g. "Answer five questions only: one question must be taken from each part and the fifth question may be taken from any part." Any such instructions must be followed.

(c) Allocate equal time to each question or apportion time according to the marks carried by each question where indicated. Remember that "diminishing returns" apply to examination answers; it is comparatively easy to get pass marks but a disproportionate amount of time has to be put in to get very high marks.

(d) Think about each question, jot down the relevant points as they come to mind and shuffle them into a tidy legible plan on the answer paper. Delete it only when you have completed the answer.

(e) Write legibly.

(f) Write your answers in essay form unless you are asked to list points or write a report or letter. Write your answer in short concise sentences without slang or unacceptable abbreviations and try to start paragraphs with "key sentences." Finally, check your answer through for inaccuracies.

(g) Do not be politically biased in your answer, and do not

waste time attempting to sway the examiner by humour or appeals.

(*h*) Do not give cross-references between questions; *e.g.* "I have already explained this in my answer to question 3."

(*i*) You are attempting to impress the examiner and should appear widely read, so give frequent examples. Also, answers may be improved by the use of economic concepts, *e.g.* elasticity and long- and short-run comparisons.

(*j*) Do not panic.

PRESENT VALUE OF £1

Year	2%	4%	6%	8%	10%	12%
1	0·980	0·962	0·943	0·926	0·909	0·893
2	0·961	0·925	0·890	0·857	0·826	0·797
3	0·942	0·889	0·840	0·794	0·751	0·712
4	0·924	0·855	0·792	0·735	0·683	0·636
5	0·906	0·822	0·747	0·681	0·621	0·567
6	0·888	0·790	0·705	0·630	0·564	0·507
7	0·871	0·760	0·665	0·583	0·513	0·452
8	0·853	0·731	0·627	0·540	0·467	0·404
9	0·837	0·703	0·592	0·500	0·424	0·361
10	0·820	0·676	0·558	0·463	0·386	0·322

INDEX

Details of some other Macdonald & Evans
Handbooks on related subjects can be found
on the following pages.

For a full list of titles and prices write for the
FREE Macdonald & Evans Business Studies
catalogue and/or complete M & E Handbook
List, available from Department B4,
Macdonald & Evans Ltd., Estover Road,
Plymouth PL6 7PZ

Business Mathematics
L. W. T. STAFFORD
The sixth impression of a popular HANDBOOK designed for the business student taking the examinations of the professional bodies, universities and technical colleges, which increasingly require a knowledge of mathematics. Also for those already in business who feel they have an insufficient grasp of the new mathematical techniques and their applications in the fields of finance, operational research and mathematical statistics.

Capital Gains Tax
VERA DI PALMA
The amount of capital gains tax legislation is substantial and makes great demands on the student already heavily committed in other subjects. This HANDBOOK is intended for such students; every area of the subject in which they are likely to be examined is included and an appendix contains sample questions from the past papers of the relevant professional bodies. For this new edition, the text has been fully revised and brought up to date.

Company Accounts
J. O. MAGEE
The primary purpose of this HANDBOOK is to show the student the basic principles underlying accountancy for limited companies. Each example is broken down into a number of stages, showing the gradual build-up of an account, entry by entry.

Commercial and Industrial Law
W. T. MAJOR & GWYNETH ROBERTS
Both mercantile and industrial law are outlined in this HANDBOOK. Full coverage is given to the *Factories and Shops Acts*, and more detail is given on the law of contract than is usually possible in a book in this field. The book will be invaluable to students and to personnel officers and others concerned with the administration of factories and offices.

Company Law

M. C. OLIVER

This is the latest edition of a HANDBOOK by an eminent lecturer which provides in full for examination requirements, while rendering this important subject interesting and easily assimilable. In this edition the author has made several amendments to the text, and the recent judicial decisions of importance have been included as well as the relevant provisions of the *Health and Safety at Work Act* 1974, the *Industry Act* 1975 and the *Employment Protection Act* 1975.

Corporate Planning and Control

R. G. ANDERSON

The prime purpose of this HANDBOOK is to provide a framework for systematically planning and controlling the operations of a business. The inter-relationships of related functions and systems are studied in detail, as are the uses of management information in providing a firm foundation on which to build an effective business structure. It has proved invaluable to students taking the various professional examinations in the subject.

Corporation Tax

B. S. TOPPLE

This HANDBOOK assumes no prior knowledge of taxation on the reader's part. It provides a basic introduction to the principles of company taxation: there are chapters covering capital allowances and losses, the treatment of income tax and close companies. The author provides typical examples of firms accounts in the text to illustrate each point. This new edition has been prepared to take account of recent relevant legislation, including the *Finance Act* 1976.

Data Processing and Management Information Systems
R. G. ANDERSON

This HANDBOOK, winner of the Annual Textbook Award of the S.C.C.A., provides a comprehensive study of the field of data processing, embracing manual, electro-mechanical and electronic systems and covering such topics as data transmission, systems analysis and computer programming. It is designed to fill the needs of students preparing for examinations in data processing and computer applications and "will also be valuable to those no longer concerned with examinations who require an understanding of the method and techniques available for the processing of data for management." *The Commercial Accountant*

Economics for Professional Studies
HENRY TOCH

This HANDBOOK draws on the author's experience over fifteen years of teaching economics to professional students, and uses topical situations and examples to illustrate a detailed survey of economic theory and practice.

General Principles of English Law
P. W. D. REDMOND

Originally designed for those preparing for intermediate professional examinations, this HANDBOOK has also proved itself immensely popular with "A" level and university students. The fourth edition includes the facts of appropriate recent cases and several important new topics.

Industrial Administration
J. C. DENYER
Industrial administration as a specialised aspect of management has become an increasingly popular examination topic for students taking the final professional examinations. They will find that this HANDBOOK gives a more logical and concise treatment of the individual topics than works on management theory can provide.

Law of Contract
W. T. MAJOR
This HANDBOOK, by an experienced lecturer and examiner, reduces a difficult subject to its essentials and will be of particular value to those studying Contract for university or professional examinations. In this edition, the *Misrepresentation Act* 1967 and the *Supply of Goods (Implied Terms) Act* 1973 are dealt with, together with the more important contract law decisions of 1972-73.

Operational Research
W. M. HARPER
This HANDBOOK explains succinctly the concepts and techniques involved in the mathematical analysis of business operations. Only elementary mathematical knowledge is assumed and the first part covers the mathematics necessary to appreciate the actual operational techniques.

Organisation & Methods
R. G. ANDERSON
This HANDBOOK gives both students of O & M and those already engaged in business a comprehensive guide to the principles and practice of business systems and procedures and office methods and organisation. The syllabuses of most examining bodies are fully covered.

Statistics
W. M. HARPER

Assuming no previous knowledge on the part of the reader, this clearly written HANDBOOK sets out to enable the student to take intermediate professional examinations in this subject with success. The second edition includes new chapters on small-sample theory and statistical quality control, and the section on frequency distribution meaures has been presented in an entirely new way.